A Critique of Anti-racism in Rhetoric and Composition

A Critique of Anti-racism in Rhetoric and Composition

The Semblance of Empowerment

Erec Smith

LEXINGTON BOOKS
Lanham • Boulder • New York • London

Published by Lexington Books
An imprint of The Rowman & Littlefield Publishing Group, Inc.
4501 Forbes Boulevard, Suite 200, Lanham, Maryland 20706
www.rowman.com

6 Tinworth Street, London SE11 5AL, United Kingdom

Copyright © 2020 The Rowman & Littlefield Publishing Group, Inc.

All rights reserved. No part of this book may be reproduced in any form or by any electronic or mechanical means, including information storage and retrieval systems, without written permission from the publisher, except by a reviewer who may quote passages in a review.

British Library Cataloguing in Publication Information Available

Library of Congress Cataloging-in-Publication Data Available

ISBN 978-1-4985-9040-2 (cloth : alk. paper)
ISBN 978-1-4985-9042-6 (pbk : alk. paper)
ISBN 978-1-4985-9041-9 (electronic)

∞™ The paper used in this publication meets the minimum requirements of American National Standard for Information Sciences—Permanence of Paper for Printed Library Materials, ANSI/NISO Z39.48-1992.

Contents

Preface vii

Acknowledgments xi

Introduction: Something "More than a Negro" xiii

1 The Primacy of Identity: Prefiguration,
   The Sacred Victim, and the Semblance of Empowerment 1

2 So What is Empowerment? 27

3 Disempowerment and Code-meshing Pedagogy 65

4 The "Soft Bigotry" of Anti-racist Pedagogy:
   Victims, Tricksters, and Protectors 87

Conclusion: Getting Over Ourselves and Centering
Empowerment 105

Epilogue: Am I Overreacting?
(A Humble Request for Your Input) 123

References 129

Index 139

About the Author 149

Preface

In Nichiren Buddhism, the term, *shakubuku*, is often heard among its lay practitioners. Although the term is used most often to denote the successful "recruitment" of a new member through one's sincere explanation of the practice, this was not its original meaning. Based on the original use of the word, *shakubuku* is an unapologetic speaking of truth to power, "the aim of which is to suppress others' illusions and to subdue their attachment to error or evil."[1] It is the act of correcting false views while not pulling punches.

People often confuse *shakubuku* with *shoju*, which is a "method of expounding Buddhism in which one gradually leads another to the correct teaching according to that person's capacity and without refuting his or her attachment to mistaken views."[2] This is an approach used when one feels an audience, of one or many, would not fully understand the elaborate truth or is not yet ready to think beyond long-held beliefs. Traditionally, *shoju* is used on people "without wisdom" who, apparently, know no better than the things they have been taught. *Shakubuku*, on the other hand, is meant for those who have wisdom but hold "perverse views" and spread misinformation, thinking critically only insofar as it benefits themselves.

Most people will see this book as one of *shakubuku*.

I have been trying to convey my thoughts on this book's topic—the nature of anti-racism in academia—for quite some time. I recall, as a graduate student, a lingering disappointment with some scholarship and methodologies meant to eradicate racism from the individual and the structural levels. I would vocalize this to some degree, but, looking back, I was much more of a *shoju* person. I did not mind rocking the boat, but I had yet to realize that the boat really needed to capsize.

Traditionally, academia was no stranger to the *shakubuku* style of refutation. Although slightly less contentious than the Buddhist concept, academic debate was framed by argumentation in the form of deliberative rhetoric or dialectic. These ideas seem to be falling away or atrophying as G. Thomas Goodnight may say. In fact, his concept of deliberative rhetoric, "a form of argumentation through which citizens test and create social knowledge in order to uncover, assess, and resolve shared problems"[3] has given way to something else. Something much less rhetorical, democratic, and, frankly, intellectual. Presently, disagreement is difficult to tolerate. Someone with an opposing ideology is not an interlocutor, but an enemy. That person is not to be engaged, but silenced. In a space like this, *shoju* would lose its efficacy. *Shakubuku* would be the go-to tactic.

At a recent conference in which I conveyed some of the thoughts on which I will elaborate in this book, an audience member spoke to me about it afterward.

"You dealt a lot of swords," he said.
"You think so?"
"Yeah, a lot of swords."

Dealing swords was not my intention. Telling the truth and doing so unapologetically was. Inspired by a ubiquitous charge within social justice and academia to speak truth to power, I wanted to do just that. When truth is considered "a lot of swords," we are in trouble.

So, I write this short prologue to let you know that I have no desire to hurt or, to extend the aforementioned metaphor, "cut" anyone. That being said, saying what I think needs to be said may cause people to feel like I am attacking. I already know that some people are taking my critiques personally. I already know that my views have been considered "hurtful."

I can only tell you that I seek truth and justice and I write this book solely from that interest. I genuinely hope people will read, engage, and critique it to their heart's content. I want to know why they agree or disagree with my conclusions. One of the main motivations for this book is to encourage a productive and generative approach to disagreement and discourage attempts to silence, shut down, or shame others into submission.

Sincerely,
Erec Smith

P.S. Yes, I know the direct translation of shakubuku is "to break and subdue." Still, I am just trying to argue my point.

NOTES

1. "*Shakubuku*," *The Nichiren Buddhism Library*, accessed 8 August 2019. https://www.nichirenlibrary.org/en/dic/Content/S/108
2. "*Shoju*," *The Nichiren Buddhism Library*, accessed 8 August 2019. https://www.nichirenlibrary.org/en/dic/Content/S/148.
3. G. Thomas Goodnight, "The Personal, Technical, and Public Spheres of Argument: A Speculative Inquiry into the Art of Public Deliberation," *Contemporary Rhetorical Theory: A Reader,* ed. Mark J. Porrovecchio and Celeste Michelle Condit (New York: Guilford Press, 2016), 199–209.

Acknowledgments

I want to thank those who have walked with me through part or all of this writing process. Michele Purdue, you were there when I needed someone to talk to after a scholar of anti-racist pedagogy approached me to ask me *not* to critique "them" in an upcoming conference presentation. You were there through the social media events that quickly devolved into a kind of degradation ceremony. You were there until I had typed the last sentence of this book. I am forever grateful.

I would also like to thank Mal-Lee Gong for encouraging me to write what I thought was right and to have faith in myself. "NMRK!"

Thank you Mal-Lee Gong and Errol Wizda for taking time to give feedback on my ideas. You don't know how much that meant to me.

I would like to thank my friends from the Uptown York Rotary Club for your fellowship and support throughout the writing of this book. You listened; you conversed; you bought me a drink or two. Your presence in my life has proven, once again, to be both fulfilling and therapeutic.

Thank you, Mom, for being so excited about my every publication that I am that much more motivated to finish the next one.

I would like to acknowledge by name all the colleagues who stood by me as I wrote this book and weathered the storm of pre-publication vitriol, but I fear they may get mobbed on social media. So, for all the people who cheered me on, listened to my struggles with this book's topic, checked in on me, offered feedback, and urged me to stand up for what I believe, I am forever grateful. You know who you are.

Introduction

Something "More than a Negro"

> "We have now sunk to a depth at which restatement of the obvious is the first duty of intelligent men."
>
> George Orwell, *Facing Unpleasant Truths: Narrative Essays*

The above quote seems to get more and more popular with each passing day in this era so many of us call "post-truth." Lee McIntyre also uses this quote to introduce a chapter in his 2017 lamentation of contemporary American society, simply titled *Post-Truth*. In the chapter titled "Fighting Post-Truth," the quote introduces a last-stand manifesto against post-truth in which McIntyre champions the power of repetition, critical thinking, and self-reflexivity as acts that will win out in the end.[1] Of course, McIntyre is speaking of a large domain: America, if not the "civilized" world. So, if he can have hope in successfully combating phenomena like confirmation bias, motivated reasoning, and other concomitants to the post-truth era, perhaps I should harbor some hope in academia, specifically the field of rhetoric and composition.

Unfortunately, I believe Orwell's quote does accurately describe a significant part of the field, including anti-racism initiatives, especially as they manifest in *National Council for the Teaching of English* events and publications. The current leadership for the *Conference on College Composition and Communication*, for example, can be seen as harbingers of a microcosmic post-truth embraced by a variety of academics in the name of fighting racism. As a black man, I am all for the eradication of discrimination against people of color, but as a scholar of rhetoric and a fan of critical thinking, I feel the need to restate the obvious, as it were.

The "obvious" of which I speak is a major motivation for this book. It is the obvious that provides the best counterargument to the anti-racist methodologies I deem problematic in the field of rhetoric and composition. Anti-racist initiatives like code-meshing *pedagogy* (not to be confused with the natural and brilliant *phenomenon* of code-meshing), and misguided attempts to empower marginalized bodies—particularly people of color—suffer from a disconnect to social and material reality.[2] In fact, McIntyre's final words in *Post-Truth* describe the situation well: "The danger of post-truth is not just that we allow our opinions and feelings to play a role in shaping what we think of as facts and truth, but that by doing so we take the risk of being estranged from reality itself."[3] Indeed, I argue generally that feelings and opinions have replaced critical thinking, or at least a robust critical thinking, in attempts to decenter whiteness and challenge hegemonic forces in academia. These feelings and opinions seem to have led to framings of the world that see violence against people of color in places where it may not necessarily exist, which works as an obstacle to dealing with actual racism. What's more, the prevalence of feelings and opinions or reason and facts leads to "strategies" that, if followed to their ultimate consequences, are more effective at enhancing group dignity and esteem than in actually making progressive changes to structural racism that can benefit our students and society at large. One cannot successfully change reality if one is effectively estranged from it.

Although I will discuss pedagogy to some degree, my main argument will be political and ideological. I argue that anti-racism initiatives and the narratives and ideologies that feed them result from a "primacy of identity" that, itself, results from a strong sense of disempowerment that leads to fallacious interpretations of texts, situations, and people; an infantalization of the field, its scholars, and its students; an overemphasis of subjectivity and self-expression over empirical and critical thought; an embrace of racial essentialism; and a general neglect of rhetoric itself, especially regarding context, audience consideration, and logos.

This introduction, then, will begin by exploring the aforementioned disempowerment through rhetoric and composition's appropriation of a prominent figure in African American thought who actually exemplifies the opposite of the unfortunate and, ultimately, counterproductive zeitgeist that describes much rhet/comp anti-racism. Then, I will show how this appropriation illustrates disempowerment and all its aforementioned offspring.

THE "DUBOISIAN" ATTITUDE

Throughout the edited collection, *Other People's English: Code-meshing, Code-switching, and African American Literacy*, Vershawn Young claims that "language is inherently tied to identity,"[4] and that students are suffering from "linguistic segregation" when taught an English dialect deemed "standard,"[5] making such instruction "tyrannical and oppressive" to them.[6] This segregation apparently induces a collective low self-image in students and, therefore, should be remedied by allowing code-meshed pedagogy (typically considered a blending of a "standard" dialect with a non-standard dialect in writing classrooms). W. E. B. Dubois' concept of double consciousness is referenced as an apt description of the emotional and psychological pain students experience when taking on a standard grapholect. In fact, Young and others go as far as to say students suffer from a kind of "racial schizophrenia," and that Dubois, himself, promoted this interpretation of his famous concept. Young references others who have taken on the "racial schizophrenia" interpretation of Dubois' terms, and finds instances of racism suffered by Dubois to strengthen this interpretation. In fact, Dubois' apparent suffering paints him as a psychologically disempowered victim that Young and others see as a kind of cautionary tale for teachers who would "tyrannize" students of color with standardized dialect instruction.[7] The taken-for-granted connection of identity to language, the "racial schizophrenia" interpretation of Dubois' double consciousness, and Dubois' assumed disempowerment can be construed as foundational concepts of anti-racist initiatives in the teaching of rhetoric and composition; to discover flaws in these concepts would do more than problematize these initiatives.

First, if one were to explore the connection of identity to language, one may find it to be much looser than initially thought. One's cathexis to a particular dialect is not a guaranteed occurrence and not everyone constructs identity in the same ways. Yet, the confluence of identity and dialect is taken for granted throughout rhetoric and composition's charge to give students the right to their own language. This connection of identity and dialect does not have the necessary theoretical backing to solidify it as the ontological phenomenon it is often deemed to be.

In *How to Think Like an Anthropologist,* Matthew Engelke explores our tacit understandings of language's relationship to identity and discovers that the idea that they are intrinsically and fundamentally linked reflects an "ideology of authenticity" underpinned by the concept of sociolinguistic naturalism:[8] the assumption that a language ideology is "Given. Just the way it is."[9] In the anti-racist work of rhetoric and composition, the ideology of authenticity seems to be the common understanding of the language/identity link. This ideology "is based on essentialism and suggests that our language expresses something integral to who we are, both individually and corporately."[10] He attributes the embrace of this ideology most saliently to "the impetus to emphasize authenticity" from a marginalized position.[11]

On the other hand, the "ideology of anonymity"[12] looks at language as something nonessential and open to anyone regardless of identity (i.e., language is not something that defines us, just something used by us). This ideology can also be attributed to the idea of sociolinguistic naturalism, but this option is less present, or less respected, in much rhet/comp anti-racism pedagogy.

Engelke concludes that, if an ideology of authenticity is to be embraced, it has to be actively cultivated and is often embraced for political, not ontological, reasons. In researching the attitudes toward language, Engelke references the autonomous community of Catalonia in Spain. In Catalonia, the regional language is Catalan, distinct from Spanish. Apparently, an ideology of authenticity gave way to a more "flexible sense of belonging and identity, one in which authenticity can be made, not given."[13]

Engelke relays the events of cultural and linguistic pride that followed an influx of Spanish speakers (called Castilian speakers) into Catalonia and their subsequent feelings of marginalization. When Catalan was slowly made the official language in schools during the 1980s, Spanish-speaking students felt marginalized due to both outsider status and language use. According to a study conducted by linguistic anthropologist Kathryn A. Woolard, *some* Spanish-speaking students felt that "when they spoke in Catalan they felt a sense of embarrassment and shame, as if they were faking it and as if they didn't really have the right to do so."[14] This may sound familiar to readers well-versed in anti-racist scholarship and code-meshing pedagogy in rhetoric and composition.

But something happened in Woolard's follow-up several years later that may problematize the aforementioned assumption about authenticity. Most of the students—who were in their 30s at the time of Woolard's revisit—had a confident ownership of Catalan. They did not feel like something about their collective identity was missing. Regarding the negative self-image that resulted from their feelings of marginalization in high school, "they put this down to the toss and turn of teenage existence."[15] Engelke writes: "For them, moreover, the uptake of a Catalan identity was not necessarily tied to larger political projects or statements; indeed, most emphasized that it was personal, and derided strong nationalistic expressions. Their approach to identity had become 'a both-and rather than either-or of being."[16] The follow-up study also looked at erstwhile teens and presented "a very different situation, one in which the rough and tumble of coming into one's own wasn't gone but wasn't about which language one spoke at home. The second time around, teenagers did not think language as constitutive of identity in the same ways that they had in 1987; Catalan and Castilian had lost that iconic role."[17]

What does this say about the subjects of Woolard's study? Do they suffer from a linguistic Stockholm Syndrome? Did they internalize Catalan ideology? These things are often lobbed at people of color who do not see language as an ontological aspect of their being and freely, and not painfully, use dialects deemed standard, nonstandard, or meshed according to the contingencies of situation, attitude, and intention. Rather than being brainwashed or "schizophrenic," they ride the fluidity of language with an identity that does not so much relate to an identification with language as it does a *use* of language. Regarding group-based "schizophrenia," the now adult former students, presumably more mature in demeanor and outlook as well as physicality, do not seem to be suffering from such a condition.

For a more homegrown take on the ideology of anonymity over the ideology of authenticity, we can look at Lisa Delpit's conclusions in her essay "No Kinda Sense." Delpit, referencing theorist Stephen Krashen, attributes the success or failure, comfort or violence of language acquisition to the concept of an "affective filter": the idea that students will learn more effectively and more comfortably when they feel respected, valued, and liked.[18] Referencing her daughter Maya's experience in smoothly acquiring and utilizing African American Vernacular English (AAVE) and standardized English (SE) from experiencing a white and then black school environment,[19] Delpit delivers an understanding of language that seems comparable to the sentiments of the aforementioned Catalonian students. Clarifying the affective filter concept through Maya's experience, Delpit writes:

> In other words, the less stress and more fun connected to the process the easier it is accomplished. When she left her previous school, Maya's self-esteem was low. She considered herself an outcast, once even referring to herself as among the "dregs" of the school. When she arrived at her new school, she was embraced by the children there. She was invited into the group, appreciated for what she brought, and she found that her interests were a vital part of these children's culture. In Krashen's words, her affective filter was lowered and she subconsciously embraced the language of her new friends, as she felt embraced by them.[20]

Maya felt empowered by the attitude of her new environment and excelled, picking up the preferred dialect easily because she was implicitly and enthusiastically invited to do so. She was not shamed into doing so and she was not pressured to be someone she was not. Thus, she felt empowered.

Maya and the Catalonians expressed no sentiments indicative of a "racial schizophrenia" and felt quite comfortable with both dialects, whether others liked it or not. Frankly, and damningly for the work of many anti-racism proponents, I do not think Dubois did either. Looking at Dubois' corpus more holistically, one may not see a suffering of "racial schizophrenia" as much as a self-reflexive black man whose strong sense of pragmatism and empowerment, not a disempowerment that would result from a kind of mental disorder, helps him negotiate an unfriendly world. Dubois is the opposite of the tyrannized student Young laments. Like Maya, Dubois' student experience was one of enthusiasm. Unlike Maya, his experience would be that of one of few black students at Harvard in the late 1800s.

It is interesting that Dubois was a student of William James, arguably the most important of American pragmatists, and other scholars that embraced material reality over metaphysics and abstractions. Dubois writes about James' influence: "William James guided me out of the sterilities of scholastic philosophy to realist pragmatism"[21] and writes that "it was James with his pragmatism and Albert Bushnell Hart with his research method who turned me back from the lovely but sterile land of philosophic speculation to the social sciences as the field for gathering and interpreting that body of fact which would apply to my program for the Negro."[22] Dubois seemed to utilize a healthy dose of empiricism and reason. Dubois is clear that progress "must start on the earth where we sit and not in the skies whither people aspire"[23] and "must start where we are and not where we wish to be."[24] What a contrast to the tacit assumptions that, I will argue, taint anti-racist initiatives in rhetoric and composition.

Surely, a lack of pragmatism and engagement with social and material reality may lead one to misappropriate the character of Dubois based on the adoption of one statement as one of the founding concepts for an entire movement. Perhaps the most important example of this is Young's use of Dubois' concept of double consciousness as "proof" that code-switching pedagogy (teaching students a standardized form of English so that they can switch as they see fit) is akin to racial segregation, a manifestation of Jim Crow in the classroom.[25] In actuality, Dubois may abide by the ideology of anonymity described by Engleke.

In 1950, toward the end of a long life as an activist and scholar of race, Dubois wrote an autobiographical account of his undergraduate days in *The Massachusetts Review* titled "A Negro Attends Harvard in the Nineteenth Century." In this narrative, Dubois relays a story about his own experience as a student in a composition class. Dubois discusses receiving a poor grade on a writing assignment, which is worth quoting at length:

> It was in English that I came nearest my Waterloo at Harvard. I had unwittingly arrived at Harvard in the midst of a violent controversy about poor English among students. A number of fastidious scholars like Barret Wendell, the great pundit of Harvard English, had come to the campus about this time; moreover, New England itself was getting sensitive over Western slang and Southern drawls and general ignorance of grammar. Freshman at this time could elect nearly all their courses except English; that was compulsory, with daily themes, theses, and tough examinations. But I was at the point in my intellectual development when the content rather than the form of my writing was to me of prime importance. Words and ideas surged in my mind and spilled out with disregard

of exact accuracy in grammar, taste in word or restraint in style. I knew the Negro problem and this was more important to me than literary form. I knew grammar fairly well, and I had a pretty wide vocabulary; but I was bitter, angry and intemperate in my first thesis. Naturally, my English instructors had no idea of nor interest in the way in which Southern attacks on the Negro were scratching me on the raw flesh. Tillman was raging like a beast in the Senate, and literary clubs, especially those of rich and well-dressed women, engaged his services eagerly and listened avidly. Senator Morgan of Alabama had just published a scathing attack on "niggers" in a leading magazine, when my first Harvard thesis was due. I let go at him with no holds barred. My long and blazing effort came back marked "E"—not passed!

It was the first time in my scholastic career that I had encountered such a failure. I was aghast, but I was not a fool. I did not doubt but that my instructors were fair in judging my English technically even if they did not understand the Negro problem. I went to work at my English and by the end of that term had raised to a "C." I realized that while style is subordinate to content, and that no real literature can be composed simply of meticulous and fastidious phrases, nevertheless solid content with literary style carries a message further than poor grammar and muddled syntax. I elected the best course on the campus for English composition—English 12.[26]

Several things can be seen from this passage beyond the insight into Dubois' ideas about English composition. One can see here, that "bad" writing was a systemic problem in a very predominately white student body.[27] Because SE is a grapholect—writing that is, usually, written and not spoken[28]—many people have trouble with its initial grasp, even middle-class white students. (My own teaching experiences can attest to this.) In the time period of which Dubois speaks, Harvard was already feeling a writing crisis throughout its entire student body as gleaned from the college's written entrance exam, for "over half the students admitted to Harvard failed this initial exam, sparking the first national crisis regarding the poor writing skills of American boys."[29] It was because of this crisis that Harvard created the first English composition course in the 1880s.[30] All of this surely suggests that standard English was something with which many struggled and, therefore, was not a specific aggression toward students of color. What's more, Dubois was not discouraged but invigorated by the challenge of acquiring this dialect.

Yes, now is a different day and acceptable modes of writing in professional and civic contexts may be more lenient, which brings me to another point regarding Dubois and pragmatism. His choice of words for describing ineffective writing (poor, muddled) is problematic if he were talking about a marginal but rule-based dialect and not real grammar errors; from Dubois' essay, we do not know what kind of writing elicited a "fail" from his instructor. We do know two things. Dubois did see the benefit of African American

Vernacular English to meet black students where they are (not where we wish them to be), but with the ultimate goal of expanding knowledge of various dialects for a more worldly and holistic knowledge.[31] Also, we do know that Dubois had less concern about "bad" writing over "good" writing and more concern for effective writing over ineffective writing.[32] Thus, pragmatism comes into play, again. (The full paragraph from which I derived much of the lengthy quote above starts with a sentence describing William James as a "friend and guide."). Dubois knew that he needed to become proficient in language that would get his words across. One can infer from the aforementioned quote that Dubois thought his writing that elicited a failing grade was fine, but not *effective*, and his sense of self was not so tied to it that his failing grade was tantamount to an assault on his character. As he writes about his reaction: "I was aghast, but I was not a fool."[33]

Lastly, this quote speaks, once again, to his sense of empowerment. In the midst of a racist society, he felt confident enough to discuss race explicitly and unapologetically, writing in a "bitter, angry, and intemperate" way, "with no holds barred." Like Frederick Douglass before him, Dubois chose to let his anger empower him toward a sense of agency so strong that the probable ill-will, if not violence, of whites was of no concern. Also, like Douglass—and perhaps most importantly—Dubois did not embrace a victimhood to induce pity or interpret his failing grade as an unfair plight of the Negro in racist America. To embody such an image is to embody disempowerment, which, psychologically and pragmatically, would not have done him any good.

With this in mind, one may not be surprised about Dubois' response to his failing grade in writing. On October 3, 1890, after taking English composition to acquire a more effective mode of writing, Dubois wrote the following theme to Barret Wendell, his apparent instructor, who liked it so much he read it aloud to the class:

> Spurred by my circumstances, I have always been given to systematically planning my future, not indeed without many mistakes and frequent alterations, but always with what I now conceive to have been a strangely early and deep appreciation of the fact that to live is a serious thing. I determined while in high school to go to college—partly because other men did, partly because I foresaw that such discipline would best fit me for life. . . . I believe, foolishly perhaps, but sincerely, that I have something to say to the world, and I have taken English 12 in order to say it well.[34]

I am not ready to say that Dubois would have laughed at the current code-meshing pedagogical movement in rhetoric and composition; he lived in a different time with different societal circumstances. However, he surely would have bristled at the attitudes some anti-racist pedagogues may have regarding students of color and the acquisition of an English dialect deemed standard, exemplified by Young's belief that, for some students of color, an effort like Dubois' to acquire SE "is virtually impossible, and makes requirements to do so appear tyrannical, oppressive."[35] Instead, Dubois' response to SE smacks of two things one may not see in current anti-racist pedagogy: pragmatism and empowerment. Dubois saw the power in writing an SE for the purposes of achieving his goals. A fragile self-esteem was not the issue, nor did he need an opportunity to code-mesh to feel, gain, or regain racial dignity. As this and other passages throughout his work clearly show, Dubois' dignity was intact. Writing was a strategy, a rhetorical and pragmatic one, that would help move him toward goals that were surely lofty for his position as a young black man at the turn of the twentieth century.

Lest you think a kind of Stockholm Syndrome took a hold of Dubois as he considered his need to write in standard English, he made it quite clear that a need to acquiesce to white sentiment in search of acceptance never took place. In the same autobiographical essay about his time at Harvard, he writes:

> Towards whites I was not arrogant; I was simply not obsequious, and to a white Harvard student of my day a Negro student who did not seek recognition was trying to be more than a Negro. . . . This cutting of myself off from my white fellows, or being cut off, did not mean unhappiness or resentment. I was in my early manhood, unusually full of high spirits and humor. I thoroughly enjoyed life. I was conscious of understanding and power, and conceited enough still to imagine, as in high school, that they who did not know me were the losers, not I.[36]

These are the words of a student who does not need the full acceptance of his hegemonic peers, as long as those peers did not make a concerted effort to squelch his progress. Their apparent interpretation of his lack of concern for their approval as "trying to be more than a Negro" did not stop Dubois' progress. Becoming distraught over their opinions would have been a waste of energy and decidedly not pragmatic. That is, his plan—to receive a quality education as his first step toward loftier goals—had nothing to do with the approval of his classmates. He had to garner the interactional skills key to both empowerment and pragmatic savvy,[37] but this was dictated by his environmental situation, and nothing more. He wrote, "I was in Harvard, but not of it, and realized all the irony of my singing 'Fair Harvard.' I sang it because I liked the music, and not from any pride in the pilgrims."[38]

Thus, I find it ironic that Dubois, who is used as a foundation for a decidedly disempowering ideology of anti-racism, actually exemplified an empowered anti-racism. Dubois was not the protagonist in a victim narrative akin to the one I will argue permeates anti-racist spaces in rhetoric and composition. He was the protagonist in a narrative of actual triumph, agency, and confidence that he would not need others to bend down to him; he would simply rise above. I think this, what I sometimes call a "Duboisian Attitude," is missing from anti-racist scholars and pedagogues in rhetoric and composition, a field that seems to speak and teach from a deficit model of empowerment. This Duboisian Attitude has the following features:

1. It is decidedly pragmatic and cognizant of social and material realities;
2. It is empowered and is not suffering from any debilitating disposition, race-based or otherwise;
3. It welcomes intellectual inquiry, debate, and counterclaims—or what some would call academic discourse (not to be confused with a "standard" English dialect);
4. It does not *embrace* a victim narrative that exalts an injured identity as a primary image, although Dubois writes of such images in his scholarship.

These components, I argue, are missing from anti-racist initiatives or, at best, are not centralized as the executive components of the movement. Considering these components and how they can alter both the attitudes of and approaches to anti-racism may look quite different from the current attitudes and approaches.

Now, I can speculate as to why these components are missing and acknowledge counterarguments. Let's revisit Dubois' statements about the attitudes of his white Harvard classmates. The fact that they felt he was trying to be "more than a Negro" by disregarding their approval is something that Young acknowledges regarding the nuances of race relations at the time.[39] The reaction of white students to Dubois' lack of concern for their approval speaks to a protectionism of white culture that, apparently, was more prevalent in Dubois' America than in contemporary twenty-first-century America, according to Young, who claims a change in racism that moves from protectionism to a demand for others to "act white" around the time of desegregation.[40] That is, racism transformed from keeping codes of whiteness away from blacks to demanding that blacks embrace them. However, I believe this to be a flawed interpretation. White protectionism did not end with desegregation. (In many ways, segregation did not end either.). As I will show later in this book, some anti-racist initiatives are flawed not just because they abide by the assumption that protectionism is gone, but because they are also conducive to this protectionism.

So, anti-racism proponents are quite clear that they believe writing in standard English is a form of "acting white" and that it smacks of an acquiescence to hegemonic norms. Foregoing the inherent essentialism in the term "acting white" (for now), one could construe the adoption of standardized modes of English as a lack of empowerment. I argue, however, that the need to take a stand for identity by, for example, embracing a certain dialect—a relationship that may already be fallacious in nature—is a sign of one's need to make a concerted effort to acquire a lacking sense of empowerment. In rhetorical terms, one's confidence in exacting an effective ethos is weak if not nonexistent. Philosophical pragmatism, the kind Dubois prided himself on embracing, transcends the need to act in ways that bolster identity; a true pragmatic take necessitates the kind of empowerment on which I will focus in this book. Empowerment involves and promotes pragmatism that transcends identity and moves us (scholars, instructors, students, everyone) toward more successful and fulfilling interactions and concrete change.

So, the pain of SE instruction, the phenomenon of racial schizophrenia, and the embrace of victimhood need not find their way into a writing classroom if writing instruction is looked at through a frame of empowerment instead of the frame of disempowerment that is most prevalent in anti-racism. Like the language ideologies of authenticity and anonymity, one can choose which frame to embrace. That choice, itself, may be pragmatic. What does one stand to gain by choosing one over the other? One can easily assume the benefits of real empowerment. However, if one were to analyze current anti-racism initiatives in the field of rhetoric and composition, one may see disempowerment as a kind of social capital. Ultimately, I will explore the detriments of disempowerment as a systemic issue in anti-racist rhetoric and composition and, often, the humanities at large; it permeates pedagogy and scholarship and infiltrates commonplaces like, classrooms, conferences, and social media.

Young, himself, admits the benefit of self-segregation while simultaneously reinforcing the embrace of race as a primary and ontological factor. He writes:

> With the end of Jim Crow and with the rise of opportunities to become middle class, the problem for people like me is not whether I'm black or not; everybody knows I'm black. Hell, most of the jobs I've had, even the one at [University of Iowa], required that I be black. What matters now is what kind of black person I am, which I must demonstrate by the brand of blackness I perform through my speech and behavior.[41]

The "kind" of black person Young promotes in subsequent publications illustrates a "brand" of victimhood. Young's statement shows the benefit—the "cash value"—of disempowerment (most likely, those jobs he refers to that resulted from a perceived need of institutions to provide empowerment to the disempowered) and the benefit of "the kind of black person" Young was and is: one who, as he and others inadvertently show in their work, thrives on essentialist notions of identity that embrace disempowerment and anti-intellectualism in order to move ahead in life.

Another counter to my thoughts on empowerment is that it smacks too heavily of the hegemonic forces, deemed inherently racist, that anti-racist initiatives are trying to combat. That is, the very notion of empowerment theory put forth in this book may be seen as a European construct and therefore racist. Notions of critical thinking, even those that embrace mindfulness and metacognition, are deemed problematically white and, hence, a kind of microaggression when they are expected from students of color. This book will address this seemingly common idea in anti-racist initiatives.

What's more, many others and I believe that the embrace of victimhood and ideologies of disempowerment result from feelings of hopelessness among the marginalized. This causes people to fall back on the fabrication of spaces in which the world they seek can be enacted, ignoring a pragmatic disposition like the one embraced by Dubois. This idealized realm is the result of what is called prefigurative politics, which is a form of political engagement that seeks to *perform* progress rather than actually construct strategies to enact change.[42] I argue in this book that much anti-racism in rhetoric and composition comes from a satisfaction with the more equitable and decolonized bubbles we create for ourselves in departments, programs, and conferences. This is not empowerment but a *performance* of empowerment in which the victim persona is lauded as heroic if not, in a way, sacred.

Following Dubois' imperative that true change necessitates seeing the world as it is and not as we want it to be,[43] Jonathan Smucker and Diana Frost and Samantha Coole invoke the metaphor of an allergy to discuss this suspicion of power and fear of social and material realities. This fear denotes the lack of what, in psychology circles, is called "reality testing": "the ability to see things as they actually are, rather than the way you wish or fear they might be," which is a key skill to successful decision-making.[44] Frost and Coole, in *New Materialisms: Ontology, Agency, and Politics*, write that they are "aware that an allergy to 'the real' that is characteristic of its more linguistic or discursive forms—whereby overtures to material reality are dismissed as an insidious foundationalism—has had the consequence of dissuading critical inquirers from the more empirical kinds of investigation that material processes and structures require."[45] Jonathan Smucker elaborates on this "allergy" in *Hegemony How-To: A Roadmap for Radicals,* and writes about the embrace of disempowerment that results from it. Referring to the Occupy Wall Street movement, which I will argue, shares many characteristics with anti-racist initiatives in rhetoric and composition, Smucker writes:

> And somehow along the way we seem to have lost faith in the possibility of really winning against these logics and systems [of oppression] in the world

beyond our little clubhouse; the possibility of gaining ground again in the terrain of society. The clubhouse becomes our starting place—the source of all of our reference points—and society is written off as a lost cause. And the logic of political strategy? We don't want to hear the logic of political strategy in our clubhouse. This is a liberated, "prefigurative" and "post-political" space. We don't need strategy or organization or leadership or money in our clubhouse. All those things remind us of the insidious logics against which we define ourselves and our projects. Such a disposition was strong, if not predominant, amongst core participants of Occupy Wall Street. And it is my view that this paralyzing allergic reaction to power was as responsible for stunting the movement's growth as any external repression that we faced.[46]

In his book, Smucker is careful to insist that he is not downgrading the need to feel empowered or suggesting that prefiguration—the performance of the world we want—is not valid. He warns that prefiguration *without* strategy and acknowledgment of the real world will lead to nothing other than a sense of belonging and, of course, a mere semblance of empowerment.

Smucker references Max Weber's concept of the "ethic of responsibility" as the foil to the overreliance on prefigurative politics—an "ethic of ultimate ends"—he sees in social activism, and I see in rhetoric and composition's anti-racist initiatives. This ethic of responsibility is a concept clearly in line with a pragmatic attitude and an acknowledgment of powerful hegemonic forces to be added into a group's "strategic calculus."[47] This attitude is opposed to some, if not most, anti-racist initiatives that, I will argue, propose scholarship and pedagogies without thinking them through to the end, that is, without thinking about the real consequences for our students and ourselves. Smucker cites Weber's words about the difference between doing things based on how things *should* be versus doing things based on how they *are*, writing that "there is an abysmal contrast between conduct that follows the maxim of an ethic of ultimate ends—that is, in religious terms, 'The Christian does rightly and leaves the results with the Lord'—and conduct that follows the maxim of an ethic of responsibility, in which case one has to give an account of the foreseeable results of one's actions."[48] To be realistic and strategic is to acknowledge an uncomfortable and daunting world to which many anti-racism proponents have some kind of "allergy." Refusing to acknowledge this world may be comforting for a bit, but it is neither beneficial nor empowering to our students or ourselves.

Again, Smucker makes clear that he is not downplaying the motivations for righteousness and equality and is not moving away from these toward "unprincipled opportunism."[49] Doubling down on the allergy analogy, Smucker expresses the need for a balance of prefigurative and strategic politics and warns us not to develop "an allergic reaction to the allergic reaction."[50] He continues: "It remains important to critique power and to keep vigilant about its dangers. Let's not do it from the sidelines! Instead, we have to engage an advanced progressive critique of power, even as we lean into the hard work of building and wielding it together."[51] I believe that current anti-racism in rhetoric and composition is working "from the sidelines" while pretending to work in the trenches. This neither expresses a present empowerment nor promotes the cultivation of empowerment in others.

I write this book, then, to add a neglected part of anti-racist scholarship and pedagogy: the exploration of empowerment and what it means to be empowered, as well as an exploration of the detriments of acts and initiatives we label as empowerment but really are not. The former purpose of the book would be taken differently if the latter purpose was not exposed and analyzed. In exploring disempowerment, I will critique canonical scholarship and pedagogy for perpetuating it. I may also be called racist against my own people—a charge whites and blacks alike have thrown at me—for dismissing initiatives they believe to be empowering and reparatory. However, I feel that *truly* empowered anti-racist scholarship and pedagogy can benefit students of all colors in exploring what it means to be empowered and its implications for negotiating the social and material realities of life.

I want to make one more thing clear before I move on. My critique of current manifestations of anti-racism does not denote an aversion to anti-racism, per se. As a black man, I would never in my right mind harbor such a thought. Racism is alive and well and still taints the minds of otherwise intelligent people (and, obviously, less intelligent people). Racism has many manifestations, from exclusionary tactics and silencing, to slanted interpretations of statistics, to all-out violence. I am no stranger to such things and do not want to come off as someone who thinks a post-racial society is upon us. However, unlike others, I do not retreat into a mode of thinking that perpetuates victimhood, prefiguration, and overall disempowerment. My take on racism would embrace effective modes of empowerment when dealing with the aforementioned manifestations of racial discrimination.

I believe that racism, too, is the result of systemic disempowerment in many situations. Staci Perryman-Clark and Collin Lamont Craig share their and others' stories of being shut down, "put in their place," for apparently racist reasons. I, too, have published such a story.[52] White supremacy is a performance spurred by disempowerment, as well. This accusation of disempowerment is inspired by Frederick Douglass' salient point in "What to the Slave is the Fourth of July," when he writes that "[black equality] is admitted in the fact that Southern statute books are covered with enactments forbidding, under severe fines and penalties, the teaching of the slave to read or to write. When you can point to any such laws in reference to the beasts of the field, then I may consent to argue the manhood of the slave."[53] In other words, if black people were inherently inferior to whites, those whites would not have to enact laws for the express purpose of stifling black dignity and education. Likewise, if white people really were supreme to blacks, there would be no need to enact the racist behaviors chronicled by Perryman-Clark, Craig, and me. Acts of racism, then, are proof that those enacting them do *not* feel superior to nonwhites. Such actions, in my mind, also are flags of disempowerment. Those staking these flags become problematic when in positions of power, and such abuses of power need to be acknowledged and dealt with

This being said, white feelings of disempowerment are not a primary focus of this book; the detriments of white racism have been explored by others, from Douglass' day to the present. My main focus is the insidious disempowerment that affects anti-racist initiatives, specifically in the field of rhetoric and composition. From scholarship to pedagogy, a tacit deficit model of empowerment fuels anti-racism in too many instances. What causes the unquestioned assumptions of language's connection to identity? What causes the cherry-picking and specific appropriations of Dubois work? What causes the embrace of victimhood as a trope? Why do these phenomena create the foundation on which anti-racist initiatives in rhetoric and composition are built? This book hopes to address all these questions for the main purpose of strengthening anti-racism, not eradicating it.

Initially, I will elaborate on the problems I see with anti-racist initiatives and their proponents—people of color and their white allies/accomplices. In chapter 1, I will explain what I mean by a "primacy of identity" and show how it results in prefigurative politics and an overarching victim narrative with premade and essentialized roles. I will then say how this primacy of identity is ultimately the result of a dearth of empowerment in anti-racist initiatives. In chapter 2, I will elaborate on empowerment theory, its confluence with emotional intelligence, and its importance in effecting true progress with anti-racism, for students and academics, alike. I will show throughout the remainder of this book that anti-racist initiatives work from a deficit model of empowerment.

The next two chapters will show how disempowerment manifests in rhetoric and composition. Chapters 3 and 4 will explore the effects of disempowerment pedagogically. Chapter 3 will focus on code-meshing pedagogy as a philosophy of education framed in disempowerment. Chapter 4 will go over the tendency to frame students as ready-made victims in need of saving, and explore the possibilities of white protectionism and a kind of "trickster" racism that impedes racial uplift under the guise of encouraging it.

In the concluding chapter, I will focus on the need to "get over ourselves" as academics. That is, I discuss ways of transcending a primacy of identity in academic commonplaces and the classroom. I invoke Buddhism, as a counter to its reference in current anti-racist scholarship, to promote an ideology that embraces social and material realities while questioning our understandings of identity. I will then briefly present problem-based learning as an empowered pedagogy that can enhance rhetorical savvy, diversity, reality testing, and true progress for ourselves and our students.

NOTES

1. Lee McIntyre, *Post-Truth* (Cambridge, MA: MIT Press, 2018), 151–72.

2. I will use the term "social and material" to denote the social dynamics and material influences that make up all aspects of reality. Specifically, this term will refer to common civic and professional contexts and consider their common interpellations. I do not use the term "sociomaterial" reality because that denotes a connection to the social and technological aspects of society. Of course, the technological is part of the material, but the term "sociomaterial" emphasizes technology's confluence with behavior that is beyond what I intend to convey in this book.

3. McIntyre, *Post-Truth*, 172.

4. Vershawn Ashanti Young, *Other People's English: Code-Meshing, Code-Switching, and African American Literacy* (New York: Teachers College Press, 2014), 3. Ebook.

5. Throughout this work, I will use the term "standard" to be synonymous with "standard written English," "Modern United States English, White English, and other terms denoting a rigid, prioritized "grapholect" of English. This English is most often written but sometimes spoken, especially when a speaker takes part in linguistic divergence. I will use Language of Wider Communication (LWC) to denote a dialect that reflects more common verbal and written modes of English that may still be coded as "white." I will not capitalize the term "standard" to reflect my acknowledgment of its status as one of many legitimate dialects of English.

6. Vershawn Ashanti Young, "Nah, We Straight," *JAC* 29:1/2 (2009), 63.

7. Vershawn Ashanti Young, "To Be a Problem," *Your Average Nigga* (Detroit: Wayne State University Press, 2007).

8. Matthew Engelke, *How to Think Like an Anthropologist* (Princeton, NJ: Princeton University Press, 2019), 179.

9. Engelke, *How to Think Like an Anthropologist*, 182.

10. Ibid., 180.

11. Ibid.

12. Ibid.

13. Ibid.

14. Ibid., 185.

15. Ibid., 185.

16. Ibid., 185.

17. Ibid., 185–86.

18. Lisa Delpit, "No Kinda Sense," *The Skin That We Speak: Thoughts on Language and Culture in the Classroom*, ed. Lisa Delpit and Joanne Kilgour Dowdy (New York: The New Press, 2018), 56. E-book.

19. It is worth noting that Maya transferred from a predominantly white school to a predominately black one. A more open-minded and truly anti-racist ambience would have had Maya thrive in her former environment. White supremacy is very real, but it, too, can be remedied with a different understanding of empowerment and empowering pedagogy.

20. Delpit, "No Kinda Sense," 56.

21. W. E. B. Dubois, "A Negro Student Goes to Harvard at the End of the 19th Century," *W.E.B Dubois: A Reader*, ed. David Levering Lewis (New York: Henry Holt and Company 1995), 272.

22. Dubois, "A Negro Student Goes to Harvard at the End of the 19th Century," 282.

23. W. E. B. Dubois, "The Negro College," *W.E.B Dubois: A Reader*, ed. David Levering Lewis (New York: Henry Holt and Company 1995), 68.

24. Dubois, "The Negro College," 71.

25. Young, "Nah, We Straight."

26. Dubois, "A Negro Student Goes to Harvard at the End of the 19th Century," 280–81.

27. Ibid., 280.

28. Patricia Bizzell, "Hybrid Academic Discourse: What, Why, How," *Composition Studies*, 27.2 (1999), 10.

29. Steven Lynn, *Rhetoric and Composition: An Introduction* (New York: Cambridge University Press, 2010), 20.

30. Lynn, *Rhetoric and Composition*.

31. Dubois, "A Negro Student Goes to Harvard at the End of the 19th Century," 70–71.

32. Ibid., 280.

33. Ibid.

34. Ibid.

35. Young, "Nah, We Straight," 63.

36. Dubois, "A Negro Student Goes to Harvard at the End of the 19th Century," 274.

37. Marc Zimmerman, "Psychological Empowerment: Issues and Illustrations," *American Journal of Community Psychology*, 23.5 (1995), 589.

38. Dubois, "A Negro Student Goes to Harvard at the End of the 19th Century," 274.

39. Young, "To Be a Problem," *Your Average Nigga*.

40. Ibid.

41. Ibid., LOC 2208.

42. Dubois, "The Negro in College," 68.

43. Ibid, 71.

44. Steven J. Stein, Howard E. Book, Korrel Kanoy, *The Student EQ Edge: Emotional Intelligence and Your Academic and Personal Success* (San Francisco, CA: Jossey-Bass, 2013), 17.

45. Diane Frost and Samantha Coole, *New Materialism: Ontology, Agency, and Politics*, (Raleigh, NC: Duke University Press, 2010), 6.

46. Jonathan Matthew Smucker, *Hegemony How-To: A Roadmap for Radicals* (Chico, CA: AK Press, 2017), 137.

47. Smucker, *Hegemony How-To*, 140.

48. Ibid. Smucker quotes Max Weber's "Politics as Vocation."

49. Smucker, *Hegemony How-To*, 140.

50. Ibid., 138.

51. Ibid.

52. Erec Smith, "A Barbarian Within the Gate: The Detriments of Insularity at a Small Liberal Arts College," *Defining, Locating, and Addressing Bullying in the WPA Workplace*, ed. Cristyn L. Elder and Bethany Davila (Louisville, CO: University Press of Colorado, 2019), 138–50.

53. Frederick Douglass, "What to the Slave Is the Fourth of July," *Teaching American History,* accessed 4 August 2019, https://teachingamericanhistory.org/library/document/what-to-the-slave-is-the-fourth-of-july/.

Chapter 1

The Primacy of Identity

Prefiguration, The Sacred Victim, and the Semblance of Empowerment

> The only adversary left is ourselves. And we have mastered the art of self-sabotage. At a time when we liberals need to speak in a way that convinces people from very different walks of life, in every part of the country, that they share a common destiny and need to stand together, our rhetoric encourages self-righteous narcissism. At a moment when political consciousness and strategizing need to be developed, we are expending our energies on symbolic dramas over identity. At a time when it is crucial to dir ect our efforts into seizing institutional power by winning elections, we dissipate them in expressive movements indifferent to the effects they may have on the voting public. In an age when we need to educate young people to think of themselves as citizens with duties toward each other, we encourage them, instead to descend into the rabbit hole of the self. The frustrating truth is that we have no political vision to offer the nation. And we are thinking and speaking and acting in ways guaranteed to prevent one from emerging.[1]
>
> —Mark Lilla, *The Once and Future Liberal: After Identity Politics*

The wastes of time and energy described by Lilla are a direct result of what is commonly known as identity politics. Although varying definitions of identity politics abound, the one Lilla laments can be described as a mode of politics and activism that involve a heavy emphasis on identity, lived experience, and feeling over other ways of knowing, like reason, critical thinking, qualitative and quantitative research, and fundamental rhetorical practices (interpersonal communication, discussion, and civil debate). Identity politics in this form are not sound politics; they are defense mechanisms, direct results of powerlessness. This powerlessness, the inability to effect change in significant and beneficial ways, leads to a need for validation and a victim mentality that either ignores or fears social and material realities of civic and professional society.

If this is the definition of identity politics deemed most dangerous, the problem is more insidious than a mere waste of time and energy. Identity politics may be a well-intentioned but misguided mode of living for some (those from all walks of life who want to empower downtrodden people), but for many it is a conscious or subconscious escape from a reality deemed too complicated and too big to be handled. The insecurity of such powerlessness has prompted a retreat into narratives, some full of egregiously fallacious assumptions and propositions that do not necessarily make sense, but do provide comfort through a palatable casting of protagonists and antagonists that can provide a sense of security and validation. This narrative is essentialist and group-oriented, and that group has only a handful of essentialized standpoints from which to choose. Ultimately, it is not a sense of empowerment, but a sense of disempowerment that is the true engine that drives identity politics.

This understanding of identity politics seems to be the one most cited as an impediment to true progress, but is this definition fair? A brief history of the term may provide some answers. "Identity politics" was originally conceived by the black lesbian activists group called the Combahee River Collective and emphasized that a standpoint that, later, would be called intersectionality was imperative to social reform and progressive politics. This concept was meant to coexist with other movements, other demographics. Ideally, each movement would authentically "see" the others in order to better work together.

But current manifestations of identity politics have embraced an insularity around group identity that neglects the collaborative nature of the group's manifesto, "The Combahee River Collective Statement." The manifesto reads, "We believe that the most profound and potentially most radical politics come directly out of our own identity, as opposed to working to end somebody else's oppression. . . . *We reject pedestals, queenhood, and walking ten paces behind. To be recognized as human, levelly human, is enough.*"[2] One can infer a disinterest in—or, at least, a de-emphasis of—the celebration of identity for its own sake, and a keen interest in using identity as an epistemological standpoint that can help situate their perspectives into a collaboration with others. This is clarified by Demita Frazier, a former member of the Collective, during an interview. She states, "We worked in coalition with community activists, women and men, lesbians and straight folks. We were very active in the reproductive rights movement, even though, at the time, most of us were lesbians. We found ourselves involved in coalition with the labor movement because we believed in the importance of supporting other groups even if the individuals in that group weren't all female. We understood that coalition building was crucial to our own survival."[3] The Collective seemed to value a pragmatic take to activism, as it worked alongside people who wanted similar change without interest in competing on a basis of identity. This is far from current manifestations of identity politics like the one Lilla gave to start this chapter, especially in rhetoric and composition's anti-racist initiatives.

To distinguish from the Collective's take on identity politics, I have named the current academic manifestation a "primacy of identity." As the name indicates, the recognition and expression of identity takes precedence over other considerations, and is almost immune to critique. I describe it below. The following components actually overlap, but I make distinctions for didactic reasons.

Primacy of selective lived experience over critical thought or the combination of lived experience and critical thought: I understand the necessity for lived experience in academia, especially when it comes to the study and understanding of marginalized people. Jacqueline Jones Royster masterfully expresses the frustration that justifies a need to take lived experience seriously in "When the First Voice You Hear is Not Your Own." Royster, a black woman, expresses how her white colleagues speak about her own people through book knowledge, not taking seriously, or even considering, her own experience as a person of color among people of color. She writes: "In metaphoric fashion, these 'authorities' let me know, once again, that Columbus has discovered America and claims it now, claims it still for a European crown."[4] This essay has become a manifesto of sorts for the importance and inclusion of lived experience in identity-based scholarship.

Unfortunately, in too many interpersonal situations, from department meetings to conferences, lived experience has become an infallible panacea of communication, especially from marginalized bodies, that is immune to critical inquiry. To question the lived experience of a minority is to either expose oneself as culturally ignorant or outright racist. At the very least, critical engagement with a person's lived experience is considered a microaggression that inadvertently downplays that person's existence.

As I will explain in the following chapter, true empowerment necessitates a serious appreciation for lived experience, and because empowerment involves successful interaction with others, it is also an important consideration in rhetoric and communication. Indeed, lived experience as "lore" has benefited many instructors in the classroom.[5] But I believe the issue with lived experience in the context of a primacy of identity is that only certain lived experiences count. The lived experience of someone deemed a victim in a particular narrative is irrefutable compared to the lived experience of a person seen as having membership in a dominant role. The lived experience of the victim is a concomitant to the primacy of identity. Open expression and academic dialogue must necessarily suffer under this ideology. I am aware that power differentials come into play as well and that the demand to have our white colleagues do a better job at listening to marginal experiences is necessary. But when we demand so much listening, especially to lived experience, that we forego the very fundamentals of academic discourse—critical inquiry, civil debate, critique, and so on—can we really call ourselves academics any longer?

The primacy of self-expression over other fundamental aspects of rhetoric, especially *kairos* and audience consideration: Rhetoric is many things. As I have argued in past publications, it can be seen as a life condition as well as a practice or object of study.[6] However, a fundamental aspect of rhetoric, whether in its *utens* or *docens* manifestations, is its suasion; it conveys information in ways that audiences can understand, or it conveys information that will sway an audience toward some kind of action. (Of course, these are comparable manifestations if one sees "understanding" as a kind of action.) However, this consideration of audience is underplayed, if acknowledged at all, in a primacy of identity. In other words, language as audience-centered persuasion gives way to a rhetoric meant to disrupt an audience to see the world in a certain way. This is different from the former understandings of persuasion in that the desire to engage an audience is replaced by the desire to disengage for a certain jarring and oppositional effect. Rhetoric in the primacy of identity is less about the audience and much more about the rhetor. The rhetorical triangle of speaker, subject matter, and audience gives way to a circle with the rhetor in the center, with subject matter and audience rotating around it. This is not to be confused with the way that, say, the Hegelian Dialectic can be rendered as a circle. In the primacy of identity, the rhetor is central and dialectic interaction with an audience is substantially subordinated.

Both takes on expression have their places (we will get to *kairos* soon), but rhetoric framed by a primacy of identity is more indicative of protest and agitation than working with the available means of persuasion. Thus it is not necessarily persuasion in its traditional sense that motivates expression in a primacy of identity; it is a separation or parsing out to emphasize difference. Again, this can be a good strategy in certain instances, especially ones in which a certain group or viewpoint has been silenced and is in need of amplification. However, when this strategy is overemphasized or when it is presented as the executive and atemporal strategy of communication, it discourages constructive dialogue, especially with apparent hegemonic voices that are considered inherently oppressive. So, an "us versus them" construct is developed and purposefully perpetuated.

So, to be clear, when I use the term "rhetoric" throughout this work, I am abiding by a definition that emphasizes persuasion over expression. Thus,

Aristotle's definition, that rhetoric is "the faculty of observing in any given case the available means of persuasion"[7] can suffice for what I mean, but may be further elaborated in ways similar to Steven Lynne's three-part definition: "'Rhetoric' refers to practical instruction in how to make an argument and persuade others more effectively. . . . 'Rhetoric' also refers to the strategies that people use in shaping discourse for particular purposes. . . . 'Rhetoric' also refers to the study of [the aforementioned definitions]."[8] One may recognize the mode of rhetoric I describe in the primacy of identity ideology in Lynne's second definition of rhetoric; one can strategize to shape discourse in a way that overemphasizes a rhetor and de-emphasizes an audience. However, my major critique is that, within a primacy of identity, the first definition is significantly neglected. (Perhaps other definitions of rhetoric necessitate qualifiers, e.g., "protest" rhetoric, "performative" rhetoric, etc.)

I consider *kairos* an integral part of this understanding of rhetoric. *Kairos*, put most simply, is the confluence of time, place, topic, and audience[9] to inform one's use of language,[10] but we must parse out the complexities to see the issue with *kairos* within a primacy of identity. Eric Charles White, in *Kaironomia,* explains that *kairos* is an understanding of the present context "as unprecedented, as a moment of decision, a moment of crisis, and . . . impossible, therefore, to intervene successfully in the course of events merely on the basis of past experience."[11] Fallacies like strawman, composition, division, and genetic all involve the act of inadequately projecting the past (or some imagined time frame) into a present situation, a result of an inadequate consideration of *kairos*. The primacy of identity generates such fallacies too often.

Michael Leff may provide a good definition of *kairos* in his talk at the University of Windsor in 2009. Although he does not actually use the term *kairos*, he is clearly defining it when he speaks of "civic humanistic rhetoric" and the pedagogical considerations of teaching it:

> To teach rhetoric within this perspective invites attention to the situated character of discourse and to the way that the context of particular situations limit and enable discursive performance. The context is a complex, interconnected network of circumstances that may be conceived in different ways generally and always assumes a different and unique configuration in each case, but normally includes recognition of the time, place, and occasion, the issues and subjects under consideration, the persona of the rhetor, the composition and the character of the audience, and the presence of opposing rhetors and attitudes. Operating within this matrix of contingent circumstances, the rhetor seeks to adapt the discourse to its end, and the end is connected somehow with influencing the audience. The goal of the teacher of rhetoric is to help the student develop the capacity to speak effectively as the situation demands.[12]

The last sentence will be relevant to discussions of anti-racist pedagogy in chapters 3 and 4. For now, perhaps the most salient aspect of Leff's description is that it is mentioned in regard to the teaching of "civic humanistic rhetoric," which he describes as "an educational program that nurtures the student's capacity (*facultas*) to use discourse appropriately—to size up the situation accurately and to discover, use, and combine the argumentative and linguistic strategies best suited to meet the demands of the situation."[13] A primacy of identity has little concern for the civic humanistic charge in pedagogy, scholarship, or academic discourse, as I hope to show throughout this book.

Civic humanistic rhetoric may emphasize *kairos,* as most rhetorics do, but it is not the only philosophical vantage point to support *kairos'* importance. *Kairos*, as it will be used in this book, is a concept comparable to mindfulness studies and Buddhist conceptions of the confluence of rhetoric and ontology.[14] All aspects of environment must go into choices in communication and interpretation. Often, those working from a primacy of identity are atemporal in their communication. For example, a white male speaking authoritatively is coupled with images of white males in past situations using their positions to demean or ignore the issues of nonwhite, non-male Others. A consideration of *kairos*, the particulars of a present environment, from human agents to ecology, may render a different interpretation. This understanding of *kairos* is often missing within a primacy of identity ideology.

Discouraging the critique of a person deemed a minority or a "victim" in some capacity. Clearly, this is a corollary of the above components but is still worth addressing on its own. When discussing lived experience, I was focusing on a more interpersonal mode of communication (i.e., department meetings, conferences). Now, I want to speak to the apparent infallibility of scholarship focused on identity or marginalized bodies written by the corresponding identities or bodies. Any text on the black experience by a black author, for example, is beyond reproach from whites and blacks, alike. So, this component is more about the dearth of open-minded academic intertextuality in which an identity-based text is questioned or critiqued by others. It is seen as a kind of bullying to engage academically with such texts in any ways short of praise.

Yes, critiques of this nature do happen, but the authors of those critiques often pay in some way. They are met with social media mobbing, threats to job security, and, too often, threats of physical violence. These "dissenters" are often silenced by students and scholars who force their respective institutions to cancel speaking events. This particular mode of anti-intellectualism is an effect of the primacy of identity, the focusing on the prevalence of identity over any other aspects of academia, including critical inquiry and debate. To be clear, this behavior springs forth from both sides of the political aisle,[15] and both sides see themselves as victims in one way or another. (More on that below.)

tradition. Postmodernism and poststructuralism are inherently antiessentialist, as is Buddhist philosophy which, as I will address a bit in this book's conclusion, is an oft-cited viewpoint for anti-racist initiatives toward the decolonization of the academy and the classroom. Like its aversion to critical inquiry, the primacy of identity ignores the unsavory aspects of these theoretical approaches—that is, the aspects that weaken its legitimacy—in an attempt to close itself off from social and material reality. Karen Kopelson, when talking about similar phenomena in Queer theory, may say that the primacy of identity performs a "disintegration of coherence" and an "especially pointed assault on any notions of *the real*."[18]

Similar sentiments have been expressed in contexts beyond rhetoric and composition, and even the United States at large. What I call the primacy of identity is similar to Gregory Fernando Pappas' 3-point description of flawed decolonialism (as opposed to decolonialism done right). In summarizing Luis Villoro's critique of decolonial activism, Pappas describes this flawed decolonialism thus:

(1) If you do not share the same beliefs or theory of domination as I do, then you are not one of us (against domination) or should be subjected to suspicion.
(2) If your philosophy is not explicitly political and about what we believe is the cause of domination, then it is not a philosophy that works on behalf of liberation.
(3) Only those that interpret the set of beliefs (that ground our movement) correctly, usually intellectual leaders, can direct the movement of resistance; and those that question the beliefs are heretics; and inauthentic philosophers.[19]

One can see the primacy of identity in Pappas' words; a fundamental narcissism is at play here. Pappas also identifies a universal mistrust of anything white and anything nonhegemonic is lauded:

* Modernity and Liberalism was and is totally bad (it is an ideology to dominate, colonize, oppress) or only it has a darker side.
* Eurocentrism (interpretation, standpoint) is bad; but philosophy from the periphery is good.
* Western concepts have been used to distort or occlude indigenous (non-Western) ones therefore all or most Western concepts distort, contaminate, or are tools of domination.
* Western epistemologies are imperialistic; the epistemologies of each of the colonialized regions are good.[20]

Despite the similarities between my concept of the primacy of identity and Villoro's (through Pappas) critique of decolonialism, especially with narcissism and essentialism, I render my own take on this to emphasize the mistreatment of rhetoric in the field of rhetoric and composition and to highlight the manifestations of lived experience, victimhood, and prefiguration that are implied but not centralized in Pappas' work. I present Pappas' work to show that the primacy of identity is nothing new nor particular to rhetoric and composition and that I am not alone in my assessment of anti-racism and decolonialist initiatives and methodologies.

This primacy of identity is the cause that leads to detrimental and counterproductive effects. Within a narrative driven by a primacy of identity, one's identity, particularly a marginalized identity, is all the ethos one needs. Any opposition to such a person's ideas is taken as an ad hominem attack, a kind of bullying. Because critique or inquiry of such a person is considered anathema, a lack of accountability from this person is seen as a symbolic gesture of empowerment. When this happens, "Because I said so" is an acceptable response to any academic inquiry or request for elaboration, especially if that inquiry or request comes from a white body. For example, a white person's inquiry or critique of a black person speaking on black issues is considered wildly out of bounds.

This silencing of traditionally hegemonic voices is seen as a move toward minority empowerment. However, an opposite, disempowering effect takes place. Allowing traditionally marginalized groups to forego intellectual accountability and well-reasoned responses to inquiry simply by virtue of being marginalized groups is not only an act of disempowerment; it is really infantilization. A member of a traditionally marginalized group is allowed to base arguments solely on lived experience and prefiguration (more on that later) while "the real grown-ups" have to actually put some arguments together. This is strongly reflected in the current demonization of critical thinking in anti-racist pedagogy.[21] Understanding and respecting the standpoints of others is a necessary endeavor, but as Henry Louis Gates, Jr., writes: "To treat black people as if they're helpless rag dolls swept up and buffeted by vast social trends—as if they had no say in the shaping of their lives—is a supreme act of condescension."[22] I prefer the term "infantilization" over "condenscension" because the assumptions of helplessness, fragility, and coddling are too salient features.

The primacy of identity is meant to provide validation and security to the traditionally marginalized. The dire need for validation and security among many marginalized circles in academia has prompted an infamous dismissal of critical thought and a refusal to acknowledge the civic and professional realities of the world. Victimhood and subjective experience provide the ethos to speak on certain issues and make certain demands; an argument is considered a weak alternative to the claim that one's experiences and injuries provide all necessary authority. To those who embrace this primacy of identity, ethos driven by victimhood provides them with a voice where they didn't have one, or an argument where they could not make one. Many people who feel marginalized and powerless in society are in need of a validating and dignifying narrative. A narrative driven by the primacy of identity provides that.

So, the primacy of identity is meant to provide agency and empowerment to those who have lacked it, traditionally. However, the provision of agency and empowerment often come off as more symbolic or contrived than actual and authentic. That is, many who embrace the primacy of identity partake in a *performance* of agency and empowerment, dubbed "prefigurative politics" by many activists and/or scholars. Prefigurative politics can be described as a politics "that seeks to demonstrate the 'better world' it envisions for the future in the actions it takes today."[23] Prefigurative politics works at "building a new society in the shell of the old"[24] and, ideally, "a strategic commitment to developing revolutionary organizations that embody the structures of deliberation and decision-making that a post-capitalist society is to contain."[25] On the surface, prefigurative politics seems to make sense; one should practice what one preaches and condition oneself for what one is simultaneously trying to develop.

Unfortunately, manifestations of prefigurative politics stop short of the aforementioned descriptions in too many contemporary activist and academic circles. According to Jonathan Smucker, author of *Hegemony How-To: A Roadmap for Radicals*, and director of *Beyond the Choir*, a non-partisan political organization, prefigurative politics often stops with the performance of a better world, harboring no real desire to develop strategies that would actually bring that world to fruition. In major activist initiatives, "prefigurative rituals came to *stand in for strategy*" for many activists.[26] Ultimately, "the prefigurative politics tendency confused process, tactics, and self-expression with political content and was often ambivalent about strategic questions" displaying "an inability or disinterest in engaging questions of political strategy."[27]

Indeed, the aforementioned inability or disinterest seems to be the salient aspect of many versions of prefigurative politics. Paul Raekstad, a research fellow at the University of Amsterdam, cites a certain kind of prefigurative politics as "problematically unstrategic in nature."[28] Distinguishing *unstrategic* prefigurative politics from more practical and effective *strategic* prefigurative politics, Raekstad says that the former, especially in the US, was a result of the "shifting emphasis from the structure of revolutionary organization to modes of life and culture, coupled with moving away from participating in such organizations."[29] In other words, to many prefigurative activists, the mere performance of change became the entirety of the movement. The manifestation of prefigurative politics lamented by Smucker and Raekstad, the kind that favors performance over substance, produces spaces in activist and academic circles that serve as incubators for narratives based on the primacy of identity. Thus, for the sake of clarity, the term "prefigurative politics" will, henceforth, denote the unstrategic, performance-based version of the term.

Prefiguration and the primacy of identity go hand in hand. Both ignore concrete concerns in order to focus on a dream. A prefigurative space performs a world where marginal identities are so empowered they need not engage in dialogue with hegemonic identities. A prefigurative space is one in which the primacy of identity can play out without anyone being reminded that the ways of the world suggest different strategies for actually improving the lives of its citizens. Prefigurative politics and the primacy of identity let us pretend we either have made more headway than we actually have or less headway than we actually have (due to oppressive forces), and prompt us to label those who point out these instances of prefiguration as tyrannical, oppressive, discriminatory, or traitorous.

In the introduction, I spoke of Smucker's and Diane Coole's and Samantha Frost's "allergy" metaphor used to articulate identity politics' neglect of social and material realities succinctly. The proponents of identity politics seem to be suffering from this "allergy" and take part in a prefigurative politics that serves as an almost ludic stand-in for the "investigation" or "material processes and structures" that are truly needed. Smucker, again, laments this tendency among those claiming to fight for social justice: "The same way a stained glass window depicts a static story at the cost of preventing parishioners from seeing outside, our narrative filter prevented us from accurately assessing reality."[30] And let us extend this metaphor to reiterate the faux empowerment taking place within a primacy of identity: the aforementioned glass is stained with a perspective stemming from a place of disempowerment.

To recap, identity politics, which can be defined as "political arguments emanating from the self-interested perspectives of self-identified societal interest groups,"[31] originated as a radical call to social and economic equality at times when policies were adamantly opposed to such things in the name of capitalism and hegemonic (straight, white, male) supremacy.[32] Embracing identity, per se, is not inherently problematic; group esteem and speaking truth to power are important endeavors for implementing changes toward social justice, as exemplified by the Combahee River Collective, whose identity politics derived from the need for black feminist lesbians to deal with the particularities of their own issues while simultaneously working with others for social justice. They had specific plans, featuring the critique and attack of capitalism, which, they believed, was the impetus for the racism and sexism from which they suffered.

Presently, however, the primacy of identity—the contemporary bastardization of the original concept of identity politics—is about protest for its own sake, "showing up and showing out," self-righteous indignation, displays of anger, and relentless individualism.[33] The primacy of identity is a performance based less on reality and more on abstractions of victimhood.[34] In essence, its proponents define themselves by their injuries and apparent enemies. This description falls in line with the components of the primacy of identity I laid out earlier. The aforementioned "showing up and showing out" could be defined as a display of true prefiguration, but too often, is the bastardized version of prefiguration that denotes mere performance.

Even some students recognize the inefficacy of prefiguration. Eboo Patel, in "Chicago's New Black Lesbian Mayor and the Power/Privilege/Oppression Paradigm," writes about what students share with him regarding social justice initiatives in general:

> I visit about 25 campuses a year, and increasingly I see situations where students know exactly which character to play when they step into the theater of 'the diversity program'. People of color talk about how oppressed they are, everyone else nods along sympathetically.
>
> But many students are smart and honest enough to know that *this is chiefly a performance*—everyone is playing a part, including the professional leading the program.... They worry whether a paradigm that was supposedly designed to advance them is having its intended effects.[35]

These students are aware of their situation: a prefigurative politics sans strategic and pragmatic planning that can actually get things done. The prefigurative performance of empowerment is the means *and* the end of their diversity programs.

I want to be clear that identity politics and prefiguration are not fundamentally detrimental. It is their contemporary manifestations in many activist and academic circles that are problematic. So, we should not throw the baby out with the bathwater. According to Kwame Anthony Appiah, those who embrace marginalized identities as important but not omnipotent treat marginalizations "not as sources of limitation and insult but as valuable parts of who they are."[36] Appiah elaborates:

> And since a modern ethics of authenticity (which goes back, roughly, to Romanticism) requires us to express who we centrally are, they move, next, to demanding society recognize them as women, homosexuals, blacks, and Catholics, and do the cultural work necessary to resist the stereotypes, to challenge the insults, to lift the restrictions. Since these old restrictions suggested substantially negative norms of identification, constructing a life with dignity entails developing positive norms of identification instead.[37]

This sentiment is both understandable and very important. Destigmatizing one's own identity is imperative if one plans to fight for the rights of that identity. Recognition as a demand for respect and dignity is a necessary first step in social justice endeavors.

However, proponents of the primacy of identity began to treat the step of recognition as the only step. The Combahee River Collective, for instance, recognized the need to advocate for themselves in no uncertain terms, but the end goal was political and social change that would benefit everyone. Recognition for its own sake, however, has become the primary goal. Again, Appiah articulates this well. While acknowledging recognition as a powerful tactic, he writes:

> But it's important to see that, while members of groups that have experienced historical exclusion, contempt, or obloquy may indeed need new social practices in order to flourish, what they are seeking is not always recognition. When blacks and women in the United States campaigned for the vote, they did so very often as blacks and as women. But they weren't asking for recognition of their identity; they were asking, precisely, for the vote. *Participation of this sort may presuppose a minimal sense of recognition, but it entails a good deal more.* Similarly, when the lesbian and gay movement in the United States pursues recognition, it does so by asking for rights—to serve in the military, to marry—that would be worth having even if they came without recognition. So not all political claims made in the name of a group identity are primarily claims for recognition.[38] (My emphasis)

Recognition as a starting point is ideal. As an endpoint, however, it misses the point. Such a demand for recognition does harm to the supposed desire for actual change because it demands—of both members of a specific marginalized group and those they address—that identity must subordinate strategy, pragmatic thought, and critical thinking.[39] Far from the ideology of the Combahee River Collective, a primacy of identity is less about practicality and progress, if about them at all.

Beyond Appiah's acknowledgment of an extreme politics of recognition as the culprit, three other reasons—perhaps subcategories of a politics of recognition—are apparent. First, the currency of prefigurative politics driven by a primacy of identity, as opposed to strategic or tactical politics, is not just about the aggrandizement of identity but, by extension, the achievement and usurpation of the moral high ground. Politics toward real change are skirted if acknowledged at all. So, the "ends" of prefiguration and the primacy of identity are at issue, and the focus on morality has overshadowed and, in some cases, eradicated the need for critical thinking and concrete progress. Second, victimhood is seen as a virtue in the primacy of identity. It is such a virtue that critical thought and social/material realities are powerless against it. For this reason, identity—especially a traditionally downtrodden identity—overpowers critical thinking and empirical information. Lastly, the primacy of identity is unapologetically narcissistic from either a group or individual standpoint. That is, what matters beyond anything else is one's embrace of the constitutive rules of a particular identity and/or the embrace of one's injured self or potentially injured self. Even ideas and strategies that could prevent further injury are thwarted, for attention to group or self is the goal, thus creating another form of oppression, this time self-imposed.[40] All three reasons derive from the fact that prefigurative politics and the primacy of identity, like other things, are ideologically, narratively driven. Abstraction, not progressive strategies based on the concrete social and material realities, are the driving forces.

Smucker attributes the aforementioned issues to the primacy of identity (although he never uses that term) when trying to make sense of his fellow activists' spending too much time debating word choice in their group mission statement. Smucker writes about the moment it dawned on him that an overemphasis on identity was the issue:

> The mission statement was contentious because it was an expression of our *identity*. It was about who we were as people—what we stood for and believed and how we expressed ourselves—much more than it was about our instrumental purpose and political goals as mobilization. Our debate about the mission statement was qualitatively different than navigating and negotiating legitimate disagreements over political goals or strategies and tactics for their achievement. This was about how we conceived ourselves and projected our identities. That made compromise very difficult.[41]

In Smucker's experience, rhetorics of identity overpowered rhetorics of civic engagement and progressive activism. Furthermore, rhetorics of identity overpowered any tactical concerns, for, according to Smucker, "It felt as if *having the right line* about everything was more important than *making measurable progress* on anything."[42]

If the primary goals of a movement are the heavily narcissistic ideas of validation and redemption over concrete social and political progress, the primacy of identity makes sense. Thus, much rhetoric within a discourse shaped by this primacy is pathos-oriented, epideictic, and, at best, forensic. Deliberative rhetoric, the rhetoric most needed to change policies, norms, and actions, is wildly underrepresented or done in ways that involve logos "only insofar as it is in the vested interest of the thinker to do so."[43] As said earlier, this is because the goals of the primacy of identity are often performative. The point is to perform the role of the victim demanding empowerment and speaking truth to hegemonic power. The protagonists in this narrative are driven not to make concrete progress but to show their injured identities, their victimhood, and their righteousness in ways that shock hegemonic figures into feelings of remorse, guilt, and placation.

The partnership of prefigurative politics and the primacy of identity becomes clear. The primacy of identity's biggest result is the construction of discourse communities in which the performance of an inverted hierarchy or an equanimity of power is enough. Those who abide by the primacy of identity—marginalized people and their hegemonic "accomplices" as well as those who feel power has been unfairly taken from them—come together to act out and practice the equality and reckoning they preach. But when the mere performance of these things are enough, the primacy of identity conflates with prefigurative politics.

Smucker writes about why the Occupy movement ultimately failed in America. Its politics were too prefigurative. The Occupiers had no strategically sound plan for making the world outside the bubble of the Occupy camps into their idea of a better world. All was good within this bubble, but the outside world had not gone away, and for many Occupiers, the bubble was all they needed. Smucker sees this satisfaction with in-group performance as a major problem in activist circles. As Mark Lilla puts it, "we are a republic, not a campsite."[44]

Slavoj Zizek makes a similar statement in the form of a warning. In *The Year of Dreaming Dangerously,* a book that analyzes social justice movements around the world, Zizek writes, specifically regarding the Occupy Wall Street participants, "one of the great dangers the protestors face: the danger that they will fall in love with themselves, with the fun they are having in the 'occupied' zones."[45] Zizek continues: "But carnivals come cheap—the true test of their worth is what happens the day after, how our everyday life has changed or is to be changed. This requires difficult and patient work—of which the protests are the beginning, not the end."[46] Lastly, and perhaps most harshly, Zizek writes that we should "avoid the temptation simply to admire the sublime beauty of uprisings that are doomed to fail."[47] The primacy of identity and its animation through prefiguration can be understood as a "falling in love" with oneself and an admiration of the sacred victimhood to the neglect of sound planning. Self-admiration is not inherently bad; even Zizek suggests that it is a necessary action in the beginning, but admiration to the neglect of the difficult, patient, and necessary work—the work that acknowledges social and material reality as opposed to ideological performance—works against the formulation of strategies that can truly affect change. (This will be more apparent when we address empowerment theory in the next chapter.)

The primacy of identity has become an executive ideology in academia quickened by prefigurative politics. From classrooms to conferences, academics teach and act out ideologies in spaces that are "largely detached socially and geographically from the rest of the country."[48] Academics have romanticized education and themselves as a saving grace against the harsh realities of a world they refuse to acknowledge directly. They work to send students out into this world equipped to handle the prefigurative space in which they were educated, not the realities of the civic and professional spaces they are entering. Students even move from discipline to discipline assuming that the lessons learned from prefigurative courses in the humanities will translate to more empirically oriented—or at least significantly less prefigurative—spaces in the social sciences and other disciplines.

Lilla addresses the prefigurative politics of academia in *The Once and Future Liberal*, claiming that such politics have replaced the faded ambitions of real change based on real life. Campuses and campus towns become a model of a desired world, not a place to work out political strategies to apply to the world at large.[49] Lilla suggests that such a stance on politics is less about strategies, tactics, and real change and more about meaning, which is usually oriented to a particular identity or intersection of identities.[50] The fact that the reciprocal relationship between prefiguration and the primacy of identity leads to an idiosyncratic and narcissistic take on meaningful politics alludes to Zizek's warning. Lilla even crafts a hypothetical narrative about some college environments and the effects of prefiguration and the primacy of identity on college students.

> Imagine a young student entering such an environment today—not your average student pursuing a career, but a recognizable campus type drawn to political questions. She is at the age when the quest for meaning begins and in a place where her curiosity could be directed outward toward the larger world she will have to find a place in. Instead, she finds that she is being encouraged to plumb mainly herself, *which seems an easier exercise.* (Little does she know. . . .) She will first be taught that understanding herself depends on exploring the different aspects of her identity, something she now discovers she has. An identity which, she also learns, has already been largely shaped for her by various social and political forces. *This is an important lesson, from which she is likely to draw conclusions that the aim of education is not to progressively become a self throughout engagement with the wider world. Rather, one engages with the world and particularly politics for the limited aim of understanding and affirming what one already is.*[51] (Emphases mine)

Lilla's hypothetical student enters into and is shaped by a prefigurative space that blinds her to the larger world and encourages a primacy of identity detached from any concern for societal progress outside of herself. We see how prefiguration and a primacy of identity do a dance in which each is both the cause and the effect of the other.

So, as a college professor, I would be part of the problem if I were to forego any acknowledgment of academic circles as prefigurative spaces and the connection between social and academic manifestations of the primacy of identity. In his article "Higher Education is Drowning in BS: And It's Morally Corrosive to Society," Christian Smith laments the pipeline of "BS" (bullshit) from academia to society at large. He begins his essay writing that "the accumulated effects of all the academic BS are contributing to this country's disastrous political condition and, ultimately, putting at risk the very viability and character of decent civilization."[52] He ends this essay by writing, "As the mounds of BS continue to pile up, the more immediate question is just how much waste, idiocy, and destruction inside and (as a result) outside the academy we will all have to suffer in the meantime."[53] From Smith, one can infer that the effects of the primacy of identity and prefiguration in academia can serve as a didactic microcosm of its societal effects.

Ultimately, regarding both academic and nonacademic spaces, my argument is that those who abide by the primacy of identity believe that creating a terministic screen, or "narrative filter" based on victim validation—which includes moral high ground, narcissism, and vested critical thinking—will provide a prefigurative space where identity-based groups are given a less arduous path toward group esteem and the semblance of societal success, but not much else. What's more, any critical thinking based on acknowledging social and material realities or pragmatic action must be strategically shunned by "primary identities," as it were, to perpetuate the narrative.

Perhaps the biggest problem with the primacy of identity is its role as an extremely effective distraction from the subjects that need to be broached and the actions that need to be made. Class warfare and the detrimental effects of capitalism seem a cause—at least an antecedent—of many of the problems that produce social injustice, especially as it pertains to individual and group rights. Both in society and in academia, we perform the resolution of these issues. This performance, this prefiguration, seems to be a defense mechanism against one's own powerlessness. That is, when one cannot reach the goal that is needed, one embraces the goal one can achieve and pretends that this goal is a panacea. The low-hanging fruit of performance is glamorized. Acts of prefiguration, which are all some people feel they have, are treated as powerful counterattacks to hegemony. The primacy of identity is a game of make-believe, and both society and academia produce sandboxes in which the "kids" can play. Referencing Zizek, these proponents of the primacy of identity have done worse than falling in love with themselves; they have convinced themselves that their performances, their games of make-believe, are real.

THE SACRED VICTIM: AN ETHOPOEIA

The primacy of identity creates a narrative of victimhood. Seemingly, this narrative is the victim's quest toward triumph, but the narrative's status as a bildungsroman of sorts is thwarted by the fact that the victim never achieves triumph because actual triumph was never the real intention in the first place. Paradoxically, the primacy of identity thrives off a politics of injury that perpetuates victimhood itself as the triumph. What's more, the "hero's journey" is replaced by the victim's usurpation of a space (e.g., an academic field) as a comforting home geared specifically to the victim's identity and ideology. The protagonist of this narrative, what some scholars have called the "sacred victim" finds the most value in the perpetual struggle itself; overcoming victimhood isn't the primary telos, if it is one at all; this is no bildungsroman.

The religiously oriented term, "sacred victim," derives from the evangelical tone of much identity-based activism in America. Lilla compares the surge of the primacy of identity (what he and most others call "identity politics" in its contemporary, post-Combahee River Collective, manifestations) in the last few decades to a religious awakening, saying that its rhetorics "sound evangelical rather than political," and that many tactics associated with the primacy of identity, especially those that have to do with the policing of speech, "have their precedents in American revivalist religion."[54] I believe this evangelical rhetoric is worth discussing.

The religiosity of much of the anti-racism movement may not come as a surprise. The "ethical efficacy" of couching ideals, missions, and goals in religious rhetoric is nothing new.[55] For anti-racist initiatives and other initiatives throughout the social justice movement, this ethical efficacy has been fashioned into a narrative. This is akin to Plato's "noble lie" but closer to DanDennet's "intentional strategy," rendered by Kwame Anthony Appiah as "[t]he strategy of prediction—the strategy we use to make sense of the behavior of all the things we can usefully treat as intentional systems," which works "to apply an idealized model, knowing that, because it *is* idealized, it won't always get things right," but may work "well enough for practical purposes."[56] The problem with the sacred victim narrative is that it jettisons the acknowledgment that it is not a perfect idealization. It is seen as infallible and universal. It is a narrative that neither can nor should apply to everything, but it is still taken as, well, sacred. Within the sacred victim narrative, roles have to be played, roles that, according to the drivers of the narrative, have a collective and synergistic purpose in bringing on a desired outcome. Within this narrative, the sacred victim is a driving force, whose own ethical efficacy is seen as the key to achieving anti-racist goals.

The sacred victim, the collective personification of nonhegemonic forces, is justified in an initial status as an injured party, but injury has gone from a predicament to a strategy. A perpetual victim expects perpetual recompense and, as is often the case, the perpetual guilt of hegemonic forces cast as the perpetrators. The victims are thus recognized, but they are validated as heroic victims. Victimhood is a lionization of sorts.

Extending the metaphor of the sacred victim may better display the religious nature of this narrative and the sanctity of its collective protagonist. The sacred victim cannot be questioned, challenged, or engaged with civil debate; to do so is tantamount to sacrilege. His or her victimhood is all the argument needed. No critical thinking is necessary, and the guilt and genuflection from hegemonic others is the proper mode of worship. Information that would end the downtrodden and unfortunate status of the victim is often shunned as sin or interpreted as a more covert and insidious oppression.

This leads to "virtue signaling," a tendency to display one's repentance through a kind of religious self-flagellation. John McWhorter extends the religious metaphor in "The Virtue Signalers Won't Change the World" when discussing the actions of contemporary proponents of the primacy of identity or what he calls the "third wave" of civil rights activism:

> The idea that whites are permanently stained by their white privilege, gaining moral absolution only by eternally attesting to it, is the third wave's version of original sin. The idea of a someday when America will "come to terms with race" is as vaguely specified a guidepost as Judgment Day. Explorations as to whether an opinion is "problematic" are equivalent to explorations of that which may be blasphemous. The social mauling of the person with "problematic" thoughts parallels the excommunication of the heretic. What is called "virtue signaling," then, channels the impulse that might lead a Christian to an aggressive display of her faith in Jesus. There is even a certain Church Lady air to much of the patrolling on race these days, an almost performative joy in dog-piling on the transgressor, which under a religious analysis is perfectly predictable.[57]

The theme of eternal repentance is decidedly ineffective and toxic for those inside and outside of hegemony; it perpetuates an embodied essentialism, a typecasting of raced bodies in premade and strategic roles. The focus on the primacy of identity has distinguished the "hero" identity (the marginalized) from the villainous one (the hegemonic), and the latter must announce his sins indefinitely to gain forgiveness. This is the cult of the sacred victim.

Prefiguration's origin in religious contexts (e.g., John the Baptist prefigured Christ) is no real coincidence. Prefigurative politics says, to use a hackneyed movie line, "If you build it, they will come." Regarding its religious origins, prefiguration denotes an inevitable future resonated backward in time and reflected in contemporary actions of the righteous.[58] That is, prefiguration, itself, derives from a sacred framing of time. For our purposes, prefigurative politics should be understood as a ritualistic acting out of the world we want so that it finally comes to fruition. Max Weber would call prefiguration of this sort the "ethics of intention," (also translated as the ethics of ultimate ends) in which concrete and productive consequences are shunned in the name of simply doing the "right" things. Comparing activist ethics to the moral absolutism of the Sermon on the Mount, Weber writes of an archetypal political activist with this religious zeal for social justice:

> The man who bases his ethics on intentions feels that he is 'responsible' only for seeing that the flame of pure intention, the flame of protest against the injustice of the social order, is not extinguished. The aim of his actions, which, considered from the point of view of its possible consequences, is totally irrational, is to keep fanning the flame; the action can and should have only the value of an example.[59]

Weber's activist is into action for its own sake. The social or political consequences, even if given lip service, are really of no consequence to him or her; it is the performance that counts. Many academics have settled for the prefiguration, having grown satisfied with the world constructed in the bubble of a particular field, campus, or even department.

McWhorter sees the connection between prefiguration and the sacred victim narrative, although he does not use the term "prefiguration":

> Antiracism as a religion, despite its good intentions, distracts us from activism in favor of a kind of charismatic passivism. One is to think, to worship, to foster humility, to conceive of our lives as mere rehearsal for a glorious finale, and to encourage others to do the same. This kind of thinking may have its place in a human society. But helping black people succeed in the only real world we will ever know is not that place.

The performance of prefiguration can be construed as a "charismatic passivism" in which nothing real gets done because the "real" is ignored. The term "slacktivism" comes to mind; rituals like acknowledging white privilege or considering anti-racist texts written by people of color as inherently infallible takes the place of real strategies for making change. Genuflection is all that is needed to expiate white guilt and dignify the marginalized.

Like strategic and pragmatic planning, critical inquiry is also missing. Academia's distinct habitus encourages the sacred victim while simultaneously being affected by it; it has made academia less academic. In academic circles, the sacred victim's status as victim is the most significant research needed. This status allows one to determine what topics can and cannot be broached. This status insists on being centralized and prioritized in circles in which those of hegemonic status are the majority. Critical thinking is subordinate to sacred victimhood if it is accepted at all; logic and reason are secular and base in comparison. This narrative has lowered the epistemic standards of academia, truncated critical thinking to laud the sacred victim. Inquiries that call the legitimacy of the sacred victim into question are not allowed and are punished through silencing and even excommunication.

Again, scholarship that pushes the sacred victim is considered infallible and dogmatic, much like actual religious texts. I am often accused of having not read anti-racist scholarship when I speak out about the inefficacy of some anti-racist initiatives. The fact that I read the scholarship but simply was not convinced never crosses my accusers' minds. These anti-racism proponents, the parishioners of the cult of the sacred victim, cannot go against "the Word." How can any kind of intertextual critique, a common and necessary aspect of academic discourse and open inquiry, exist when certain texts are deemed untouchable?

Some construe academic disciplines in the humanities as sects especially dedicated to the consecration of the sacred victim. Within these disciplines, all is predicated on uplifting—but not necessarily empowering—the sacred victim, for true empowerment would significantly weaken any identification as a victim. In this context, to empower the sacred victim is to desecrate the sacred victim. To atone for past sins, academics seen as beneficiaries of societal privilege, even if they are allies of minority causes, must see the sacred victim as perfect and pure in her/his/their victimhood.

This extended and admittedly dramatic metaphor is meant to take a more and more common term, the "sacred victim," and emphasize its metonymical relationship to dogmatic belief systems in which dissent—that is, speaking against sacred images and ideals—is demonized. The sacred victim narrative works against any ideas of practical, tactical strategies toward empowerment that may come with acquiring tools that will most likely come in handy in civic and professional contexts. It works against ideas that open dialectic, a bastion of democracy, is a societal good.

THE VICTIM AS RIGHTFUL KING

I would be remiss to not acknowledge that, although the primacy of identity is mostly associated with minority groups, it manifests in hegemonic contexts, as well. The Alt-Right and the Incel movements, peopled mostly, if not entirely, by white males, house apparent victims that have been deprived of their birthright. They are the "rightful kings" that have had their crowns usurped by lesser characters. Like Odysseus, they are lost in a sea of diverse and multicultural happenings while, at home, lesser suitors try to take what is theirs.

In this narrative, the victim has been "left behind." He or she has been deprived of the advantages of gainful employment, attractiveness, and clout by those less deserving. He or she has been all but ignored by women, who neglect their place as damsels in order to "steal" societal prowess, if not assist or join the usurpers. He or she desires a reckoning in the form of societal recognition of his or her prowess and the willful submission of those he or she deems inferior: the current usurpers of his or her crown.

This victim is of noble blood, but, in his has been exiled to the margins. His rightful claim to authority is replaced by the wants and desires of those less pure and less virtuous. This victim's erasure is the ultimate transgression that has gone unpunished by those ignorant of the erasure and its dastardly motivation. This victim must make a stand, against diversity, against women's rights, against the #metoo movement, against African American literature, and so on. Right makes might, and the rightful heir to the hegemonic throne is always right.

Although I find it important to acknowledge the other prominent narrative in identity politics, the "rightful king" narrative, I will focus on the sacred victim narrative most prominently in this work. I have two reasons for this. First, as a proponent of civic engagement and an academic, I have more at stake with the sacred victim narrative than I do with the rightful king narrative, although some of my thoughts on the primacy of identity are informed by the intents of the latter narrative. Indeed, as I will relay in this book, my negative experience as a WPA of color can be attributed to a version of the rightful king narrative. However, my goal for this book is not to combat that narrative, but to rescue anti-racism from the sacred victim narrative. Secondly, unlike the rightful king narrative, in which its protagonists want to re-acquire power they have apparently lost, thus doing harm to the Other while uplifting themselves, the protagonists of the sacred victim narrative are doing harm to *themselves* by taking refuge in a prefigurative politics instead of working to actually instill beneficial change. These reasons make for a substantial focus on the sacred victim over the rightful king.

With this goal in mind, I want to parse out a detailed understanding of empowerment. The next chapter will not only define empowerment, but will also elaborate on its inherent necessity in a field like rhetoric and composition and, especially, the anti-racist endeavors therein. Empowerment is not only a necessary foundation for addressing inequality and injustice; it is imperative to effective and productive communication and actual change.

NOTES

1. Mark Lilla, *The Once and Future Liberal: After Identity Politics* (New York: Harper Collins, 2017), 102. E-book.
2. Combahee River Collective, "Combahee River Collective Statement," *Available Means: An Anthology of Women's Rhetorics* (Pittsburgh: University of Pittsburgh Press, 2001).
3. Demita Frazier, "Rethinking Identity Politics: An Interview with Demita Frazier," Interview by Karen Kahn. *Sojourner: The Women's Forum* 21.1 (1995), 12.
4. Jacqueline Jones Royster, "When the First Voice You Hear Is Not Your Own," *College Composition and Communication* 47.1 (1996), 31.
5. Richard Haswell and Min-Zhan Lu, *Comp Tales: An Introduction to College Composition Through Its Stories* (New York: Longman, 2000).
6. Erec Smith, "Buddhism's Pedagogical Contribution to Mindfulness," *Journal of the Assembly for the Expanded Perspectives on Learning*, 21 (2016), 36–46.
7. Aristotle, *Aristotle on Rhetoric: A Theory of Civic Discourse*, Trans. George Kennedy in *The Rhetorical Tradition: Readings from Classical Times to the Present*, ed. Patricia Bizzell and Bruce Herzberg (New York: Bedford/St. Martin's Press, 2001), 181.
8. Steven Lynn, *Rhetoric and Composition: An Introduction* (New York: Cambridge University Press, 2010), 14.
9. Carol Lea Clark, *Praxis: A Brief Rhetoric*, 3rd ed. (Southlake, TX: Fountainhead Press, 2016), 14.
10. Like other theorists, I conflate the concept of *kairos* with *to prepon*, which is an attention to the appropriateness of place and audience. I take *to prepon* to be a tacit aspect of *kairos* and, therefore, will abide by the definition I put forth in this book.
11. Eric Charles White, *Kaironomia* (Ithaca, NY: Cornell University Press, 1987), 14.
12. Michael C. Leff, "What is Rhetoric?" in *Rethinking Rhetorical Theory, Criticism, and Pedagogy* (East Lansing, MI: Michigan State University, 2016), 476.
13. Leff, "What is Rhetoric?" 478.
14. Smith, "Buddhism's Pedagogical Contribution to Mindfulness."
15. Jarret T. Crawford and Jane M. Pilanski, "Political Intolerance, Right *and* Left," *Political Psychology* 35.6 (2014), 841–51.
16. Royster, "When the First Voice You Hear Is Not Your Own," 36–37.
17. Ibid., 37.
18. Karen Kopelson, "Dis/integrating the Gay/Queer Binary: 'Reconstructed Identity Politics' for a Performative Pedagogy," *College English* 65.1 (2002), 19.
19. Gregory Fernando Pappas, "The Limitations and Dangers of Decolonial Philosophies: Lessons from Zapatista Luis Villoro," Academia.edu, accessed 19 August 2019. https://tamu.academia.edu/gregorypappas.
20. Pappas, "The Limitations and Dangers of Decolonial Philosophies: Lessons from Zapatista Luis Villoro," 15–16.
21. Asao Inoue, "Afterward," in *Black Perspectives in Writing Program Administration: From the Margins to the Center* (Urbana, IL: NCTE 2019), 150.

The Primacy of essentialist notions of identity or an authentic/inauthentic dichotomy of identity based on embodiment. In the aforementioned Jacqueline Jones Royster essay, the author relays an incident with a well-meaning white coworker about linguistic authenticity. When doing a presentation, Royster decided to read a passage out loud, apparently rendering black characters in the vernacular and intonation intended by the author. Royster then describes an exchange with her white colleague after the presentation:

> One, very well-intentioned response to what I did that day was, "How wonderful it was that you were willing to share with us your 'authentic' voice!" I said, "My 'authentic' voice?" She said, "Oh yes! I've never heard you talk like that, you know, so relaxed. I mean, you're usually great, but this was really great! You weren't so formal. You didn't have to speak in an appropriated academic language. You sounded 'natural.' It was nice to hear you be yourself." I said, "Oh, I see. Yes, I do have a range of voices, and I take quite a bit of pleasure actually in being able to use any of them at will." Not understanding the point that I was trying to make gently, she said, "But this time, it was really you. Thank you."[16]

Royster goes on to express her frustration about the incident and incidents like it. After referencing a similar sentiment from bell hooks, Royster writes: "I claim all my voices as my own very much authentic voices, even when it's difficult for others to imagine a person like me having the capacity to do that."[17] Not only does Royster shirk an apparent expectation and "responsibility" to perform a certain kind of blackness, but she speaks against the common lore in rhetoric and composition that to acquire a secondary dialect, one has to relinquish a primary dialect. Many people of color can attest to the falsity of such a myth, but its staying power is formidable.

This incident speaks to a tendency and, as I will argue, a *need* for essentialized raced bodies, especially marginalized bodies. Within the primacy of identity, anti-racism perpetuates this phenomenon. White people and black people, alike, render black bodies as a collective identity that embraces oppositional culture, shares a language coded as "black," feels uncomfortable in spaces deemed "white," and suffers from a perpetual victimization.

Royster, just one person who has experienced a projection of identity, wrote that essay over twenty years ago, and the issue, per se, is even older than that. Yet, this essentialization of bodies is a necessity within a primacy of identity. In fact, refusing to take on the role seen as authentic to one's body is seen as scandalous by many. Skirting the role one has been cast to play in a preferred narrative of anti-racism or decolonization can be met with vitriol and attempts at ostracism by both people of color and their white allies.

Beyond the "no two snowflakes are alike" counterargument, essentialism of this kind is debunked philosophically in both Western and Eastern

22. Henry Louis Gates, Jr., "Breaking the Silence," *The New York Times*, 24 August 2004, accessed 17 July 2019. https://www.nytimes.com/2004/08/01/opinion/breaking-the-silence.html.

23. Jonathan Matthew Smucker, *Hegemony How-To: A Roadmap for Radicals* (Chico, CA: AK Press, 2017), 103.

24. Paul Raekstad, "Revolutionary Practice and Prefigurative Politics: A Clarification and Defense," *Constellations* (2017), 362. https://onlinelibrary.wiley.com/doi/epdf/10.1111/1467-8675.12319.

25. Raekstad, "Revolutionary Practice and Prefigurative Politics: A Clarification and Defense," 363.

26. Smucker, *Hegemony How-To*, 105.

27. Ibid., 112.

28. Raekstad, "Revolutionary Practice and Prefigurative Politics: A Clarification and Defense," 363.

29. Ibid, 362.

30. Smucker, *Hegemony How-To*, 30.

31. Howard J. Wiarda, *Political Culture, Political Science and Identity Politics: An Uneasy Alliance* (Farnham, Surrey: Ashgate, 2014), 148.

32. Combahee River Collective, "Combahee River Collective Statement," *Available Means: An Anthology of Women's Rhetorics*.

33. Asad Haider, *Mistaken Identity: Race and Class in the Age of Trump* (Brooklyn, NY: Verso Press, 2018), LOC 383–95. E-book.

34. Haider, *Mistaken Identity*, LOC 191.

35. "Chicago's New Black Lesbian Mayor and the Power/Privilege/Oppression Paradigm," *Inside Higher Ed*, 11 April 2019. https://www.insidehighered.com/blogs/conversations-diversity/chicago%E2%80%99s-new-black-lesbian-mayor-and-powerprivilegeoppression.

36. Kwame Anthony Appiah, "The Politics of Identity," *Daedalus* 135. 4 (2006): 20.

37. Appiah, "The Politics of Identity."

38. Ibid.

39. Ibid, 21.

40. Ibid.

41. Smucker, *Hegemony How-To*, 27–28.

42. Ibid., 28.

43. Richard Paul, *Critical Thinking: What Every Person Needs to Survive in a Rapidly Changing World* (Tomales, CA: The Foundation for Critical Thinking, 2012), 47.

44. Lilla, *The Once and Future Liberal*, LOC 136

45. Slavoj Zizek, *The Year of Dreaming Dangerously* (Brooklyn, NY: Verso Books, 2015), Loc 1390–95. E-book.

46. Zizek, *The Year of Dreaming Dangerously*, Loc 1395

47. Ibid., Loc 1412.

48. Lilla, *The Once and Future Liberal*, Loc 453.

49. Ibid., Loc 603–35.

50. Ibid., Loc 619–35.

51. Ibid., Loc 635–51.

52. Christian Smith, "Higher Education Is Drowning in BS," *Chronicle of Higher Education*. January 9, 2018, https://www.chronicle.com/article/Higher-Education-Is-Drowning/242195.

53. Smith, "Higher Education Is Drowning in BS."

54. Lilla, *The Once and Future Liberal*, Loc 883.

55. Anthony Appiah, *As If* (Cambridge, MA: Harvard University Press, 2017), 25.

56. Appiah, *As If*, 45.

57. John McWhorter, "Virtue Signalers Won't Change the World." December 23, 2018. https://www.theatlantic.com/ideas/archive/2018/12/why-third-wave-anti-racism-dead-end/578764/.

58. Uri Gordon, "Prefigurative Politics Between Ethical Practice and Absent Promise," *Political Studies,* 66.2 (2018): 521–37.

59. Max Weber, "Politics as a Vocation," in *Max Weber: Selections*, ed. W.G. Runciman (New York: Cambridge University Press, 1978), 218.

Chapter 2

So What is Empowerment?

So far, I have identified a devolution of identity politics I have called a primacy of identity and have given a general description of the "sacred-victim" narrative it seems to fuel. In the end, however, I attribute both phenomena to a fundamental lack of true empowerment. The power (e.g., senses of dignity, recognition, agency) achieved through a primacy of identity and the performance of the sacred victim narrative is really a disempowerment that, through the performances of prefigurative politics, is made to look like actual empowerment. In reality, the performance is a veritable game of make-believe that ignores social and material reality and does not effect progressive and beneficial change. In this chapter, I want to parse out why this is antithetical to real empowerment by explaining what I mean by "empowerment."

As you will see, my use of "empowerment" will synthesize standard empowerment theory with Emotional Intelligence. The two overlap substantially and could plausibly be synthesized with aspects of Stoicism, Buddhist philosophy, and rational emotive behavioral therapy.[1] However, for our purposes, a concentration on empowerment theory and Emotional Intelligence will do; Buddhism, will be touched on in the book's conclusion. For now, I will explain empowerment theory, show its implicit synthesis with Emotional Intelligence, and identify a rhetoric of empowerment that can benefit anti-racism initiatives in rhetoric and composition.

EMPOWERMENT THEORY

So, what is empowerment? "Some define it as a categorically individualistic and personal phenomenon, a depoliticized word, acceptable to 'people changers' but not to those who seek institutional change."[2] Throughout this work, however, empowerment will be discussed in the context of its theoretical use in disciplines like social science, social work, and psychology. I hope to take the initial steps toward a working rhetoric of empowerment. That is, I hope to show how empowerment theory can provide a terministic screen that is more beneficial to anti-racism in the field of rhetoric and composition, if not the humanities as a whole. I will argue here and throughout this book that "empowerment" should be as much of a god-term as "diversity" (if not more so) and one that should commingle with diversity for the most positive outcomes for all involved.

In current empowerment theory, empowerment is defined by psychologist Marc Zimmerman as "a process by which people, organizations, and communities gain mastery over issues of concern to them."[3] Empowerment "is a multilevel construct in which each level of analysis is interdependent with the others" and is typically at the "individual level of analysis."[4] This last description is worth emphasizing, especially since empowerment involves substantial communal interaction. At the end of the day, all this is about individuals. Whether individual students, instructors, scholars, administrators, or individual citizens, empowerment starts with the individual and, ideally, grows into collective experience and collective action, and "includes active engagement in one's community and an understanding of one's sociopolitical environment."[5] Empowerment needs a primary spot in this work because I argue that it is the executive concept for individual and social progress and, unfortunately, the missing component in current anti-racist initiatives in rhetoric and composition. Without it, the field inadvertently disempowers those it claims to care about the most: faculty and students.

Empowerment is both a process and an outcome. That is, empowerment includes both the means of acquiring power and agency and the production of things that can better ensure power and agency for individuals and/or communities.[6] As a process and outcome, empowerment is an imperative aspect of civic engagement and problem-based learning, which I will touch upon in the book's conclusion. For now, its manifestations in the field of rhetoric and composition is the primary subject.

Ultimately, empowerment consists of three main components[7] or levels.[8] Theorists label the components differently, but the meanings are consistent. For now, I will go with Zimmerman's labeling in "Psychological Empowerment: Issues and Illustrations."[9] According to Zimmerman, empowerment "is expected to include a sense of and motivation to control; decision-making and problem-solving skills, and critical awareness of one's sociopolitical environment; and participatory behaviors," labeled the "intrapersonal component," the "interactional component," and the "behavioral component," respectively.[10] All components have to actualize for true empowerment to take place. Zimmerman writes: "[T]hese three components of [empowerment] merge to form a picture of a person who believes that he or she has the capability to influence a given context (intrapersonal component) understands how the system works in that context (interactional component), and engages in behaviors to exert control in the context (behavioral component).... All three components must be measured to fully capture [empowerment]."[11] An exploration of each component in the context of rhetoric and composition[12] may illustrate my critique of anti-racist endeavors and my claim that, actually, they are exercises in disempowerment.[13]

The intrapersonal component of empowerment, the most subjective of the three components, arguably could be the most important for my critique of anti-racist initiatives in rhetoric and composition. It is defined most specifically as the component that "refers to how people think about themselves and includes domain-specific perceived control and self-efficacy, motivation to control, perceived competence, and mastery."[14] Zimmerman emphasizes the term "perceived" in his descriptions, stressing that the first step of empowerment is having the confidence, at least perceived confidence, that one can accomplish specific goals or can actually enact change. I believe some central tenets of anti-racist work in rhetoric and composition are a result of a lack of perceived confidence in our ability to make real change, thus falling back either on performative change or the silencing of supposed dissenters while having no real or practical plan for social or institutional progress. Zimmerman writes: "It is unlikely that individuals who do not believe that they have the capability to achieve goals would either learn about what it takes to achieve those goals, or do what it takes to accomplish them."[15] This echoes sentiments by political theorists offering reasons why individuals or groups stop short of enacting strategies for real change; as activist Bob Wing said, "If winning feels impossible, then righteousness can seem like the next best thing."[16] Applying this to the executive narrative in anti-racist circles, one could revise Wing's statement to "If being the hero seems out of reach, then playing the victim in need of retribution is the next best thing." As Zimmerman writes, "perceptions of social isolation, powerlessness, and normlessness" are thought to correlate negatively with empowerment.[17] This aligns with Smucker's observations about the tendency for the alienated and psychologically needy to flock toward social justice activism to *feel* empowered.[18] (I will discuss this further in an upcoming section.) The lack of the intrapersonal component leads to many things I consider detriments in anti-racist work.

I want to reemphasize the centrality of the individual in the intrapersonal component. Judith A. B. Lee cites the empowerment approach to social work as the building of a "Beloved Community" as "both the process and the hoped for outcome" of empowerment.[19] However, this beloved community must start with the individual. This is by no means an endorsement of a primacy of identity; the other components that make up the whole of empowerment theory would not allow that. Nor is it what Asao Inoue might call "hyperindividualism," a characteristic he attributes to whiteness.[20] In empowerment theory, individuality is an important step in the successful acquisition of empowerment. Lee writes, when applying empowerment theory to social work: "The social worker is concerned with the client's individuality and her right to be who she is as a unique person. . . . The emphasis on uniqueness is especially important as there is a dangerous tendency to generalize about members of stigmatized and oppressed groups. The value on individuality is central to empowerment practice."[21] As mentioned above, staunch individuality has been frowned upon in anti-racist circles for reflecting whiteness; that is, it is seen as a Eurocentric value and, therefore, racist when applied to nonwhites.[22] However, even if one were to abide by this interpretation of individuality, empowerment theory necessarily adds communal components. The intrapersonal is an imperative first step in the process of empowerment, but if the other components of empowerment, communal components, are weak or missing, empowerment cannot ensue.

So let us explore those other components, starting with the one that should follow the intrapersonal. The interactional component of empowerment is the most analytically rhetorical of the three, and "refers to the understanding people have about their community and related sociopolitical issues. This aspect of [empowerment] suggests that people are aware of behavior options or choices to act as they believe appropriate to achieve goals they set for themselves."[23] As I will show throughout my book, I think communication indicative of an academic domain—civil debate, critical inquiry, dialectic—are squelched by anti-racist scholars who do not harbor enough of the intrapersonal component to feel they can confidently hold forth against scrutiny, thus hindering the interactional component at a fundamental level.

Looking at the interactional component from all angles is important and could explain the primacy of identity and sacred victimhood as a primary aim of anti-racism proponents. The ideal understanding of rhetoric for an empowered person is indicative of the definition I gave in the previous chapter, but it also is indicative of Plato's concept of "good" rhetoric: a fair-minded and genuine attempt at mutual understanding and audience consideration. Unfortunately, from a "bad" rhetoric that some would call sophistic, the interactional component also could be firmly embraced. Consider Zimmerman's description:

> Individuals must learn about their options in a given context in order to be able to exert control in their environment. This suggests that they need to understand the norms and values of a particular context. Relevant norms and values might include cooperative decision making, commitment to collective (versus personal) interests, or mutual assistance. Individuals may also need to develop

a critical awareness of their environment, including an understanding of the resources needed to achieve a desired goal, knowledge of how to acquire those resources, and skills for managing resources once they are obtained.[24]

The acquisition of these skills suggests "environmental mastery," which can be achieved regardless of the spirit in which it is attempted. For example, the left-leaning space that is general academia is open and quite sympathetic to the tribulations of marginal bodies and very cognizant of the need to "make up" for past wrongs. What's more, the embrace of political correctness, for better or for worse, has created spaces in which hegemonic bodies tiptoe around marginalized bodies so as not to inadvertently commit acts of emotional violence, microaggressions, or white hegemony that, apparently, could do mental and emotional harm. This space was ripe for those lacking true intrapersonal power to seek agency by embracing victimhood. Being cognizant of this, being able to "understand the norms and values of a particular context" is necessary to take advantage of such a space.

So, we have two sides to consider. The critical thinking involved in the interactional component could be that which philosopher Richard Paul calls "fair-minded" critical thinking or "sophistic" critical thinking, rendered below.

Fair-Minded Critical Thinking:
   a) Skilled thinking which meets epistemological demands regardless of the vested interests or ideological commitments of the thinker
   b) Skilled thinking characterized by empathy to diverse opposing points of view and devotion to truth as against self-interest
   c) Skilled thinking that is consistent in the application of intellectual standards, holding one's self to the same rigorous standards of evidence and proof to which one holds one's antagonists
   d) Skilled thinking that demonstrates the commitment to entertain all viewpoints sympathetically and to assess them with the same intellectual standards, without reference to one's own feelings or vested interests, or the feelings or vested interests of one's friends, community, or nation.[25]

Sophistic Critical Thinking:
   a) thinking which meets epistemological demands insofar as they square with the vested interests of the thinker
   b) skilled thinking that is heedless of assumptions, relevance, reasons, evidence, implications, and consistency only insofar as it is in the vested interest of the thinker to do so
   c) skilled thinking that is motivated by vested interest, egocentrism, or ethnocentrism rather than by truth or objective reasonability[26]

Clearly, a person could use either format to effectively enact the interactional component, given one's telos. I argue that the primacy of identity as defined in the previous chapter requires a sophistic model of critical thinking that centers victimhood over a robust participation with all involved, including hegemonic bodies. Nevertheless, we begin to see distinct teleological trajectories, here. Full enactment of the intrapersonal component leads to an interactional component that fully embraces "fair-minded" critical thinking. A weak or nonexistent intrapersonal component may lead to "sophistic" critical thinking. My argument, as it will be throughout this book, is that the powerless feel they only have truncated dialectical tactics, tricks even, at their disposal. Sophistic critical thinking is the tool of the disempowered. (Throughout this work, when I mention critical thinking as an academic value, I am referring to fair-minded critical thinking.)

Returning to the ideal version of the interactional component, which, as established earlier, is commiserate with fair-minded critical thinking, Zimmerman continues by writing that "the interactional component provides the bridge between perceived control and taking action to exert control."[27] That is, the interactional component connects the first component of empowerment, the intrapersonal, to the third component, the behavioral.

The behavioral component[28] "refers to actions taken to directly influence outcomes."[29] Throughout this book I will reference theorists who insist that true political strategy, cognizant of social and material reality, is often dismissed for performance—prefiguration—in which the "lifeworld" created by a particular group is enough; no real action for real change is necessary. Mentioning the aforementioned trajectories, the trajectory of disempowerment would have the faux-intrapersonal component move into the "sophistic" interactional component and, finally, into a prefigurative or performative behavioral component, where nothing but the semblance of productive interaction and change is accomplished. That is, from a teleological standpoint, a lack of perceived self-efficacy and a "sophistic" (disempowered) way of interacting with one's environment will likely result in little to no progressive accomplishments in the real world. The insular world of academia, however, too often basks in prefigurative glory. Some academic spaces in rhetoric and composition, be they departments or conferences, seem to settle for performative outcomes. That is, in *their* space, the victim is lauded as the hero, hegemonic bodies are marginalized or only centered if accompanied[30] by a minority, and anything deemed Eurocentric is frowned upon at best. The empowered, fair-minded trajectory actually seeks to make real change by acknowledging social and material reality and then making strategic and pragmatic moves to affect that reality in positive and empowering ways. This is how empowerment is both a process and a product.

To change gears for a moment, the relationship of anti-racism to empowerment theory is not entirely negative. I have been focusing on the foundations of empowerment and its weak embrace by anti-racism proponents in rhetoric and composition, but those proponents are carrying out another aspect of empowerment quite well. In social work theory, a next tier of empowerment exists that speaks to the considerations that have been embraced successfully by proponents of anti-racism in rhetoric and composition. This tier is called the multifocal vision of empowerment. Judith B. Lee, DSW, articulates the vision thus.

1. Historical view
2. Ecological View
3. Ethclass perspective
4. Cultural/Multicultural perspective
5. Feminist perspective
6. Global perspective
7. Critical perspective[31]

These components of the multifocal vision have been embraced and centered by anti-racism initiatives and are clear aspects of decolonialism.[32] Length of oppression is considered when considering the very real systemic aspects of oppression. The ecological view takes into consideration the material influences of the world on behavior and outlook. "Ethclass" is synonymous with intersectionality and takes into consideration the various demographics one person can embody. The feminist component focuses on the political aspect of seemingly personal tribulations, that is, the personal is political. The critical denotes a challenge to hegemonic forces. The cultural and global recognizes how certain forces affect both our local considerations and those of other cultures and countries.

These are all important considerations, but like anything else, their true quality depends on the foundation on which they sit. If the foundation is one of empowerment, these considerations can go a long way in affecting societal change in ways that align with progressive social justice. However, as Gregory Pappas tacitly shows in "The Limitations and Dangers of Decolonial Philosophies: Lessons from Zapatista Luis Villoro,"[33] if the foundation is one of disempowerment (i.e., insufficient manifestations of the proponents of empowerment that lead to the primacy of identity and victimhood), these components, too, can reflect what Richard Paul may call a sophistic take on change. That is, without a strong foundation of the three components of empowerment, the multifocal vision can be done "insofar as it is in the vested interest of the thinker to do so" and can be "motivated by vested interest, egocentrism, or ethnocentrism rather than by truth or objective reasonability."[34]

It would seem that Lee's second tier of successful empowerment has been used more to fill out the sacred victim narrative than to actually enact change.

EMPOWERMENT AND EMOTIONAL INTELLIGENCE

Perhaps the difference between empowerment and disempowerment that may result in sophistic critical thinking can be found in the role played by what psychologists call Emotional Intelligence. The relationship of Emotional Intelligence to empowerment is easily discernible, but exactly how relevant Emotional Intelligence is to the embrace of disempowerment in anti-racist initiatives deserves to be parsed out a bit.

Emotional Intelligence (also known as EQ, the emotion quotient, as opposed to IQ, the intelligence quotient) is a form of intelligence that "displaces a natural or emotional inclination with one that will lead to a better outcome."[35] Of course, in an almost circular line of reasoning, a definition of "better" in the prior quote may depend on one's level of Emotional Intelligence and correlated sense of empowerment. Disempowered people may take the semblance of power and progress, or the embrace of a prefigurative activism that values performance over actual change, as a form of a "better" outcome. However, according to the empowerment theory just articulated, especially regarding its third "behavioral" component, strategic cooperation and concrete change, not the semblance of those things, is a necessary outcome. Also, a strong manifestation of the intrapersonal component of empowerment involved in self-efficacy may also prompt someone to strive for a more concrete "better," whereas someone with a weak grasp of this component may settle for the empty "better" I am associating with disempowerment.

Daniel Goleman, the psychologist most associated with EQ, talks about it in relation to what he calls "Social Intelligence." He writes: "Emotional Intelligence, a different way of being smart, is a key to high performance at all levels, particularly for outstanding leadership. It's not your IQ; it's how you manage yourself and your relationships. It's not usually taught in schools. You learn it in daily life—at home, on the playground, or in the office."[36] We see here that EQ is a key to outstanding leadership, which relates to a strong sense of empowerment. Empowerment and EQ are tightly intertwined. Thus, a parsing out of EQ's components, as we did earlier with empowerment, is necessary. EQ has four major components: Self-Awareness, Social Awareness, Self-Management, and Relationship Management. I will explain these and then illustrate their connections to empowerment theory.

Self-Awareness is "the ability to understand your own emotions and their effects on your performance."[37] Think about this statement in relation to Goleman's claim that EQ is not usually taught in schools, where IQ is emphasized. We often study theories and even modes of practice in ways that are isolated from reality, where a testing of these theories and practices would induce a need for Emotional Intelligence in the form of Social Awareness, which we will get to shortly. Regarding Self-Awareness, Goleman continues with a second-person description of the socially aware individual:

> You know what you are feeling and why—and how it helps or hurts what you are trying to do. You sense how others see you and so align your self-image with a larger reality. You have an accurate sense of your strengths and limitations, which gives you a realistic self-confidence. It also gives you clarity on your values and sense of purpose, so you can be more decisive when you set a course of action. As a leader, you can be candid and authentic, speaking with conviction about your vision.[38]

With this component of EQ, alone, we can see some salient connections to empowerment, specifically the intrapersonal and interactive components. Sensing how others see you and working with that observation is key to the interpersonal component of empowerment, which emphasizes a keen awareness of one's environment and how to negotiate that environment rhetorically. Regarding the intrapersonal component, having an accurate assessment of your strengths and limitations induces a self-confidence in line with the perceived self-efficacy imperative to empowerment.

Social Awareness involves the competencies of Empathy and Organizational Awareness. (In this section, I will capitalize these and other competencies as they are rendered in the literature on Emotional Intelligence). Regarding the former, Social Awareness emphasizes both emotional and cognitive Empathy, that is, the ability to put oneself in the shoes of another. People with a sound sense of Empathy "get along well with people from very different backgrounds and cultures, and can express their ideas in ways the other person will understand."[39] This is an important statement for the general purpose of this book for obvious reasons, but regarding the differences between empowerment and disempowerment, Empathy could be used, to refer back to Richard Paul, "sophistically" from the standpoint of the latter. Goleman clarifies that "empathy doesn't mean psyching out the other person so you can manipulate them, but rather knowing how best to collaborate with them."[40] One may be reminded of the concepts of victimhood and liberal guilt when thinking of the competency of Empathy as a "psych out" tool. It is implied, then, that Empathy from the standpoint of empowerment would embrace Paul's "fair-minded critical thinking." Hence Goleman's claim that "being skilled at empathy is necessary to fully engage with the full range of human experience."[41]

The other competency of Social Awareness, Organizational Awareness, actually implies Empathy in a distinct group context, like a specific civic or professional space. Goleman writes:

As an Emotional Intelligence Competency, Organizational Awareness means having the ability to read a group's emotional currents and power relationships, and identify influences, networks, and dynamics within an organization. Leaders who can recognize networking opportunities and read key power relationships are better equipped to navigate the demands of their leadership role. Such leaders not only understand the forces at work in an organization, but also the guiding values and unspoken rules that operate among people. People skilled at the Organizational Awareness Competency can sense the personal networks that make the organization run and know how to find the right person to make key decisions, and how to form a coalition to get something done.[42]

The issue with Organizational Awareness is the very definition of "organization." For our purposes, we could ask if the organization is an academic discipline (rhetoric and composition), a particular association within that discipline, (e.g., National Council for the Teachers of English), or a subgroup within that organization (e.g., proponents of anti-racism). However, one can see that the more steeped a person is in the competency of Organizational Awareness, the better that person would be in negotiating the dynamics of all these groups.

With the Social Awareness component of EQ, we can see the interactional and behavioral components of empowerment at play. According to Zimmerman, the interactional component involves understanding community and the issues therein, learning one's options in a given environment for bringing projects to fruition, and developing a critical awareness to understand the resources and skills necessary for success in a particular environment.[43] From the perspective of a social worker focusing on oppressed and marginalized groups, Judith A. B. Lee relates the interpersonal component to "biculturality," the ability to live in two cultures: the nurturing culture of one's own group and the wider culture that oppresses even as it offers some opportunities for actualization."[44] Combining Zimmerman and Lee, one can see that empowerment is a resilient and decidedly rhetorical navigation of the world that leads toward the behavioral component, indicated by Goleman's statement that sound Social Awareness can show us "how to form a coalition to get something done"[45] even in a hostile environment.

The component of Self-Management involves several competencies: Emotional Self-Control, Adaptability, Achievement Orientation, and Positive Outlook. Emotional Self-Control, according to Goleman, is "the ability to keep your disruptive emotions and impulses in check, to maintain your effectiveness under stressful or even hostile conditions."[46] This may remind us of Lee's take on the interactional component of empowerment but it also overlaps with resilience studies, a close companion to both empowerment and EQ.[47] Repressing one's emotions is not the goal of emotional Self-Control. "Rather, it is not being swept away or overwhelmed by disturbing emotions."[48]

In an attitude reminiscent of Stoic philosophy—also misunderstood as a movement that supports the suppression, not the proper handling, of emotion—Self-Control reminds us that "Men[49] are disturbed not by things, but by the views which they take of things."[50] This is a tall order for anyone, but necessary to gain Emotional Intelligence and empowerment. What's more, as psychologist Vanessa Druskat points out, that tall order is shortened a bit if structures are put in place to ensure group belonging.[51] In what can be called social pragmatism, John Dewey echoes this notion in addressing social problems and the need for progress as a society. He proposed that we alter social conditions, not individuals, suggesting that "the positive means of progress lie in the application of intelligence to the construction of proper devices." That is, we can collaborate to create an environment in which the stoicism inherent in emotional Self-Control is manageable because our communities are conducive to such management. Dewey continues:

> Theoretically, it is possible to have social arrangements which will favor the friendly tendencies of human nature at the expense of the bellicose and predatory ones, and which will direct the latter into channels where they will do the least harm or even become means of good. . . . [The problem of human progress] is a problem of discovering the needs and capacities of collective human nature as we find it aggregated in racial or national groups on the surface of the globe, and of inventing the social machinery which will set available powers operating for the satisfaction of those needs.[52]

So, Self-Control can be enhanced if the proper "social machinery" is put into place, preferably one that takes into consideration collective (not selective) human nature.

I think that anti-racist initiatives in rhetoric and composition are trying to construct this social machinery by decentering Eurocentric hegemonic ideals and giving voice to the traditionally silenced. However, their new social arrangements, as I will show throughout this work, are misguided endeavors to create social machinery not conducive to an empowered Self-Control promoted by Zimmerman, Goleman, and others, but a disempowered Self-Control associated with a lack of "reality testing"—the ability to see the world as it is and not as we want or fear it to be.[53]

Overcoming this lack of reality testing, a key aspect of Emotional Intelligence having to do with effective decision-making,[54] necessitates a take on Self-Control that incorporates all three components of empowerment, but focuses on the behavioral component as a teleological guide. Psychologist Richard Boyatzis, working closely with Goleman, writes: "On a very basic level, emotional Self-Control has the underlying intent of being able to control impulses and feelings *for the good of the group, or for the good of the task, mission, or vision.*"[55] (My emphasis). Thus, Self-Control, when it comes to Emotional Intelligence and empowerment, is very pragmatic. If the purpose of the behavioral component is to "directly influence outcomes,"[56] Self-Control is motivated by a need to acquire concrete results outside of oneself as efficaciously as possible. In a statement tacitly shunning prefigurative politics, Lee (who calls the behavioral component of empowerment the "Political Level") writes: "Ultimately, oppression is a political problem that requires political solutions. Workers and clients alike must develop the knowledge and skills needed to affect political process."[57] Synthesizing these ideas about EQ and empowerment, the end goal of actually concrete, political solutions in an eclectic and elaborate society necessitates the competency of emotional Self-Control.

The competency of Adaptability overlaps with Self-Control substantially. It means "having flexibility in handling change, being able to juggle multiple demands, and adapting to new situations with fresh ideas or innovative approaches. It means you can stay focused on your goals, but easily adjust how you get there."[58] According to Goleman, for attaining the competency of Adaptability, Self-Awareness and Self-Control are necessary prerequisites. They are the first step toward Adaptability, which is tantamount to improvisational skill and extemporaneous communication. In this sense, the Adaptability competency is heavily rhetorical and kairotic. After being socially aware of one's surroundings and being mindful of one's emotions, one can adequately gauge a situation and act, speak, or write accordingly.

Regarding fair-minded critical thinking, Adaptability is key. One may come across thoughts or research that is disquieting and may even cause some cognitive dissonance, but how does one step back well enough to continue a dedication to, for instance, "skilled thinking that demonstrates the commitment to entertain all viewpoints sympathetically and to assess them with the same intellectual standards, without reference to one's own feelings or vested interests, or the feelings or vested interests of one's friends, community, or nation"?[59] Adaptability is a necessary competency for this, and is key in fair-mindedness; those with a firm grasp of the Adaptability competency are not afraid of the loss of beliefs or even values.

The fear of loss, too, is the opposite of Adaptability, especially when it comes to a loss of power. However, those with high Adaptability competency do not fear the unknown or, in the context of the aforementioned fair-minded critical thinking, do not fear coming across knowledge that weakens an embraced stance. Adaptability is a contrast to what psychologists call "cathexis": a deep, affective connection to an object, a person, or even oneself. Ideas and concepts can also be objects of cathexis. Cathexis can be an obstacle to change. However, those with high Adaptability embrace change. According to George Kohlrieser, "High-performing leaders are not afraid of loss. They think, 'I'm willing to go through the pain for the benefit.' By seeing change as positive, Adaptability becomes a process of exploration, creativity and discovery. By welcoming change, we are not held hostage to the fear of the unknown."[60]

(The lack of Adaptability is not just an anti-racist phenomenon. White culture in almost all aspects of life has lacked this competency when dealing with race and equality throughout American history. For the purposes of this book, I want to focus on its lack in circles in which anti-racism is the said goal.)

Perhaps what is most unsettling about Adaptability, besides its virtual absence in some anti-racism initiatives, is that the power anti-racism proponents fear losing is not real power. It is disempowerment in the guise of power, that is, prefiguration and performance. The lack of Adaptability results in actions done to protect this semblance of empowerment. Shutting down ideas, shouting down those with opposing views, and other such behaviors associated with current anti-racist initiatives are signs of rigidity, not the flexibility necessary to embrace the Adaptability competency. Adaptability can also be seen as what can be called a kairotic disposition, that is, one's ability to gauge the time, place, people, topic, and one's subject position to adequately communicate and interact. However, if the *kairos* is consistently a prefigurative space, one does not develop the Adaptability to deal with larger social and material realities.

Lastly, when taking Adaptability as a kind of kairotic disposition, a person with strong competence in the adaptability that comes with Self-Management would not feel oppressed or inflicted with "racial schizophrenia" for writing in standard English. Such a person would feel that the acquisition of the tool was an expansion of skills, an enhancement of Adaptability. To be adaptable does not mean one has to give up one tool for another for evermore; Adaptability is not necessarily an erasure of skill brought from home or one's community. (Remember Lisa Delpit's daughter, Maya.) How many scholars who see the acquisition of one dialect as a necessary relinquishing of another simply do not have or understand the Adaptability competency?

Achievement Orientation surely involves all three components of empowerment. One can see the relation to the intrapersonal, interpersonal, and behavioral in Goleman's words:

> When we're strong in the Achievement Orientation competency, we strive to meet or exceed a standard of excellence and appreciate metrics for and feedback on our performance. We look for ways to learn how to do things better. We set challenging goals and take calculated risks. And we can balance our personal drive to achieve with the needs and goals of an organization.[61]

Meeting a standard of excellence implies the perceived self-efficacy of the intrapersonal component. Taking calculated risks and balancing personal and organizational goals reflect aspects of the interactional component. Lastly, the behavioral component is reflected in this competency's name itself; "Achievement" denotes the acquisition of a goal, the concrete and/or political outcomes that round out empowerment.

Achievement Orientation can become a detriment if the other competencies of EQ do not accompany it. Achievement Orientation implies Adaptability to a large degree, but without Organizational Awareness, Empathy, Self-Control, etc., we could be looking at a tyrannical figure.[62] So, although someone steeped in this competency may *feel* empowered, his or her inability to reach goals because of his or her inimical personality and lack of cooperative skills will stifle both the interactional and behavioral components of empowerment.

Proponents of anti-racism may take issue with the terms "standard of excellence" and "metric for success." They may hear the adjective "Eurocentric" or just plain "White" preceding each term. Thus, they would say that Achievement Orientation was just an insidious tactic to further supremacy.[63] The thing is, someone who embraces the Achievement Orientation competency does not see it that way. This person is focused on success and acquiring potential tools to ensure its achievement. This person is focused on a finish line that will lead to success, hopefully for this person *and* others. Think of Dubois' thoughts and experiences discussed in this book's introduction. The "Duboisian Attitude" is definitely one steeped in Achievement Orientation.

The group form of Achievement Orientation, called "performance orientation" involves several people working together toward a particular goal. The aforementioned anti-racism proponents exhibit a performance orientation in their initiatives and, as is typical, leaders have emerged. However, this group equivalent of Achievement Orientation may have a group equivalent of the achiever sans other important EQ competencies, which results in toxic leadership.

Lastly, people with Achievement Orientation look for thorough feedback so that they can improve and get things right. This, too, seems inimical to proponents of anti-racism, whose ideology of a primacy of identity often shuns critical inquiry, especially from outsiders. An achievement-oriented person, especially one harboring other competencies in EQ, has an adequate amount of emotional resilience and grit. In fact, "grit" is what results from the combination of Achievement Orientation with Self-Control and the final competency in Self-Management, Positive Outlook.[64]

Positive Outlook can give much insight regarding anti-racist initiatives, their proponents, and implications of empowerment and Emotional Intelligence. The definition Goleman gives may have red flags for those cognizant of hegemonic idealism. However, in the context of EQ and empowerment theory, Positive Outlook is redeemed as an inevitable aspect of both. Goleman's definition follows:

Positive Outlook is the ability to see the positive in people, situations, and events. It means persistence in pursuing goals, despite setbacks and obstacles. You can see the opportunity in situations where others would see a setback that would be devastating, at least for them. You expect the best from other people. It's that glass-half-full outlook that leads you to believe that changes in the future will be for the better.[65]

This definition, especially with its glass-half-full platitude, may induce eye rolls from people who recognize such statements as excuses to justify inequality and discrimination. That is, people who are truly victimized in society are seen as people who only need to think positively for their lives to change. Taken alone, this definition seems to fall in line with that shortsighted sentiment. However, Goleman saves Positive Outlook for last because, like he did for other competencies, prior competencies must act as foundations for subsequent ones. Positive Outlook is the final competency of the Self-Management component because without the prior competencies it is just wishful thinking.

Those with a strong grasp of Positive Outlook will, through Self Awareness and Self-Management, know how to stave off knee-jerk negative reactions to a situation. Thus, Positive Outlook can enhance interpersonal communication and civil debate because actions are not automatically labeled negative. With this outlook, behavior that seems like microaggression is explored, opening the door for critical inquiry and dialogue fueled by fair-minded critical thinking. This is not to say that true transgressors would be let off the hook; it is to say that the necessary conversations are more likely to take place instead of an automatic shunning of an alleged culprit.

Again, the Positive Outlook competency is often mistaken as a synonym for wishful thinking. In addressing the equivocation of Positive Outlook and wishful thinking, Goleman shows that Positive Outlook is more aligned with the self-efficacy of empowerment's intrapersonal component than something like wishful thinking, or what he calls "Don't worry, be happy" statements.[66] A pessimistic explanatory style attributes negative outcomes to personal failings or inevitably negative circumstances.[67] People with an optimistic explanatory style recognize that negative outcomes are minor setbacks, not categorical descriptions of a situation, and they "trust their ability to deal with stressful situations." We see in this statement all the prior components of EQ along with a general acknowledgment of rhetoric and finding in any given case, the available means of (self) persuasion.

Clearly, a person with a strong intrapersonal component will lean toward the optimistic explanatory style, but one could construe such a person, in a given context, as being unrealistic.

Here is where Kenneth Burke's concept of the terministic screen comes into play. According to Burke, the way we speak about things, the discourse in which we speak about them, directs attention to some things and not others. All sincere language use is a reflection of reality, but "[e]ven if any given terminology is a *reflection* of reality, by its very nature as a terminology it must be a *selection* of reality; and to this extent it must function also as a *deflection* of reality."[68] Burke continues: "Here the kind of deflection I have in mind concerns simply the fact that any nomenclature necessarily directs the attention into some channels rather than others."[69] Positive Outlook, then, is a recognition of the arbitrary nature of these selections and deflections when reflecting on reality.

The intrapersonal component in empowerment theory may select and deflect in ways that promote self-efficacy, but its partnership with the interactional component, with its critical awareness of situations and adequate reality testing when considering ideal outcomes, will temper these selections and deflections toward necessary change. So, there is something inherently pragmatic and teleological about the Positive Outlook competency when discussed along with terministic screens. That is, one who wants concrete change will have different deflections and selections than one who will settle for prefiguration. Someone with strong empowerment and Emotional Intelligence will have different deflections and selections than someone who is disempowered.

Getting back to Goleman, the confluence of the intrapersonal and interactional components of empowerment denote what he calls the optimistic explanatory style's most mature explanation, "dispositional optimism," which denotes the willingness to achieve goals one values and sees as realistic. Goleman writes that "rather than advocating for an 'optimistic under all circumstances' perspective, what might be most effective is cultivating a generally optimistic outlook that is tempered by realistic pessimism."[70] This concept, closely related to reality testing, further distinguishes Positive Outlook from wishful thinking or an unrealistic take on things.

Goleman does admit that cultural differences may come in when we consider the Positive Outlook competency, which clearly speaks to my incorporation of Burke into the argument. Goleman writes: "When I read the research literature [on Emotional Intelligence], I'm aware that many of the studies I'm reading have been conducted in North America with people of European descent."[71] This is a relevant and necessary consideration when discussing the importance of Positive Outlook in anti-racist initiatives. Is the Positive Outlook competency of EQ antithetical to discourses, terministic screens, and reflections of people of color in America? If so, which ones? If so, is this a good thing or a fallacious appeal to tradition? I plan on addressing these questions later in this book.

So far, we have discussed three of the four major components of EQ: Self-Awareness, Social Awareness, and Self-Management. Last, we will explore

Relationship Management and its competencies: Influence, Coach and Mentor, Inspirational Leadership, Conflict Management, and Teamwork.

Influence is reflected in all three empowerment components; one has to perceive one's own ability to influence, one has to exercise that influence by being critically aware and interactional, and one has to show the manifestations of that influence by behavioral or political change. "Influence as a competency refers to the ability to have a positive impact on others, to persuade or convince them to gain their support. With the Influence competency, you're persuasive and engaging, and you can build buy-in from key people."[72] This competency, then, is closely related to actual agency and the ability to stimulate a movement. The term *zeitgeist* even comes to mind. Thus, the empowered and disempowered alike can have a strong grasp of the Influence competency.

Of course, ethos comes into play, here. Ethos looks different through a lens of empowerment than through a lens of disempowerment. Ethos in a primacy of identity favors one's identity as a member of a certain group over the logos one presents to display competence, critical thought, and generally good ideas. Empowerment recognizes the value of experience, but its interactional component would necessitate a welcoming of critical inquiry and criticism, the better to hone a clearer path to a goal. That is, lived experience should be an adequate commingling of outside critique and self-reflexivity to ensure the avoidance of solipsistic thinking. Where critical thinking and the attempted avoidance of solipsism is frowned upon or punished, we may find a strong influencer in a disempowered discourse community: one driven by a primacy of identity.

Clearly, Influence is heavily rhetorical. After ethos is established, one must gauge things kairotically, an act indicative of the critical awareness imperative to the interactional component of empowerment, and speak/act accordingly. According to Boyatzis, Influence involves a consideration of *kairos* and rhetorical appeal to get things done: "The core intent of the Influence competency is a desire to get someone to agree with you. The behavior that demonstrates this competency is doing things that appeal to their self-interest and anticipating the questions they would have."[73] This is rhetoric in its simplest form. The basics are there: message, speaker, audience. Influencers, then, are consummate rhetors and dialecticians.

But, again, we can discern a distinction between empowered Influence and disempowered Influence. Rhetoric and Composition is a large field, with various subfields. In order for a paradigm shift to take place, a subfield has to speak to more people than just those in their particular discourse communities. Empowered people may have a "home" community, but are more cosmopolitan when it comes to the interactional component. They branch out into the world, read social and material realities as kairotic, and take on the behavioral component toward strategizing and bringing about change. Disempowered influencers, on the other hand, stay insular and prefigurative. They influence their in-group and work to silence those who would naysay them, even if those people have good ideas or have resources and positions necessary for change in broader settings. Disempowered Influence is a contained Influence.

The next competency is Coach and Mentor. Like other competencies, it builds on the prior competency as it manifests in a specific, interpersonal way. The Coach and Mentor competency is "the ability to foster the long-term learning or development of others by giving feedback and support." Goleman continues: "You have a genuine interest in helping others develop further strengths. You give timely constructive feedback. You understand the person's goals, and you try to find challenges for them that will provide growth opportunities."[74] One may notice a similarity to what can be called a Teacher competency. This is where this competency is most salient with regard to the purposes of this book.

Goleman's definition centers the mentee, as it were. It shows a strong consideration for the mentees' goals while giving them beneficial strengths. Antiracist pedagogues surely do this when teaching students about the realities of English dialects and abiding by what is called "Critical Language Awareness," which is the study of all dialects as equal in themselves while exploring the political implications of each and how they relate to each other. The problems come when agendas in which students are uninterested are thrust upon them in likely well-intentioned attempts to raise student consciousness. Boyatzi's research finds "that if you coach to people's dreams and values, those coached are able to change for the better."[75] However, "If you coach for compliance—how you want them to be—rather than toward their own goals, you have a negative impact on the person you are coaching."[76] Many anti-racist pedagogues see the learning of English deemed "standard" as "compliance" to the norms of the colonizer. Thus, to decenter that hegemony is to move toward having the student elude the demand to comply. What is ignored often is that anti-racist endeavors are their own compliances, and students of color who see the power of standard English as a valuable skill for their personal goals—and not a violence toward identity—may not need or want to experiment with code-meshing, for example. (More than likely, they already know how to code-mesh. They already have rhetorical skill.)

This speaks to the apparent partnership between language and identity I question in this book's introduction. Antiracist pedagogues abide by the ideology of language authenticity and project it onto students in an attempt to empower them. However, real empowerment, especially when taking the Coach and Mentor competency into consideration, is giving students the tools to reach their goals, rather than what a teacher may think is good for them.

Goleman writes: "Getting someone in touch with their dreams and values creates more potential pathways to the future for them, while trying to get them to fall in line with compliance closes those doorways to possibility."[77] Of course, people have been accused of this very compliance precisely for having students write in standard English. Is that not what sparks anti-racism initiatives in rhetoric and composition the most? However, and as I will show in a later chapter, Dubois' student pragmatism is alive and well in our contemporary students. Many need not be awoken or saved in their First Year Composition courses. Thus, I will address pedagogues who come across resistance from students and, at times, academics of color and how an "I know what's good for you" attitude seems to take shape.

Lastly, regarding Coach and Mentor, some anti-racist proponents may suggest that teaching anything is, in a sense, forcing students to comply. To this, I have several answers. Acknowledgment of social and material realities that suggest certain skills need to be systematically taught for students to reach their goals will be addressed in upcoming chapters. My immediate response in this chapter, a chapter on empowerment, is that pedagogues in rhetoric and composition often undervalue what students want. Most students enter college classrooms expecting to learn a certain thing. When that thing is muddled (meshed?) with what the teacher wants the student to know on a social and political level, the teacher may feel more empowerment than the actual student; the former speaks truth to power through pedagogy, the latter gets something for which he or she may not have asked.

The next competency, Inspirational Leadership, is what I call the "mission and vision" competency. To be clear, "mission" and "vision" are different from goals; they provide the motivational factor for goals. Boyatzis writes: "Goals are important, but goals are not purpose. Purpose, vision, mission—each is bigger and, in fact, fuzzier—often more philosophical or nobler—than a particular goal."[78] This kind of motivation often feeds off tacit understandings of what people already want. For this reason, this competency is closely related to that of Influence. It is the motivating factor to solidify the habitus in which leaders and followers coexist.

The "fuzzy" description of Inspirational Leadership is worth discussing. Activist Jonathan Smucker sees fuzziness, or what he simply calls ambiguity, as a key rhetorical tactic in motivating groups. When motivating a community, ambiguity "can open the door"[79] to inspiring people, for too much detail loses the ability to create intrinsic motivation. Details are often counterproductive when trying to create a *zeitgeist*.

Anti-racist proponents have been successful in this because, like Smucker, they tend to think in terms of activism more than theory or pedagogy. In fact, their activism, when put through the ringer of the pedagogical imperative, can result in the pedagogy I explained in the Coach and Mentor section. However, this activism-oriented mode of action, which embraces ambiguity, works precisely because it is not academic in the sense of meticulous critical thinking that embraces constructive skepticism and parsed reason. Academia's content in "reveling in the lucidity of its own analytic critique"[80] will not get the job done.

Smucker argues that, when trying to create a movement, meticulous analysis may stifle any mobility.[81] For this reason, he embraces ambiguity at the expense of critical thinking (including critical awareness and pragmatism) at *initial* stages, when working to inspire and spark a movement. Once again invoking the concept of an activist circle as a "clubhouse," Smucker writes:

> The notion that there is positive strategic value in ambiguity may offend some progressive sensibilities. We tend to want clarity. And there are certainly times when clarity is precisely what is called for. It may be important for a group's leaders, organizers, and core participants to have clarity about their campaign goals and about the political terrain that they need to cross in order to reach those goals. We may also want clarity in our own thinking about complex, social, economic, and political systems. However, if you want to organize and mobilize people *outside the clubhouse*, you have to also befriend ambiguity. If you can't turn off your need for clarity in some moments, you may well succeed in painting a clear analytical picture for yourself, but you're unlikely to attract the social forces we need, if we're to start turning this thing around.[82] (My emphasis)

I think anti-racist proponents in rhetoric and composition have done a good job at foregoing specificity and embracing ambiguity to get people on board with a movement. They seem to have a firm handle on Inspirational Leadership, in that sense. However, the italicized words in the above quote concern me the most. The words, "outside the clubhouse" refers to those outside academia, that is, "laypeople," those not aware of the movement and who need to be made aware before the intricacies of analysis are introduced. The existence of laypeople implies the existence of experts and professionals, those who do and, as their positions in academia necessitate, should embrace the intricacies of analysis, critical thinking, constructive skepticism, critical inquiry, etc. *We* should not need the ambiguity of which Smucker speaks, that which is used to pique the interest of newcomers and laypeople. So, in the anti-racism movement in rhetoric and composition, the experts and the laypeople are intermixed *within* academia. The necessary ambiguity of the Inspirational Leaders never stopped once people got into the "clubhouse." This neglect of critical thought is normal in prefigurative spaces, where the zeitgeist is not an energizer for arrival at a *telos*, but is the *telos* itself. The "calm and cool" of academia is dismissed, often because it is seen as inherently Eurocentric.[83] But, although societal conversations can be contentious, academics are supposed to rise above it into a fair-minded, open-minded critical thinking. This does not happen in many anti-racist circles.

The last two competencies of EQ's Relationship Management component can be addressed together: Conflict Management and Teamwork. It may be best to provide definitions of both in full before elaborating.

> The Conflict Management Competency involves having the ability to help others through emotional or tense situations, tactfully bringing disagreements into the open, and defining solutions that everyone can endorse. Leaders who take time to understand different perspectives work toward finding a common ground on which everyone can agree. They acknowledge the views of all sides, while redirecting the energy toward a shared ideal or an agreeable resolution.[84]

Conflict Management necessitates many competencies, especially Self-Awareness, Emotional Self-Management, Empathy, and Organizational Awareness. Its skill in leadership is imperative.[85] Thus, in a truly empowered move, people skilled in this competency see conflict as potentially positive. "If we step toward conflict instead of stepping back into passivity, we can take it as a challenge, a problem to be solved, and, ultimately, an opportunity."[86]

Let us now turn to the competency of Teamwork. "Teamwork is the ability to work with others toward a shared goal, participating actively, sharing responsibility and rewards, and contributing to the capability of the team. You empathize and create an atmosphere of respect, helpfulness, and cooperation." Goleman quotes the Japanese saying "All of us are smarter than any of us"[87] to drive home the idea that teamwork is imperative to the success of a movement. Teamwork also puts the onus on individual teammates to illustrate the aforementioned competencies in a purposeful way. "Being skilled in teamwork could entail modeling good collaborative behavior yourself, or suggesting that everyone comes together to discuss how they see a particular problem, and to brainstorm, collectively, how to resolve it going forward."[88] Both Conflict Management and Teamwork overlap to promote a healthy community and evade dysfunctional interaction.

The field of rhetoric and composition, particularly the study of anti-racism, has illustrated a severe lack of both these competencies. Regarding conflict, the field would rather silence or ostracize people who don't abide by its favored ideology or narrative. George Kohlrieser's definitions of "conflict" and "bond" can further illustrate the dearth of the Conflict Management" and "Teamwork" competencies in the anti-racism movement.

> Conflict can be defined as a difference between two or more persons or groups where there are tension, emotionality, and disagreement and when bonding is lacking or broken. By bond, I mean an emotional connection, *even with someone you do not like*. It is a relationship that seeks to understand the other

person's needs and maintain the relationship despite difference. *You can have a big difference and keep the bond, and a small difference where the bond is broken or creates big conflict.*[89] (My emphasis)

The italicized words suggest that disagreement alone should not necessitate the perpetuation of a conflict or the interpretation of a conflict as inherently negative; even dislike should not endanger civil debate or a possible synthesis of ideas. These considerations are missing from prominent anti-racist initiatives in rhetoric and composition due to a lack of true empowerment and the Emotional Intelligence needed to acquire it. When anti-racist initiatives are met with critique, even inadvertent critique, the "perpetrator" is met with hostility if not outright vitriol. The Teamwork competency is never realized because this naysayer is surely jettisoned from the team for critical inquiries and opinions that come nowhere near being beyond the pale. Conflict, then, is the only way of dealing with critique from "Others."

All the components of EQ and their respective competencies shed light on the issues in anti-racist rhetoric and composition initiatives in ways that argue that empowerment theory should be synthesized with these initiatives to make for more real, concrete outcomes while assuaging possible conflicts. Throughout this book, I judge anti-racist initiatives for not being pragmatically sound and for perpetuating an allergy to the real, but these judgments derive from the foundational judgment that true empowerment is missing from anti-racism. Disempowerment is either embraced as empowerment or settled for by those who lack the components of EQ and empowerment, themselves. Although I will show the effects of this disempowerment, I hope to work with others to find ways to empower anti-racism without being derailed by conflict.

Ultimately, high IQ is a regular characteristic in academic circles, but low EQ may be what plagues those circles. Anti-racist initiatives in rhetoric and composition are no exemptions by any means, but neither are insular white spaces, as I and others show in other publications. I argue that it is low EQ mixed with the astuteness that comes with high IQ that is responsible for a primacy of identity and its resulting victim narrative as well as narratives that truly perpetuate white supremacy. It is a low EQ but high IQ that represents the acquisition of English deemed standard as a necessary cause of a veritable mental disorder among students of color. It is low EQ and high IQ that fuel resistance to multiculturalism and racial equality. One can say, then, that high IQ and high EQ are the necessary prerequisites to empowerment, while high IQ and low EQ (or both low IQ and low EQ) are the prerequisites to disempowerment.

For the sake of clarity and brevity, my use of the term "empowerment" should be understood henceforth as the confluence of empowerment theory and Emotional Intelligence discussed in this chapter. So, to be truly empowered, one abides by the intrapersonal, interactional, and behavioral components of empowerment theory that house, in varying configurations, the Emotional Intelligence components of Self-Awareness, Self-Management, Social Awareness, and Relationship Management as well as the corresponding competencies of each. As one can see, "empowerment" is a powerful concept.[90]

A RHETORIC OF EMPOWERMENT

I think it is clear at this point that empowerment is a kind of rhetoric, and I argue that it is a rhetoric tragically absent in anti-racist initiatives in general. At this point, I want to parse this rhetoric for both clarity and didactic reasons. A clear understanding of the discourse of empowerment will better expose the inherent disempowerment in current anti-racism initiatives. Anti-racism is an important and imperative endeavor; within a rhetoric of empowerment, we can better ensure productive outcomes.

First, what is *a* rhetoric? As I often do, I cite James Gee's description of Discourse, which denotes, in addition to language or grammar, "saying (writing)-doing-being-valuing-believing combinations" and is capitalized to distinguish it from its common understanding as a synonym for dialogue.[91] Gee describes Discourse as a way of being in the world that incorporates language use, but more importantly (especially for our purposes), ways, beliefs, behaviors, attitudes, and values.[92] Based on the understanding of empowerment in this chapter, we can describe the "identity kit" of an empowered individual or group. Based on the concept of Discourse and Zimmerman's explanation of empowerment theory at this essay's start,[93] we can come to an understanding of a truly empowered proponent of anti-racism. I will explain the rhetoric (Discourse) of empowerment by describing the idealized empowered person.

First, an empowered individual values self-efficacy and a self-perception as competent and agential. This self-perception may be acquired through experience, education, or upbringing. This person does not feel the need to cut corners or sabotage a situation for the best outcomes, and so fair-minded critical thinking is the preferred approach. This person abides by a high epistemological standard, generally, and does not shy away from incidents that may prove a held belief false; fallibility in ideas and viewpoints is an accepted fact of life. This person's identity cannot be thwarted by the acknowledgment or acquisition of other worldviews, other ways of communicating, and other values; these things are seen as aspects of an ever-growing repertoire and an ever-changing, nonessentialized identity.

An empowered individual acknowledges social and material reality. That is, this person sees the world for what it is, not how one would like the world to be. This person is immune to the "allergy" of the real and takes the world at face value to better ensure a proper handling of actual circumstances. Of course, this includes an acknowledgment of all aspects involved—people, places, times—and interaction according to one's goals or intentions. To the best of one's ability, speculative projections are avoided and something akin to James Berlin's social-epistemic rhetoric is adopted., a rhetoric that "is self-reflexive, acknowledging its own rhetoricity, its own discursive constitution and limitations" and "is aware of its own historical contingency, of its limitations and incompleteness, remaining open to change and revision."[94] The empowered person sees the significance and value of *kairos* and has the adaptation skills to work with it.

Thus, the empowered person is comfortable with interpersonal and group interaction and embraces the idea of never being in the wrong place at the wrong time.[95] Emotional and cognitive empathy is not just a moral imperative but a necessary aspect of effective communication. If conflict does ensue, it is seen as an opportunity to improve on a situation—to build something new or enhance something old, not necessarily a violence perpetrated against oneself. Community is valued in a cosmopolitan, not insular, way. A positive outlook is embraced not merely as wishful thinking, but as a pragmatic and necessary aspect of fair-minded critical thinking, for it opens the person to consider various ideas and viewpoints, whereas a negative outlook would close one off to new and innovative possibilities.

The empowered person is pragmatic and values the knowledge of lived experience tempered by reason and situational observation. Thus, lived experience is understood as an aspect of fair-minded critical thinking, not its replacement. This person does not succumb to egregious solipsism, but gauges a situation—with its available means of persuasion—to achieve sought goals. Concrete outcomes are sought and prefiguration is only a motivator and primer, never an end in itself. The empowered person works well with others to achieve these goals; liking others is ideal but less relevant than effectively collaborating with others to meet desired ends.

The empowered person is resilient not because of an avoidance or repression of emotions, but because of an acknowledgment of emotions, why they are happening, and what can be done to channel them in productive ways. The empowered person takes responsibility for these feelings and does not interpret them as necessarily direct reflections of reality. In other words, the empowered person knows that *feeling* a certain way does not necessarily reflect actual circumstances. (For example, feeling silenced does not actually denote *being* silenced.)

Compare this rhetoric of empowerment to that of a primacy of identity, in which lived experience, self-centeredness, and an aversion to critique are primary components. The empowered person, with all the values and behaviors that go with the intrapersonal, interactive, and behavioral components of empowerment, can go beyond subjectivity and self-interest, giving himself or herself over to the situation, and embracing critique as opportunistic conflict. The empowered person sees that situations are beyond the scope of oneself and that the emotions induced by those situations can be studied, critiqued, and transformed. Ultimately, the empowered person has a level of fortitude that cannot be damaged easily, even if experiences ranging from microaggressions to more egregious forms of discrimination are met. The empowered person's pragmatism and teleological outlook are primary motivators; dignity and esteem are not the primary goals, especially since the empowered person already has a healthy sense of both.

What is most interesting and most damning for many scholars and pedagogues who insist that academia is a space that perpetuates injury onto students and scholars of color is that people of color—especially African Americans and Latinx people—score very high, if not the highest, on Emotional Intelligence tests.[96] What's more, in a recent study of over 3,000 diverse college students done by Gallup, the Knight Foundation, and the Newseum, researchers discovered that most students of color never felt uncomfortable in college settings, including classrooms, living areas, or public spaces. (Black students felt the most uncomfortable, but even these students were a minority compared to the black students that did not.)[97] Of course, this does not mean that emotionally difficult things do not happen to this population, and it definitely does not mean that emotionally charged racist incidents do not occur. However, it does make one question the legitimacy of charges of psychological injury done to students by, for example, having to learn a dialect other than the ones they bring with them to First Year Composition courses. Students so emotionally resilient probably are not cowing to the "tyranny" of composition studies.

Ultimately, one can glean the source of disempowerment from an important aspect of the Conflict Management competency of Emotional Intelligence: the lack of a secure base. A secure base is "a person, place, goal or object that provides a sense of protection, safety and caring and offers a source of inspiration and energy for daring, exploration, risk taking and seeking challenge."[98] Many people, especially traditionally marginalized people, do not see academia as a secure base. Thus, a primacy of identity and a sacred victim narrative arise as defense mechanisms to handle profound feelings of disempowerment. This is understandable and will be touched on throughout the book. In this chapter, I wanted to show how empowerment theory can potentially help us, as a field, co-create a secure base without succumbing to rhetorics and outlooks of disempowerment.

THE NEED FOR TRUE EMPOWERMENT

The sacred victim becomes a symbol of resistance that results from an insidious lack of empowerment. I argue that creating an environment where traditionally marginalized groups are cast as untouchable authorities of everything pertaining to their respective groups is meant to hide feeling powerless to actually bring about change and eradicate discrimination. Disempowerment motivates us to demand genuflection instead of finding real ways to bring about change. The world is scary, vast, and difficult to alter. In a move indicative of disempowerment, academia is refashioned as a stage on which anti-racist sentiments can be acted out. The world beyond the gates surrounding the ivory tower is of no real concern. The disempowered settle for make-believe.

Clearly, a driving motivation of anti-racism proponents is validation, recognition, and recompense. These things are important for individuals and groups to have. However, from a place of disempowerment, this validation is "achieved" through a primacy of identity and a demand for obeisance from those considered privileged. The disempowered must prohibit critical inquiries that can expose the sacred victim narrative as the quasi-religious movement it is, one in which logic, reason, merit, and open inquiry are considered hegemonic constructs and inherently discriminatory toward people of color.

It may also be the impetus for confirmation bias and the purposeful embrace of irrational beliefs that have come to define "post-truth" America. Hannah Arendt's work on Totalitarianism addresses this tendency to knowingly embrace falsehoods for the greater good, that is, staving off erasure and further marginalization.[99] The desperation of embracing fallacious reasoning suggests that disempowerment is a, if not *the*, primary antecedent to a primacy of identity that demonizes any questioning of that particular identity.

As opposed to disempowerment, empowerment suggests that people are aware of behavioral options or choices to act as they believe appropriate to achieve goals they set for themselves. Within a sacred victim narrative fueled by a primacy of identity, I think communication indicative of an academic domain—civil debate, critical inquiry, dialectic—is squelched by anti-racist scholars who do not feel empowered.

The primacy of identity and the corresponding sacred victim narrative seem to be attached to two concepts that may shape the overall discourse of disempowerment I am trying to parse out: negative emotionality and the stimulus-response model of interpretation. Psychologist Scott O. Lilienfeld defines negative emotionality (NE) as "a pervasive temperamental disposition to experience aversive emotions of many kinds, including anxiety, worry, moodiness, guilt, shame, hostility, irritability, and perceived victimization."[100] Citing studies spanning from 1984 to 2009, Lilienfeld continues to write: "[I]ndividuals with elevated levels of NE tend to be critical and judgmental of both themselves and others, vulnerable to distress and emotional maladjustment, and inclined to focus on the negative aspects of life.... They also tend to be vigilant and overreactive to potential stressors" and are "prone to interpreting ambiguous stimuli in a negative light."[101] Could NE be both the cause and effect of the kind of environment in which critical thinking is squelched, that is, an environment driven by a primacy of identity?

An affirmative answer would imply that a majority of the anti-racist leadership in rhetoric and composition exudes NE, which would seem to work well with sacred victimhood. But is this a fair assessment? Smucker, in his work on analyzing social justice movements in the last twenty years, has made observations about the kinds of people that gravitate to social justice activism, a category under which anti-racism easily fits. Smucker writes that a therapeutic subtext always operates under the mission of an activist group. Finding likeminded souls with whom to fight against oppressive hegemonic forces is an understandable relief.[102] But there is more to this. As I do, Smucker understands and empathizes with those in need of a therapeutic space and sees that as part of an activist circle's charge. A problem arises when serving as a therapeutic space is the primary charge of activist groups. Smucker's assessment is worth quoting at length.

> Let's be frank. I suspect that anyone who has meaningfully participated in contemporary social movements in the United States would have a hard time denying that movements often attract some very alienated individuals who sometimes arrive with overwhelming psychological needs. There is even a logic to the pattern: by publicly challenging aspects of the status quo, movements may unsurprisingly become a kind of "magnet" that attracts people who feel especially alienated from that status quo. And movements often provide a space where such individuals can meaningfully participate and feel empowered. It can be highly problematic to psychologize the motivations of individual participants in political movements, but given that we have to practically navigate—toward political ends—the consequential social psychological level within social movements, it behooves us to candidly assess this level, including the pathologies. We might lean toward structuralist explanations for social, economic, and political problems, but if we want to build functional political vehicles run by actual human beings, we cannot afford to be disinterested in the psychological level of collective action. This level is an important part of the terrain that we have to learn to navigate.[103]

Before we dismiss Smucker's assessment as pop-psychology or the flippant complaints of a frustrated community organizer, we should realize that other characteristics common to social justice activists steeped in a primacy of identity resonate with "cognitive distortions that cause depression and anxiety," according to cognitive behavior therapy.[104] Educator and social psychologist George Lukianoff and Jonathan Haidt, respectively, notice several distortions on college campuses that include and build upon NE and the upcoming stimulus-response model.[105] They suggest that these distortions are becoming the insidious components of the social atmosphere of many college campuses. Smucker, then, has a point; ignoring the psychological significance of activist cultures, on and off campuses, may be a mistake.

I do not write this to downplay phenomena like microaggression or all-out racism. I do not write to deny the power of institutional racism. I have written about my own experiences with such things in academia, as I will discuss below. I definitely do not write to demonize people with true trauma from discriminatory experiences. However, I am concerned with the ecological effects of those phenomena. I think Smucker's assessment is understandable; it is not unreasonable to imagine that movements built to enhance and perpetuate feelings of empowerment would attract the disempowered. What is at issue here is that the disempowerment is not processed in productive ways. It grows into an overarching narrative that drives movement, silences threats to the integrity of that narrative, and sees everything through a terministic screen of victimhood and injury. Smucker speaks to the need for critical awareness of environment indicative of the interactional component of empowerment when urging that, although institutional structures are major culprits of oppression, we need to pay attention to the individual bodies who make up our environments if we are to build networks of true empowerment and effectively bring about change.

This brings us to the second concept related to the construction of a victim-based (and, therefore, disempowered) mode of antiracism: "the stimulus-response model." Closely related to NE, stimulus-response denotes a broad assumption that every member of a specific group interprets actions or situations in exactly the same way.[106] In reality, the idea that certain behaviors, even if deemed microaggressions by all, elicit the same response by its "victims" has not been substantiated and is "highly doubtful."[107] This is part of the essentialism I identify as a key component of a primacy of identity.

The inherent fallacy of the stimulus-response model can be gleaned through its almost synonymous relationship to the fallacy of composition: a part represents the whole the way a fractal might be a smaller manifestation of a larger pattern. Yes, a relationship between a part and a whole may have important overlap; this is what would be called "semi-fiction" by Hans Vaihinger—cited by Appiah in a chapter titled "Useful Untruths"—who wrote that such constructions "deliberately substitute a fraction of reality for the complete range of causes and effects."[108] Stimulus-Response, in the context of a primacy of identity, is a fallacy self-imposed by those embracing identity to create a "useful untruth": the narrative of the sacred victim.

Apparently, this was not lost on the psychology community. After explaining that the stimulus-response model has been highly debunked and is highly inimical to the literature in both social and health psychology, Lilienfeld writes of a different model: "Instead, the experimental literature better accords with a *transactional model*, in which individuals vary in their responses to racially tinged statements as a function of their traits and states, including their personality dispositions and strength of minority group identification."[109] Lilienfeld says that psychology and allied fields favor that move from stimulus-response to "more multifactorial *cognitive transactional models*" that consider how "individual differences shape people's subjective reactions to potentially stressful events."[110] With the transactional model, we move from group think to individuality and contextuality, a move I think needs to be taken more seriously in many anti-racist circles. Of course, working together as a community is imperative to success, but recognizing that an affinity group is not a monolith but is made of individuals can only enhance the critical awareness crucial to successfully acquire and utilize true empowerment. Along with having a vigilant eye on NE, the hold of a primacy of identity can be loosened enough to better ensure the fair-minded critical thinking necessary to bring on true change.

But, I think the motivation for the embrace —consciously or unconsciously—of something like a stimulus-response model should be explored. Anti-racism initiates, in order to exist, need something to combat. Because a sense of belonging is a strong motivator for many anti-racism proponents, anti-racism represents a secure base from which to operate and wherein marginalized people can feel safe. So, if racism causes and perpetuates anti-racism, and anti-racism creates a safe space for those who feel discomfort in hegemonic spaces, then eradicating racism would eradicate those safe spaces. Thus, one's NE ensures the reproduction of racist incidents and the stimulus-response ensures an autonomous home base where dissenters are ostracized as heretics or a scandalous threat.

In *The Ethics of Identity*, Kwame Anthony Appiah calls this the negation of affirmation, explaining that members of a group derive meaning from mission; without it, a profound insecurity ensues. Appiah provides an illustration of this phenomenon with his fictional affinity group, the Dyspeptics:

> Imagine, then, a cultural group, the Dyspeptics, that thrives on rejection. Perhaps it had its origins in some sixteenth-century heresy, and ever since the heretics were expelled from the community they once belonged to, they have sought to remain aloof and isolated. Accordingly, the Dyspeptics behave in ways odious to others, ensuring that they will be constantly rejected, gaining strength from the hostility of outsiders, and so keeping their way of life uncorrupted by external influence. Now, however, they find themselves within a regime that welcomes them and lavishes governmental largesse upon them; and as a result

the younger members of the group are beginning to question the basic tenets of the Dyspeptic creed. Of course, you might think this was a good thing. You might even take it as a vindication of your hug-a-Dyspeptic-today initiative. But such a policy cannot have as its rationale the *protection* of Dyspeptic culture. You haven't protected it; you've eroded it. The way to preserve its character would have been to encourage your non-Dyspeptic citizens to treat them with contempt. For it was under such conditions that the Dyspeptic culture arose, and under such conditions that it will best perpetuate itself.[111]

Appiah's tongue-in-cheek labeling of the group is surely meant to reflect the antagonism against hegemony that works to solidify identity. Many people in marginalized societies find themselves "gaining strength from hostility of outsiders." Smucker also writes of this phenomenon, in which working with outsiders, even if ultimately beneficial, is considered a traitorous act.[112] If marginalization caused the fortification of the group, a threat to that marginalization through interaction may be daunting.

Other aspects of Appiah's passage parallel real-life phenomena. Appiah's description of the Dyspeptic youth that begin to question the efficacy of Dyspeptic ways echoes an incident relayed in Eboo Patel's work. His short essay on how Chicago's Mayor, Lori Lightfoot, achieved success through a firm grasp of empowered thinking ends with a college student noticing the disempowered actions of her student diversity club. She says, "I've been involved in lots of diversity activities here. I've built lots of safe spaces and done lots of healing work. But the more I think about it, the more I wonder what good all of it is doing me."[113] Typically such a voice would be condemned or silenced by members of the group that embrace a primacy of identity and the secure base it affords them.

Lastly, Appiah alludes to the "white liberal" role in current anti-racist movements by mentioning the person who has created and/or takes part in a "hug-a-Dyspeptic" initiative. This person, by showing such affection to this marginalized group, thinks of such an act as good. However, the act threatens the distinction between oppressed and oppressor, a distinction that frames the comforting identity the oppressed have come to see as the very definition of who they are. This may be why virtue-signaling is such a strong and common phenomenon. "Woke" allies, because of people like the "hug-a-Dyspeptic" group, need to let the marginalized group in question know that they are not *one of them*.[114]

The sacred victim narrative and its animating primacy of identity work together to give voice and meaning to marginal groups. This meaning, unfortunately, seems to lose any kind of efficacious mission once it props up a distinct identity and a space (academia, the humanities, the field of rhetoric and composition) that can provide a secure base. The empowerment felt here is merely the comfort of safety. A sense of safety is important, but it is just the beginning. As a *telos,* it has no bearing on the other modes of well-being on which we should focus.

Of course, one's identity as a victim can be an objective fact and one that has to be acknowledged before plans to remedy this status can be made. This is not the issue; the centralization of victimhood to the point of sanctification is the issue. In "A Barbarian at the Gate," I reference my experience at a small, conservative, and predominantly white liberal arts college as a double-marginalized identity. I was both African American and a scholar of rhetoric and composition, which were two atypical things in the context of this particular institution. I did not write that essay to demand recognition or recompense for my injuries. I wrote it to show the detriments of insularity, where such insularity stems from, and how such insularity can be remedied. Discussing my role and embodiment juxtaposed to the aforementioned conservative, white discourse community is a means to an end, not the end itself. Thus, that essay is not an offshoot of the primacy of identity outlined in this book.

It is in my experience conveyed in "A Barbarian at the Gate," where I find a clue to an antidote for the primacy of identity. A primacy of identity that results in the creation of a sacred victim is detrimental. Citing identity for the sake of transcending it to talk about a larger issue is not the same as the primacy of identity. The use of identity to address the concept of general insularity in academic contexts is a microcosm of what should happen in civic and academic contexts. Getting outside of ourselves, an act strongly promoted by pragmatism, Buddhism, and mindfulness (prosoche), is both an antidote to the disempowerment that drives the primacy of identity and a more productive way to acquire a sense of empowerment and create positive and progressive change by acknowledging social and material realities and tactical necessities.

Ultimately, I claim that anti-racist endeavors in rhetoric and composition operate from a deficit-model of empowerment. That is, whether consciously or inadvertently, we frame our students and ourselves as powerless victims fighting hegemonic forces for power. This is not necessarily the case. Power is something that can be developed, enhanced, and perpetuated on an individual and group basis. Empowerment, itself, is a skill that can be self-cultivated. Yes, structural restrictions exist in academia and society at large, but in order to adequately and actually (not prefiguratively) combat those restrictions, we must come from an already empowered attitude.

What's more, empowerment theory is a morality of sorts. Unapologetic individualism is often dichotomized with communality.[115] However, with empowerment theory, these things combine within the three components. The intrapersonal constitutes the self-awareness and self-management concomitant to individualism while the intrapersonal and behavioral components emphasize an awareness of and engagement with community, respectively. The sovereign individual lauded in Eurocentric Enlightenment thinking is combined with the emphasis on community that seems to be centered in decolonial thought. Empowerment theory seems to emphasize a more holistic human experience.

The following chapters will address the detrimental effects that follow a lack of empowerment and how a rhetoric of disempowerment has driven anti-racism initiatives in the field of rhetoric and composition. First, I use codemeshing pedagogy as an example of good intentions thwarted by rhetorics of disempowerment. Then, I will show how a rhetoric of disempowerment drives theories and pedagogies that perpetuate the very injustices anti-racism proponents seek to reverse. By showing the detriments of disempowerment, I hope to expose the need to embrace a rhetoric of empowerment in both scholarly and pedagogical endeavors.

NOTES

1. The exploration of how all these connect to empowerment theory is beyond the scope of this chapter and the mission of this book. For more, see Edward Marguia and Kim Diaz, "The Philosophical Foundations of Cognitive Behavioral Therapy: Stoicism, Buddhism, Taoism, and Existentialism," *Journal of Evidence-Based Psychotherapies,* 15.1 (2015).

2. Judith A. B. Lee, *The Empowerment Approach to Social Work: Building the Beloved Community*, 2nd ed. (New York: Columbia University Press, 2001), 32.

3. Zimmerman, "Psychological Empowerment: Issues and Illustrations," 581.

4. Ibid.

5. Ibid., 582.

6. Douglass Perkins and Marc Zimmerman, "Empowerment Theory, Research, and Application," *American Journal of Community Psychology* 23.5 (1995), 570.

7. Zimmerman, "Psychological Empowerment: Issues and Illustrations."

8. Lee, *The Empowerment Approach to Social Work Practice.*

9. It is important to know that some scholars reconfigure the components while maintaining the general theory behind empowerment. See Brian D. Christens, Christina Hamme Peterson and Paul W. Speer, "Psychological Empowerment in Adulthood," *Encyclopedia of Primary Prevention and Health Promotions,* ed. T.P. Gullotta and M. Bloom (New York: Springer Science+Business Media, 2014), 1766–76. Zimmerman, himself has labeled the intrapersonal, interactional, and behavioral components the "psychological," the "organization," and the "community," respectively. (See Marc A. Zimmerman, "Empowerment Theory: Psychological, Organization, and Community Levels of Analysis," *Handbook of Community Psychology* (New York: Plenum Publishers, 2000), 43–64.)

10. Zimmerman, "Psychological Empowerment: Issues and Illustrations," 588.

11. Ibid., 590.

12. These components are called different things throughout scholarly publications, even by Zimmerman himself. I choose the rendering in this book—the intrapersonal, interactional, and behavioral—because I believe they fall in line with key concepts in rhetoric and composition more than other terms and capture the Buddhist concepts of "interbeing" and "dependent origination" as rhetorical concepts that I will discuss in a later chapter.

13. Again, t is important to know that some scholars reconfigure the components while maintaining the general theory behind empowerment. See Christen, Hamme Peterson and Speer, "Psychological Empowerment in Adulthood," 1766–76. Zimmerman, himself has labeled the intrapersonal, interactional, and behavioral components the "psychological," the "organization," and the "community," respectively. (See Zimmerman, "Empowerment Theory: Psychological, Organization, and Community Levels of Analysis," 43–64.) Lastly, it is important to note that Zimmerman initially used the term "psychological empowerment" to denote empowerment theory as a whole but would later use the term to denote the intrapersonal component, specifically. Thus, I will simply use the term "empowerment" here even when referring to publications in which "psychological empowerment" is used as an all-encompassing term.

14. Zimmerman, "Empowerment Theory: Psychological, Organization, and Community Levels of Analysis."

15. Ibid., 589.

16. Jonathan Matthew Smucker, *Hegemony How-To: A Roadmap for Radicals* (Chico, CA: AK Press, 2017), 142.

17. Zimmerman, "Psychological Empowerment: Issues and Illustrations," 589.

18. Smucker, *Hegemony How-To*, 80–81.

19. Lee, *The Empowerment Approach to Social Work Practice*, 2.

20. Asao Inoue, *Labor-Based Grading Contracts: Building Equity and Inclusion in the Compassionate Writing Classroom.* Perspectives on Writing (Fort Collins, Colorado: The WAC Clearinghouse and University Press of Colorado, 2019). Accessed August 19, 2019. Available at https://wac.colostate.edu/books/perspectives/labor/, 27.

21. Lee, *The Empowerment Approach to Social Work Practice*, 41.

22. Asao Inoue, "Chapter One: The Function of Race in Writing Assessment," *Antiracist Writing Assessment Ecologies: Teaching and Assessing Writing for a Socially Just Future* (Fort Collins, CO: The WAC Clearinghouse and Parlor Press, 2015), 49. Ebook. https://wac.colostate.edu/books/perspectives/inoue/.

23. Zimmerman, "Psychological Empowerment: Issues and Illustrations," 589

24. Ibid.

25. Richard Paul, *Critical Thinking: What Every Person Needs to Survive in a Rapidly Changing World* (Tomales, CA: The Foundation for Critical Thinking, 2012), 47.

26. Paul, *Critical Thinking.*

27. Zimmerman, "Psychological Empowerment: Issues and Illustrations," 589.

28. Although Zimmerman, arguably, is one of the most influential empowerment theorist, not everyone agrees with his rundown of empowerment components. More contemporary theorists consider the behavioral component of empowerment as less of

a component and more as a process variable and a predictor of outcome. (See Christens, Hamme Peterson, and Speer. "Psychological Empowerment in Adulthood," 1766–76) That is, it is better understood as an aspect of the other components, or a "final product" of the other components Considering this, I still see the term "behavioral component" as a placeholder for the productive participation and the successful acquisition of desired outcomes of a group: policy changes, institutional changes, etc. In other words, where the interactional component is rhetoric in theory and analysis, the behavioral component is rhetoric in action as productive collaboration.

29. Zimmerman, "Psychological Empowerment: Issues and Illustrations," 590.

30. I hope the double-meaning of "accompanying a minority" is not lost on the reader. The implied infantilization of minorities in anti-racism will be discussed later in this book.

31. Lee, *The Empowerment Approach to Social Work Practice,* 49–50.

32. Pappas, "The Limitations and Dangers of Decolonial Philosophies: Lessons from Zapatista Luis Villoro," 2–5.

33. Pappas, "The Limitations and Dangers of Decolonial Philosophies: Lessons from Zapatista Luis Villoro."

34. Paul, *Critical Thinking,* 47.

35. Frances Kay and Neilson Kite, *Understanding Emotional Intelligence: Strategies for Boosting your EQ and Using it in the Workplace.* (Philadelphia: Kogan Page, 2011), 13.

36. Daniel Goleman, "Emotional Intelligence Competencies: An Introduction," *Emotional Self-Awareness: A Primer* (Florence, MA: More Than Sound, 2017), Loc 33.

37. Goleman, "Emotional Self-Awareness: An Introduction," Loc 201.

38. Ibid.

39. Daniel Goleman, "Empathy: An Introduction," *Empathy: A Primer* (Florence, MA: More Than Sound, 2017), Loc 117.

40. Goleman, "Empathy: An Introduction."

41. Ibid., 265.

42. Daniel Goleman, "Organizational Awareness: An Introduction," *Organizational Awareness: A Primer* (Florence, MA: More Than Sound, 2017), Loc 112.

43. Zimmerman, "Psychological Empowerment: Issues and Illustrations," 589.

44. Lee, *The Empowerment Approach to Social Work Practice,* 51.

45. Daniel Goleman, "Organizational Awareness: An Introduction," *Organizational Awareness: A Primer* (Florence, MA: More Than Sound, 2017), Loc 121.

46. Daniel Goleman, "Emotional Self-Control: An Introduction," *Emotional Self-Control: A Primer* (Florence, MA: More Than Sound, 2017), Loc 117.

47. See Diane Coutu, "How Resilience Works," *Resilience: HBR Emotional Intelligence Series* (Boston, MA: Harvard Business Review Press, 2017).

48. Coutu, "How Resilience Works."

49. The term "Men" is used here to maintain the accuracy of the quote. I would prefer the more appropriate "people" in its stead.

50. Epictetus, *Enchiridion,* Trans. Thomas Wentworth Higginson, *Project Gutenberg,* March 10, 2014, https://www.gutenberg.org/files/45109/45109-h/45109-h.htm.

51. Vanessa Druskat, "Emotional Self Control in Teams," *Emotional Self-Control: A Primer* (Florence, MA: More Than Sound, 2017), Loc 173.
52. John Dewey, *The Philosophy of John Dewey*, ed. Joseph Ratner (New York: Henry Holt and Company, 1928), 464.
53. Steven J. Stein, Howard E. Book, and Korrel Kanoy, *The Student EQ Edge: Emotional Intelligence and Your Academic and Personal Success* (San Francisco, CA: Jossey-Bass, 2013), 17.
54. Stein, Book, and Kanoy, *The Student EQ Edge: Emotional Intelligence and Your Academic and Personal Success*.
55. Richard Boyatzis, "Emotional Self-Control: What It Looks Like, How to Develop It," *Emotional Self-Control: A Primer* (Florence, MA: More Than Sound, 2017), Loc 199.
56. Zimmerman, "Psychological Empowerment: Issues and Illustrations," 590.
57. Lee, *The Empowerment Approach to Social Work Practice*, 52.
58. Daniel Goleman, "Adaptability: An Introduction," *Adaptability: A Primer* (Florence, MA: More Than Sound, 2017), Loc 19
59. Paul, *Critical Thinking*, 47.
60. George Kohlrieser, "A Mindset of Adaptability," *Adaptability: A Primer* (Florence, MA: More Than Sound, 2017), Loc 307.
61. Daniel Goleman, "Achievement Orientation: An Introduction," *Achievement Orientation: A Primer* (Florence, MA: More Than Sound, 2017), Loc 116.
62. Goleman, "Achievement Orientation: An Introduction," Loc 119–26.
63. See Asao Inoue, "Afterward," *Black Perspectives in Writing Program Administration: From the Margins to the Center* (Urbana, IL: NCTE, 2019), 150.
64. Inoue, "Afterward," Loc 155.
65. Daniel Goleman, "Positive Outlook: An Introduction," *Positive Outlook: A Primer* (Florence, MA: More Than Sound, 2017), Loc 114.
66. Goleman, "Positive Outlook: An Introduction," 223.
67. Ibid, 227.
68. Kenneth Burke, *Language as Symbolic Action,* in *The Rhetorical Tradition: Readings From Classical Times to the Present* 2nd ed., ed. Patricia Bizzell and Bruce Herzberg (New York: Bedford St. Martin's Press, 2001), 1341.
69. Burke, *Language as Symbolic Action*.
70. Goleman, "Positive Outlook: An Introduction," Loc 248.
71. Ibid., 248–54.
72. Daniel Goleman, "Influence: An Introduction," in *Influence: A Primer* (Florence, MA: More Than Sound, 2017), Loc 117.
73. Richard Boyatzis, "Influence in Action," in *Influence: A Primer* (Florence, MA: More Than Sound, 2017), Loc 154.
74. Daniel Goleman, "Coach and Mentor: An Introduction," in *Coach and Mentor: A Primer* (Florence, MA: More Than Sound, 2017), Loc 122.
75. Goleman, "Coach and Mentor: An Introduction," 144.
76. Ibid.
77. Ibid., 149.
78. Richard Boyatzi, "The Basis for Inspirational Leadership," *Inspirational Leadership: A Primer* (Florence, MA: More Than Sound, 2017), 143.

79. Smucker, *Hegemony How-To*, 190.
80. Ibid., 219.
81. Smucker, *Hegemony How-To*, 60–61.
82. Ibid., 191.
83. Inoue, "Afterward," 54.
84. Daniel Goleman, "Conflict Management: An Introduction," in *Conflict Management: A Primer* (Florence, MA: More Than Sound, 2017), Loc 107.
85. Goleman, "Conflict Management: An Introduction," Loc 102.
86. Ibid., Loc 130–36.
87. Daniel Goleman, "Teamwork: An Introduction," in *Teamwork: A Primer* (Florence, MA: More Than Sound, 2017), Loc 122.
88. Goleman, "Teamwork: An Introduction," 138.
89. George Kohlrieser, "How Secure Base Leaders Maintain Differences Without Breaking Bonds," in *Conflict Management: A Primer* (Florence, MA: More Than Sound, 2017), Loc 136.
90. It is important to distinguish between EQ and what are called "noncognitive" competencies. A major issue with the latter term is that the distinction between cognitive and noncognitive is not clear. Cognition processes can be understood as "the processes by which we acquire knowledge through perception and learning; store knowledge in memory; use, transform, and generate knowledge through reasoning, problem-solving, judgement [sic], and decision-making; and share knowledge through language." (See *Oxford Companion to Consciousness*, ed. Tim Bayne, Axel Cleeremans, and Patrick Wilken [New York: Oxford University Press, 2009], 136.) EQ is not divorced from most, if not all, aspects of cognitive processes. What's more, noncognitive processes involve "attitudes, motivation and personality traits" as well as "openness to experience," "conscientiousness," and "agreeableness." These traits, too, are not necessarily separate from cognitive processes. The very distinction between cognitive and noncognitive may need to be parsed out a bit. Thus, the components and corresponding competencies of EQ are not to be confused with what are considered "noncognitive" traits.

Assuming that the cognitive/noncognitive binary is a real one, the dichotomy is not a salient aspect of what is understood as EQ. EQ does not really see cognitive and noncognitive traits as mutually exclusive, as one can see from competencies like Organizational Awareness, Conflict Management, etc. EQ necessitates a confluence of the cognitive and noncognitive.

What's more, contrary to Inoue's general take on the cognitive/noncognitive dichotomy, success in communication and, therefore, the world also necessitates a confluence of the two. All good writing is a confluence of cognitive and noncognitive skills as they are explained above, especially when one considers that EQ competencies like Empathy, Positive Outlook, and Social Awareness are imperative to successful persuasion in written or oral communication. When it comes to writing, one can and should cultivate the cognitive and the noncognitive simultaneously.

Lastly, if, as Inoue writes, traits like "openness," "agreeableness," and "coping and resilience" are major noncognitive competencies, one could say that a lack of noncognitive awareness is significantly responsible for the lack of empowerment in anti-racist initiatives. Thus, they can alleviate the primacy of identity and victim mentality Inoue inadvertently utilizes in justifying his brand of anti-racist pedagogy. If students had these traits, would labor-based grading be so direly needed?

    For the aforementioned descriptions of noncognitive traits, see Asao Inoue, *Labor-Based Grading Contracts: Building Equity and Inclusion in the Compassionate Writing Classroom. Perspectives on Writing* (Fort Collins, CO: The WAC Clearinghouse and University Press of Colorado, 2019), accessed August 20, 2019. https://wac.colostate.edu/books/perspectives/labor/, 244–47.

    91. James Gee, *Social Linguistics and Literacies: Ideology in Discourses*, 3rd ed. (New York: Routledge, 2008), 154.

    92. Gee, *Social Linguistics and Literacies: Ideology in Discourses*, 155.

    93. Zimmerman, "Psychological Empowerment: Issues and Illustrations," 590.

    94. James Berlin, *Rhetorics, Poetics, and Cultures: Refiguring College English Studies* (Urbana, IL: NCTE, 1996), 81.

    95. This sentiment is inspired by DanDennet's concept of "intentional strategy" brought up by Kwame Anthony Appiah in Anthony Appiah, *As If* (Cambridge, MA: Harvard University Press, 2017), 45. The "intentional strategy" is one that is understood to be imperfect and, at times, a mode of self-deception to better motivate. I consider this a recognized "noble lie" to oneself and is not synonymous with the kind of prefiguration I argue weakens anti-racism initiatives.

    96. Steven J. Stein, Howard E. Book, and Korrel Kanoy, *The Student EQ Edge: Emotional Intelligence and Your Academic and Personal Success* (San Francisco, CA: Jossey-Bass, 2013), 22–24.

    97. Knight Foundation, *Free Expression on Campus: What College Students Think about First Amendment Issues: A Gallup/Knight Foundation Survey* (Washington, DC: Gallup, 2018), 19.

    98. George Kohlrieser, Susan Goldsworthy, and Duncan Coombe, *Care to Dare: Unleashing Astonishing Potential Through Secure Base Leadership* (San Francisco, CA: Jossey-Bass, 2012), 8.

    99. Hannah Arendt, *The Origins of Totalitarianism* (New York: Meridian Books, 1960), 382.

    100. Scott O. Lilienfeld, "Microaggression: Strong Claims, Inadequate Evidence," *Perspectives on Psychological Science* 12.1 (2017): 163.

    101. Lilienfeld, "Microaggression: Strong Claims, Inadequate Evidence."

    102. Smucker, *Hegemony How-To*, 80–81

    103. Ibid, 81.

    104. Bradley Campbell and Jason Manning, *The Rise of Victimhood Culture: Microaggression, Safe Spaces, and the New Culture Wars* (New York: Palgrave Macmillan, 2018), LOC 697. E-book.

    105. Jonathan Haidt and George Lukianoff, "The Coddling of the American Mind," *The Atlantic* (September 2015). https://www.theatlantic.com/magazine/archive/2015/09/the-coddling-of-the-american-mind/399356/#Cognitive%20Disorders.

    106. Lilienfeld, "Microaggression: Strong Claims, Inadequate Evidence," 147.

    107. Ibid.

108. In Kwame Anthony Appiah, *As If: Idealization and Ideals* (Cambridge, MA; Harvard University Press, 2017), 9.

109. Lilienfeld, "Microaggression: Strong Claims, Inadequate Evidence," 163.

110. Ibid.

111. Kwame Anthony Appiah, *The Ethics of Identity* (Princeton, NJ: Princeton University Press, 2005), 140.

112. Smucker, *Hegemony How-To*, 71–101.

113. Patel, "Chicago's New Black Lesbian Mayor and the Power/Privilege/Oppression Paradigm."

114. John McWhorter, "Virtue Signalers Won't Change the World."

115. Inoue, *Labor-Based Grading Contracts: Building Equity and Inclusion in the Compassionate Writing Classroom. Perspectives on Writing*, 35.

Chapter 3

Disempowerment and Code-meshing Pedagogy

So far, we have gone over the primacy of identity, its corresponding sacred victim narrative, and the underlying disempowerment that supports it all in popular anti-racist initiatives. Because I am talking about academia and the field of rhetoric and composition specifically, I want to illustrate the detriments of disempowerment in those contexts. This chapter and the next will focus on pedagogy and faculty attitudes toward anti-racist pedagogy.

In addressing the detrimental effects of a primacy of identity in academia, we may see some academic spaces as prefigurative spaces akin to those in activist contexts outside of academia, like the Occupy Movement addressed in the previous chapter. The classroom is no stranger to prefiguration; the world anti-racist pedagogues wish to see is often enacted in such spaces through discussion, activities, and assignments. This, I believe, has many benefits. However, like manifestations of prefiguration in other spaces inside and outside of academia, reality testing (the ability or desire to acknowledge the world as it is) suffers a dearth. As I will argue, the prefigurative world of anti-racist proponents infiltrates college classrooms in ways that are beneficial from a critical language analysis standpoint but detrimental from a "real world" perspective. The classroom is not immune to the "allergy" to reality lamented by Smucker and Coole and Frost.

Code-meshing, the confluence of academic and "home" modes of speaking, seems to be the flag of diversity in rhetoric and composition, driven by a primacy of identity staked firmly in the writing classroom. Its charge is to rid academia of its focus and favoring of an English dialect considered too Anglocentric, and, therefore, too oppressive to have a primary place within writing classrooms. Let me remind you that Vershawn Young has gone as far as insisting that teaching an Anglocentric dialect of English deemed "standardized" "replicates the same phony logic behind Jim Crow legislation"[1] and calls the encouragement of code-switching—the practice of changing dialects based on rhetorical contexts—"segregationist,"[2] likening a student of color's tendency to code-switch to a kind of "racial schizophrenia."[3] This implies that people should write however they want and expect an audience to cater to the writer's preferred dialect. Expecting students to write in any other dialect is considered, metaphorically, "chopping off folks' tongues."[4] It would seem that the very fundamentals of rhetoric, that is, one's "ability, in each particular case, to see the available means of persuasion," are inherently antithetical to a primacy of identity and implicitly oppressive to nonhegemonic groups and dialects. This is a problem.

Before I go any further, I want to express my respect for code-meshing as a rhetorical phenomenon. Combining dialects to produce intelligent and innovative ideas is a legitimate phenomenon that has many intriguing implications about cultural rhetoric, social construction, and the sociology of language. I, myself, code-mesh when I feel like doing so. My issue is with the *pedagogical* manifestation of code-meshing that results from a primacy of identity that is relatively unrhetorical (see chapter 1 for the definition of rhetoric put forth in this book) and antithetical to fair-minded critical thinking.

Lastly, the code-meshing movement suggests a political reality that has yet to fully actualize, thus increasing the danger of preparing students for a world that does not exist. Many rhetoric and composition scholars proudly aggrandize code-meshing as a sign of progress and behave as if those outside the field are already following suit. The academic bubble that some of us act out in conferences, symposia, and classrooms—the one that sustains the embrace of code-meshing—has not overtaken the world beyond the institution of higher education sufficiently enough. Yes, spaces exist in which such an ideology is favored, but what I call "civic and professional" contexts have not adequately followed suit. Thus, many seem to advocate preparing students to successfully navigate a college climate, if not a departmental climate, while neglecting to prepare them for the social and material realities (i.e., actual societal conditions containing multifaceted manifestations) of the outside professional and civic world.

One argument given by code-meshing pedagogues is that professional contexts already use code-meshed language. They site ESPN,[5] the Obama administration,[6] and Twitter posts[7] as examples. Two responses come to mind. First, these "professional" spaces are novel in that they speak to a very wide and diverse audience. Obama's use of African American Vernacular English (AAVE) is a result of his speaking, as a black man, to a diverse American audience. Secondly, the oral communicators in these contexts bring a specific ethos that allows their use of code-meshed language. Our students are coming out of college and into more standard professional and civic contexts; they are not coming from the NFL or Rock and Roll Hall of Fame and into another entertainment-based context. This makes Asao Inoue's argument that the success of Hip Hop music is a sign of code-meshed language's ubiquitous acceptance[8] especially short-sighted. First, people listen to Hip Hop for a variety of reasons (e.g., the music, social clout) and some do not even understand the lyrics if they listen to them at all. Secondly, no one would recommend that anyone rap their quarterly progress report to their chief officers. The use of code-meshing by celebrities, entertainers, and even a President is simply a bad argument for its pedagogical efficacy.

For clarity's sake, I want to explain what is meant by the term "code-meshing" throughout this book. What some people call code-meshing is actually just slang. Certain colloquialisms peppered into an otherwise standard discourse is not code-meshing in the way that Young's "Should Writers Use They Own English," for example, is. Nor is code-meshing seen as akin to multimodal forms of communication. Young's code-meshing, the kind of writing to which I refer when I use the term, is at issue. For example, when critiquing Stanley Fish's justification for teaching standard English, Young writes: "Lord, lord, lord! Where do I begin, cuz this man sho tryin to take the nation back to a time when we were less tolerant of linguistic and racial differences. Yeah, I said racial differences, tho my man Stan be talkin explicitly bout language differences."[9] Argument aside, let this quote serve as an example of what I mean when using the term "code-meshing."

Likewise, we would do well to explain what the term "standard English," or its variations (e.g. "standardized English") denote. Because I have given good grades to papers that would make Strunk and White turn over in their graves, deriding code-meshing for current traditional standardized English would make no sense. What I really mean, and what is more realistic, is what Geneva Smitherman calls "Language of Wider Communication,"[10] a language in which contractions, singular "they," split infinitives, and other aspects of language may exist with no controversy. Although much code-meshing scholarship has Strunk, White, and Stanley Fish as the metonymical antagonists, as is clear in essays like "Should Writers Use They Own English," I believe that "Language of Wider Communication," though not standard in a strict sense, would also be antithetical to the code-meshing put forth by pedagogues and scholars currently leading anti-racist initiatives in the field. So, henceforth, I will be using the term "Language of Wider Communication" (LWC) to refer to English *deemed* standard or English typically expected in professional and civic contexts. This book is not a defense of current traditional, standard English.

Many academics, including proponents of code-meshing, say that LWC, itself, is code-meshed English.[11] That is correct; LWC is not the prescriptive vernacular put forth by Strunk and White, for example. However, LWC, even if a meshed code, is also considered oppressive by proponents of code-meshing.[12] LWC, then, is a meshed code that has taken the place of more traditional understandings of standardization. LWC is becoming the new standard and, according to proponents of code-meshing pedagogy, a tool of linguistic tyranny for many proponents of code-meshing.

An LWC moves away from the grapholect of standardized academic English. Slang is not completely taboo in student writing if used and presented effectively, which is to say kairotically. Based on the civic and professional world into which our students enter, meticulous policing of English is rather unnecessary. However, I do try to instill what I, like many others, regardless of race, see as the *Lingua Franca* of professional and civic spaces, a writing that comes closer to the mechanics, punctuation, syntax, and register of a style deemed standard in most of these circles. So, my issue is not with the phenomenon of code-meshing, but its falling victim to a pedagogical imperative: the tendency to force a theory or phenomenon into a mode of teaching.

My main argument is that code-meshing pedagogy is motivated by a primacy of identity, a rhetoric of disempowerment. That is, what seems like empowering students by giving them the "the right to their own language," is done in a way that ignores the efficacies of the three components of empowerment (intrapersonal, interactive, behavioral) as well as the very fundamentals of rhetoric, specifically *kairos*, which is an inherent part of empowerment.

THE MINORITY WRITER AND "SACRED VICTIMHOOD"

Writing instruction at the college level can serve as an excellent case study for the aforementioned manifestations of a primacy of identity in academia. The teaching of written communication is fraught with issues of hegemonic standardization, the marginalization of nonhegemonic dialects, and the chasm between hegemonic and nonhegemonic standpoints that fuel the fires of the primacy of identity. Again, the primacy of identity often manifests in writing studies as pedagogy that centers on or encourages the confluence of hegemonic and nonhegemonic writing styles in one document or speech. Code-meshing happens organically in many contexts and has proven to be very effective in conveying information. However, when made into a rhetorical pedagogy, an educational philosophy for teaching effective written and oral communication, many ignore the concepts of rhetorical context and audience consideration—two things that are supposed to be central to rhetoric and composition—and promote an acontextual self-expression. Thus, code-meshing is less about effective communication—commonly considered the central point of rhetorical studies—and more about the validation of the writer's or speaker's "authentic" voice (or something closer to authentic than a standardized dialect). Thus, rhetorical savvy (which need not exclude social issues as subject matter) is not the goal of code-meshing pedagogy; dignity and validation seem to be its true goals.

As we've established, validation and the handling of disempowerment are primary motivations of prefigurative politics. Considerations of social and material reality that normally would dictate a need to learn an LWC are ignored. Trusting that our students will code-switch or code-mesh as they see fit—that is, as *kairos* dictates—is de-emphasized. Prefiguration is, by definition, not based securely in reality, so one can conclude that a prefigurative pedagogy will not adequately prepare students for the civic and professional social realities that await them after graduation or even during their college years.

It is here where the marginalized writer as "sacred victim" comes into play, in all its religiosity. In rhetoric and composition, specifically, the sacred victim manifests as a writing student oppressed by the expectation to acquire skills indicative of standard English, the oppressive force of choice for the pharaoh-like hegemonic forces of first-year composition. Expecting students from marginalized groups to add another tactical dialect to their home dialects is considered tantamount to asking them to denounce religion or spirituality. In such a context, to insist that one's identity and preferred dialect transcends rhetorical context and audience consideration is to be a martyr for a noble cause, and to learn and retain a standardized dialect is indistinguishable from being possessed by an evil spirit.

Even code-meshing, a compromise of sorts, is dogmatic in its manifestations. Like religious dogma, the efficacy of its use is considered universal and omnipotent, not contingent and kairotic. Code-meshing, reminiscent of the confluence of spirit and matter in some modes of theology, is to be worshipped as a messianic power, hallowing composition pedagogy and giving rhetoric and composition scholars and instructors, especially white ones, a way to atone for their "original sin": being agents of hegemony. Of course, code-meshing also serves as a "road to Damascus" for white writing pedagogues who have "seen the light" and changed their ways to better serve the sacred victim. Their "ally" status puts them at the level of clergy.

To be clear, the following is not so much a thorough analysis of code-meshing pedagogy as it is the use of code-meshing pedagogy to exemplify the detriments of a primacy of identity in rhetoric and composition. A thorough critique of code-meshing pedagogy would require reference to more authors and more texts, which is beyond the mission of this chapter. For now, to illustrate a primacy of identity's manifestations in rhetoric and composition, I will reference only a limited but salient set of code-meshing scholars to explain the detriments of a primacy of identity, sacred victimhood, and prefiguration in general.

I teach first-year composition and have done so for two decades (at the time I write this text). I want to be clear about my perceived mission when teaching composition and how that informs my critique of code-meshing pedagogy. For one, my focus in the classroom is more on writing than speaking. Writing as a grapholect, in particular, is at issue, here. Orality, due to its immediacy (one rarely, if ever, goes back to copy-edit a verbal statement), and its relative acceptance in mainstream contexts, makes it a different creature compared to written communication, which can be revised a number of times and can work with the rhetorical tendencies of a relatively assumed audience. Thus, I am more lenient when grading oral presentations when it comes to codes.

In addition, I want to express that I am not naïve enough to think that the acquisition of an English dialect considered standard will guarantee acceptance into hegemonic contexts. Some of my own life experiences are enough to debunk that myth. What I am talking about here is not acceptance by the white mainstream, but of rhetorical strategies geared toward the social and material realities of contemporary society. This is about rhetoric and *kairos*, not the eradication of racism. I am definitely interested in the eradication of racism, and I work toward that in various civic engagement endeavors, but this work is about rhetoric—particularly *kairos* and its relationship to professional and civic contexts—and our ability to give our students the tactical knowledge they need.

Of course, the history of Anglocentric oppression in general, and the use of standardized English as a gatekeeping strategy in particular, is fraught with historical and contemporary injustice. This is unfortunate and morally reprehensible, but is having students of color refrain from acquiring a tactical skill, regardless of its history, the remedy to this injustice? This is not a new question by any means, but it is one that either goes ignored or is presented with less than adequate arguments (e.g., the use of code-meshed English in entertainment contexts). Other questions are less hackneyed. Is neglecting the realities of the present going to alter our past? As Gregory Fernando Pappas argues in his work, true and useful are not synonymous terms, theories and accusations of past misdeeds, and they are certainly misdeeds, are not empowerment, which is necessarily a "here and now" concept. Of course, it is accurate to say that non-Western cultures were wrongly marginalized, their histories erased. It is true that these "non-Western, peripheralized rhetorics" can and should reemerge to effectively serve as "an avenue of radical critical practice."[13] This is truth. However, when discussing truth versus usefulness, Pappas writes that truth "may lead to analysis or diagnosis that while true at some level may actually have very little to offer in terms of more specific diagnosis and solutions that can be of any help to someone suffering an injustice."[14] Yes, it is true that standard English and even LWC derive from colonizers, but is it useful to ignore the pragmatic benefit of acquiring efficiency in these dialects?

Other questions abound. What does all this suggest about racial authenticity? Is the confluence of a particular dialect with a genuine understanding of one's authentic self a reality for everyone? Are we our dialects? Are black people, for example, who use an English dialect deemed "standardized" inauthentically black or merely performing? What of the logistics of even assessing the detriments of code-switching? Where is the line that separates "racial schizophrenia" from rhetorical savvy? What separates suffering from the tyranny of language oppression from an acquisition of a useful skill for most professional and civic contexts? I believe that code-meshing's pedagogical efficacy has been grossly exaggerated, and its detrimental implications for racial or ethnic authenticity have been all but ignored.

So code-meshing's pedagogical effects and its implications for rhetoric and composition as a field suggest that those who embrace a primacy of identity are not instructors of rhetoric and composition doing anti-racist activism; they are anti-racist activists doing rhetoric and composition. As identity politicians, as it were, these academics follow the same patterns as those outside of academia. Politics of recognition (which includes victimhood, narcissism, and the inducement of hegemonic guilt) and prefiguration motivate their actions in both scholarship and pedagogy. These things subordinate critical thinking and pragmatic thought, which indicates the subordination of empowerment theory. For many proponents of antiracism, the field of rhetoric and composition, itself, is subordinate to a primacy of identity.

THE LOGISTICAL PROBLEM IN A PRIMACY OF IDENTITY: HOW DOES ONE "TEACH" CODE-MESHING?

With code-meshing being explained and illustrated, we can begin to speak of the logistics (or lack, thereof) of code-meshing pedagogy. First, even if a student comes into a first-year composition classroom and likes the idea of incorporating home discourse into his writing, he has to acknowledge LWC. That is, in order to code-mesh, codes with which to mesh are required. Some will say that the dialects are so similar that LWC need not be considered; it is all a "common language."[15] However, if that is the case, why dedicate so much time and energy to this topic at all? If the languages are already so close, how are these students being so oppressed and tyrannized by their composition courses? The very existence of code-meshing necessitates knowledge of more than one code. Even if one allows students to write solely in code-meshed English, including final drafts of final assignments, teaching LWC is in order.

All this being said, if code-meshing is to be a part of the classroom at all, it is more of a heuristic than a pedagogy—more of a transitional concept than a rhetoric for its own sake, for rhetoric is always for the audiences' sake. (Even self-centered messages meant to agitate audiences are done after gauging that audience to better ensure that outcome.)[16] Clearly, styles deemed nonstandard have consistent structures and phonologies of their own, and code-meshing can be a powerful mode of communication, but code-meshing for its own sake misses the point: *kairos*—the simultaneous consideration of audience, topic, place, subject position, and time—should dictate the nature of one's style. Examples of code-meshing by prominent voices in the media and popular culture only manifested because *kairos* brought forth the opportunity.

Even in academia, when code-meshing is used, it is taking advantage of a kairotic moment to show the efficacy of code-meshed language. Young's "Should Writers Use They Own English" exists because his audience was aware enough of sociolinguistic issues of race. Of course, there are times when audiences can be interpellated to some extent by a rhetor. Nevertheless, we need to help our students acquire tools for occasions when their audiences expect something akin to LWC; contexts of protests, entertainment, or epideictic rhetoric are more conducive to audience interpellation than most professional or civic contexts.[17] The point is that code-meshing—and language in general—is such a saliently kairotic mode of persuasion that it may transcend measurable mastery. Code-meshing works when it is called forth by a particular situation, thus deeming its *pedagogical* efficacy mostly artificial. Students can say the same of a standardized grapholect, hence my preference for LWC, which is more kairotically flexible than both standardized and code-meshed English. Students will gauge a rhetorical situation and write accordingly. To mesh or not to mesh is a kairotic consideration.

Further logistical consideration complicates the issue and shows how a primacy of identity skirts any material and critical thought that goes against it. As one may glean from code-meshed scholarship, specifically the meshing of AAVE with LWC, the meshing involves more than merely mechanics, syntax, and punctuation; register and style also come into play. Yes, AAVE has a solid syntactical foundation, but do we expect all professors to assess the proper mix of its style and register with LWC?

This problem is articulated by Gerald Graff. In "Code-meshing Meets Teaching the Conflicts," an otherwise supportive essay about code-meshing, he writes: "What does competent code-meshing look like in student writing and speaking, and how will teachers determine the difference between successful and effective code-meshing and awkwardly cobbled together mixes of formal and vernacular English?"[18] This question, asked by a man who claims to adamantly support code-meshing, raises one of the many elephants in the room when it comes to code-meshing pedagogy: What is the distinction between style and error? Is an exorbitant number of periods in an ellipsis subject to scrutiny, or would such a critique be seen as a stifling of the student's authentic self? What semantic significance does an alternative spelling—for example, "rite" for "write"—really have, and whose call is it to determine that significance? The alternative spelling could be used to let readers know the author wants to identify as decidedly nonhegemonic, but even the efficacy of this move would depend on an audience's knowledge of the alternative spelling and knowledge of its use as an act of defiance and not an error. What are we really doing when assessing code-meshed writing?

That question becomes even trickier when we see critiques of hegemony among proponents of code-meshing pedagogy. Two examples come from the collection of essays, *Writing Centers and the New Racism.* In "The 'Standard English' Fairy Tale," Laura Greenfield rightly points out that the English we deemed standard is as nebulous as any other dialect and rightly suggests that we should help students think critically about privileged dialects. However, her observation about the inherent oppression in teaching LWC is stifling to anyone attempting to teach a composition course. She writes: "Ultimately, until our institutionalized racism is eradicated, practices that advocate the teaching of any privileged language will be—*by definition*—contributing to a system of inequity."[19] (my emphasis). So, what are we to do? First, Greenfield's charge could be reduced to a semantic one. If we replace "privileged" with another adjective that denotes the more lenient LWC, it will still be privileged in most civic and professional contexts. Secondly, the only way to not be racist as a composition instructor is to allow complete code-meshing without grading or critiquing and to the neglect of the tools typically beneficial in professional and civic contexts.

Asao Inoue's concept of anti-racist writing assessment actually moves in this direction.[20] In his ideal writing classroom, grades are based on labor and not adherence to any writing standard. However, whether one incorporates grades or not, the civic and professional contexts outside of academia exist, and writing considered most persuasive in those contexts can easily be gleaned by sample documents and presentations. What's more, Inoue openly admits that his labor-based grading contracts, meant to evaluate students based on effort and not quality, is about *his* agenda for social justice and the dismantling of white language supremacy,[21] (pragmatism and *kairos* be damned). Reality testing does not seem to be a strong consideration in his pedagogy. (I will address Inoue's assessment theory a bit more later in this book.)

Yes, teaching LWC is steeped in a long history of racism, but at this point in our history, that fact contributes to a genetic fallacy. The history of English deemed standard or LWC does not erase its benefit from a pragmatic and strategic standpoint. The historical connections of teaching standardized English and racism are true, but they are relatively banal truths if actual progress is the goal; basing pedagogy upon it is more symbolic than pragmatic, more protest-oriented than progressive. I argue that considerations of pragmatism in social and material realities are the only rational practices in composition pedagogy. The traditional correlation between writing instruction and racism is, indeed, a truth, but it is not a truth that should de-emphasize LWC in composition classrooms.

In "Should Writers Use They Own English," itself written in code-meshed English, Young doubles down on Greenfield's point by writing that code-switching, the idea that dialects should be utilized based on context, often deeming one's home language as "inappropriate" in contexts deemed academic or professional, is just another form of segregation. He prefers the concept of code-meshing, which is more egalitarian in his eyes. The issue most salient to my current argument (for there are many) is his concluding description of code-meshing: "Code-meshing use the way people already speak and write and help them be more rhetorically effective. It do include teaching some punctuation rules, attention to meaning and word choice, and various kinds of sentence structures and some standardized English. This mean too that good writing gone look and sound a bit different than some may now expect."[22] First, when he references the need to teach punctuation, meaning, word choice, and sentence structures, one can assume he means those of a marginalized dialect—in this case, AAVE. This is suggested by ending the respective sentence with "and some standard English," suggesting that the previous aspects of writing are meant to be indicative of a nonstandard English. If this is not the case, he is admitting that standardized modes of punctuation, word choice, etc., still need to be taught. Either way, a glaring problem arises, one already articulated by the above Graff quote: How does one accurately grade code-meshed English? What word choices are not wrong but simply "black"? What word choices are wrong from an AAVE perspective? What does AAVE punctuation look like? And what do we make of "some standard English"? How much standard English surpasses "some" and moves into "too much"? Like much scholarship promoting code-meshing pedagogy, the logistics are lacking.

Again, Inoue's labor-based grading, which jettisons grades and an emphasis on quality of writing, ignores social and material reality and does not go beyond the "ecology" of the writing classroom adequately enough. The freedom of expression allowed in a grade-less classroom is an understandably attractive idea, but, again, it lacks sufficient reality testing. What's more, labor should be a consideration in all grading, but making it the primary consideration in a writing classroom, subordinating a text's proximity to the rhetorical expectations of civic and professional cultures, is tantamount to "everyone getting a trophy"; it is not an adequate representation of the demands of civic and professional cultures.

Even with grade-less writing assessment, students still need feedback, and feedback, alone, is a problematic situation in code-meshing pedagogy.

Perhaps the specific issue of register will solidify this point. Register—the degree of formality or appropriateness of a word choice—is a recognized aspect of code-meshing. Young, for example, uses the term "homie" to refer to his academic colleagues in the 2019 call for papers for the Conference of College Composition and Communication.[23] The use of this term, a common synonym for "friend" that is prevalent in African American communities, is used by Young to display how code-meshing can look. Presumably, to take issue with this use is to take issue with his identity. But what if an African American student uses another synonym, the word "Nigga," to express his identity while referring to a friend? What does an instructor do? If an instructor says the word is inappropriate, then, based on the logic of Young, Laura Greenfield, and other proponents of code-meshing, is not the instructor saying that the student, himself, is inappropriate? If the instructor explains to the student that he can code-mesh, but certain terms, like "Nigga," are off-limits, is the instructor not, in effect, perpetuating the segregationist attitude that is vilified by anti-racist proponents?

In *The N-Word: Who Can Say It, Who Shouldn't, and Why,* Jabari Asim gives a take on the N-word that clashes with the salient aspects of code-meshing pedagogy. He writes:

> Alone with our thoughts, impulses, and emotions, we are at liberty to weigh the arguments and make a choice at a protective remove from the clamor and heat of Orwellian crusades. The primacy of individual choice and the esteem with which we Americans regard freedom of expression complicates our attitudes toward the N word. Like most of us, I embrace the sanctity of personal space. The thought of language police (or any other kind of police) patrolling our kitchens, bedrooms, and parlors for evidence of rude chatter chills me to my marrow. No speech is improper under one's own roof.[24]

Asim's justification of using the N-word flies in the face of code-meshing's claim that restricting certain words within a discourse is inherently segregationist. That is, according to code-meshing pedagogy, Asim's claim that "no speech is improper under one's own roof," should be revised as "no speech is improper anywhere. To say otherwise is oppressive." This point makes clear a need to discuss the complexities of a code-meshing pedagogy in more detail before presenting it as a rallying call for social justice in writing instruction.

Code-meshing is clearly a real phenomenon, but it comes about organically. This is a fact that Young, himself concedes, even if inadvertently.[25] Code-meshing happens when a person with knowledge of two or more vernaculars is interpellated into combining them. Otherwise, one is not being rhetorical (i.e., cognizant of *kairos*). Instead, one is being monological, self-expressive, and, at worst, narcissistic. This is why, as a pedagogy, code-meshing falls flat. Nothing exists to master, nothing is there to be taught. That is, effective code-meshing depends on the writer or speaker gauging audience, subject matter, timing, and location before writing or speaking accordingly. Students can and, perhaps, should add as many discourses as possible to their rhetorical repertoires, and our job is to help them add a discourse more closely aligned with most professional and civic expectations. Sometimes, code-meshing *will* be the best tactic to use. Sometimes—maybe most of the time in professional and civic contexts—it will not. Code-meshing is going to happen on its own. When the time comes, students will know when to mesh or not to mesh.

So, code-meshing is a phenomenon that should be discussed. It should be a heuristic for considerations of rhetorical choice. But code-meshing should be a kairotic means to a rhetorical end, not the end itself. Code-meshing pedagogy echoes a neglect of logistically sound strategies for the sake of idealized, prefigurative dreams. Smucker's prefigurative Occupiers, for example, spoke truth to power but had no real ability to put sound strategies into practice. Like code-meshing pedagogues, they were righteous, but not right.

As we see from code-meshing pedagogy's manifestations in academia, a primacy of identity works the same in different contexts. Outside of academia, proponents of a primacy of identity do not have a collective firm grasp of social and material realities, opting, instead, for assumptions and misguided appropriations that sound good but, at heart, are ill-conceived or fallacious. We see in code-meshing pedagogy and other anti-racist initiatives, as with a primacy of identity at large, that victimhood and hegemonic guilt are necessary ingredients. We may see in code-meshing, as with a primacy of identity, that incentivizing victimhood also incentivizes impracticality over rhetorical skill acquisition. When it comes to real-life effectiveness, the sacred victim narrative only goes so far before diminishing returns set in.

Perhaps the issue equally detrimental to academic and nonacademic spaces is the necessary neglect of the very rhetorical fundamentals we seek to teach as rhetoricians. In order for a primacy of identity to work, rhetoric has to be writer/speaker-based, and not reader/listener-based. Yes, the concept of *kairos* involves both parties, but the primacy of identity, by definition, is all about the identity of the communicator. When it comes to civic spaces, proponents of a primacy of identity may have the audience cow to the injured identity of the speaker, regardless of whether what is spoken is logically sound.[26] When it comes to academic spaces, especially first-year writing classrooms, the reader is not as important as the writer in code-meshing pedagogy. That is, the writer's expression of his or her identity overrides the need to be rhetorically effective, that is, consider *kairos* and act accordingly. Thus, code-meshing pedagogy, like a primacy of identity, is un-pragmatic, a-material, and, therefore, significantly a-rhetorical.

The search for esteem and a sense of empowerment that drives a primacy of identity brings up the age-old issue of good and bad rhetoric. In the *Gorgias*, Socrates warns that empty rhetoric (i.e., rhetoric with no logical or material backing) can appeal to people because it feels good. He equates truth (material reality, actual circumstances) to medicine, and flattery (abstractions meant to elicit certain feelings) to cookery; food that tastes good but is not necessarily good for health or ailments. Plato writes that flattery "cares nothing for what is best, but dangles what is most pleasant for the moment as a bait for folly, and deceives it into thinking that she is of the highest value. Thus, cookery assumes the form of medicine, and pretends to know what foods are best for the body."[27] A primacy of identity has a *telos* that rests not on progress but the semblance of progress, not empowerment but a semblance of empowerment. Groups can "feel" like progress is being made and empowerment is being acquired by basking in prefiguration, but such tendencies alleviate emotional and esteem-based concerns and not much else. Thus, it flatters identity-based groups without abiding by social and material circumstances that may dictate more practical strategies.

Those who point this out are considered discriminatory or, if one critiques such politics from within a marginalized identity group, traitorous. Like the situation Socrates laments in the *Gorgias*, threatening to dissolve the prefigurative illusion crafted by a primacy of identity is a thankless and often punishable endeavor. Sticking with the medicine/cookery metaphor, Plato writes that "if a cook and a doctor had to contend before boys, or before men as foolish as boys, as to which of the two, the doctor or the cook, understands the question of sound and noxious foods, the doctor would starve to death."[28] In other words, the components of good rhetoric, based on social and material realities, *kairos*, and an avoidance of fallacious reasoning are shunned in exchange for feeling good. A primacy of identity and code-meshing pedagogy are manifestations of this "cookery" and proponents of both may play the role of Plato's "men as foolish as boys."

In the meantime, social realities are not going away. According to a survey of over 63,000 business managers done by PayScale, 44 percent said the hard skill most lacking among college graduates is writing. Public speaking follows with 39 percent. The National Association of Colleges and Employers did a study in 2018 that displayed "communicative skills (written)" and "communicative skills (verbal)" as the third and seventh most sought-after attributes by employers, respectively.[29] In his textbook on public relations, Tom Kelleher identifies five reasons for writing well: Relationships (audience consideration); Influence and Persuasion; Goals and Objectives (beyond self-expression); Reputation Management (for one's organization); and Impression Management (writing for context).[30] All of Kelleher's reasons are closely linked to *kairos*, as well as the synthesis of empowerment and emotional intelligence described in the previous chapter. This is why the argument that acquisition of LWC does not guarantee professional success[31] falls flat. Of course, LWC alone doesn't guarantee success, but based on the aforementioned statistics and the confirmed correlation of emotional intelligence/empowerment with professional upward mobility, it is a necessary component of success.[32] Thus, without true empowerment and everything that goes with it (emotional intelligence, rhetorical savvy), the likelihood of success drops substantially.

I want the world to progress, become more inclusive, and recognize the richness of a variety of languages and dialects. However, we have a duty to prepare our students, regardless of race and ethnicity, for the world *we currently have*. We have a duty to help them see "the available means of persuasion" in as many situations as possible, but especially the ones they are less likely to already know and most likely to encounter in the civic and professional world. Are we really doing that? At the end of the day, my responses to code-meshing are not just rhetorical, but decidedly pragmatic. More accurately, it is a confluence of rhetoric and pragmatism that plays into a kairotic disposition inherent in empowerment theory (especially the interactive and behavioral components) and various components of emotional intelligence (Organizational Awareness, Achievement Orientation, Conflict Management, etc.), the confluence of which makes for productive empowerment unattached to a primacy of identity or a victim narrative. The social realities neglected by code-meshing pedagogy can be acknowledged while simultaneously empowering our students as rhetors and citizens. From this standpoint—a standpoint of empowerment—acquisition of LWC is not so much an acquiescence to a particular culture as it is an acknowledgment of the confluence of pragmatism and rhetoric and its efficacy in professional and civic contexts; it is a strategy. William James may agree with this assessment. In "Pragmatism's Conception of Truth," he writes:

> [S]ince almost any object may some day become temporarily important, the advantage of having a general stock of *extra* truths, of ideas that shall be true of merely possible situations, is obvious. We store such extra truths away in our memories, and with the overflow we fill our books of reference. Whenever such an extra truth becomes practically relevant to one of our emergencies, it passes from cold-storage to do work in the world and our belief in it grows active.[33]

By no means would it be a stretch to say that LWC may become important in a future situation for a person wanting to navigate professional and civic contexts with some ease and success. Rosemary Robinson Jackson refers to it as a "linguistic spare tire" that is there when one needs it.[34] Acquisition of LWC need not be a jettisoning of one's identity.[35] LWC need not be one's "executive" mode of writing.[36] But, if one abides by a pragmatic attitude or a kairotic disposition—a stance that acknowledges and works with social and material realities—one will have such "*extra* truths," and "linguistic spare tires" at hand.

So why ignore these realities in the first place? From where does the "allergy" brought up by Smucker and Coole and Frost derive? Again, a pragmatic attitude may lead us to an answer. In *Philosophy as Cultural Politics*, Richard Rorty alludes to the tendency to ignore reality for a preference of the exorbitantly abstract. He writes:

> Both the prospect of a fully unified system of scientific explanation and that of a world civilization in which human rights are respected is inspiring. But inspirational value is obviously not a reliable indicator of validity. Both the appeal to something overarching and invulnerable and the appeal to something ineffable and exhaustibly deep, are advertising slogans, public relations gimmicks—ways of gaining attention.[37]

Although I would use a word stronger than "inspirational" regarding the prospect of a world respectful of human rights, I cannot help but infer from Rorty's charge that an evasion of validity may be inspired by "gimmicks" to gain attention, for example, career opportunities or political power. (Keep in mind, Rorty wrote this well before the current manifestations of social politics in the form of a primacy of identity took hold; this was written in opposition to erstwhile theorists who dismissed their own social and material realities). Are proponents of code-meshing pedagogy engaging in "gimmick" scholarship or what Henry Giroux may call academic entrepreneurship: the tendency to emphasize careerism over authenticity?[38] If not, is our only option that proponents of code-meshing pedagogy are the new "lotus-eaters" of rhetoric and composition, so unable to wake up from a dream chocked with "overarching and invulnerable," "ineffable and exhaustibly deep," ideas of righteousness that they cannot acknowledge reality? Is being "woke" just another kind of unconsciousness? Perhaps. Call it neo-somnambulism.

Finally, like a primacy of identity in a colloquial sense, the ends of code-meshing pedagogy aren't pedagogical at all. The ends are individual or group esteem and the use of victimhood and hegemonic guilt to acquire a semblance of power in lieu of real empowerment. It is a powerless grab for power. What strikes me as most painful is that the confidence in staking a powerful position through critical thinking, pragmatic thought, and a firm appreciation of strategy is not identified as an option. The genetic fallacy strikes again; these things were put forth by people of European origin, so they must be decentered if not shunned, outright.

And what does this say about the overall opinion of minority students in rhetoric and composition? I am taken aback and offended by statements that strongly suggest an inferiority in the intellectual capacity of minorities from proponents of code-meshing. To them, having minority students learn LWC is not just "cruel," but also nearly implausible.[39] So, not only are minority students incapable of doing something I and other minority scholars have done with relative ease, but having faith in their ability to do so is tyrannical and oppressive. Why are thoughts like these tolerated? Why are members of a minority group confidently stating that their own group can only succeed if the powers that be change the rules? Why is the confidence to win not only nonexistent, but reprehensible as well? What is really going on here?

In the essay, "Your Average Nigga," Young expresses a similar sentiment. Referencing me, Keith Gilyard, and a former student named Cam, Young catalyzes a discussion on the disconnect between minority identity and composition pedagogy in which he writes that "as long as the only debate we can imagine ourselves having is the debate between BEV and WEV [White English Vernacular], it doesn't matter who wins, because no one wins—a few Cams will make it, a few Erec Smiths, and a few Keith Gilyards. But millions will continue to lose, particularly 'those who,' Cam writes, 'stand on the sidelines and hope.'"[40] Young bases his thoughts on the idea that most students, "millions," apparently, will inevitably suffer from cognitive dissonance whenever they try to write in a code other than the ones they bring to the classroom. This statement is not only egregiously false, but self-defeatist and reeking of low group self-esteem.

I found Young's statement about the sidelines to be as ironic as it is problematic, especially given Jonathan Smucker's take on the concept of "the sidelines" as a space for prefigurative politics.[41] Embracing victimhood as a power play, playing up the narrative of the sacred victim, may seem like speaking truth to power, but rest assured that it is indicative of Smucker's "sidelines," where all that gets done is the *performance* of triumph. The paradoxical play of embracing defeat to have hegemonic forces hand over a win presents the sidelines as if they are centralized spaces. They are not.

So these are the pedagogical manifestations and effects of a lack of empowerment and its subsequent embrace of a primacy of identity. Low group esteem and no confidence to accomplish goals deemed normal in American society leave that group with few strategies other than playing up victimhood in an attempt to be exempt from those societal goals. Those who speak against this exemption must be demonized. Those within the group who attempt to let the cat out of the bag are not considered confident and intelligent men and women, but boys and girls who have simply internalized the hate of the oppressor. Again, let me be clear about my own perceptions: code-meshing is a good thing, and when the *kairos* is right, can make for very effective writing—just like any other dialect. However, code-meshing's current and popular pedagogical manifestations are not about *kairos* or rhetorical savvy. If a primacy of identity and current scholarship on code-meshing are any indication, code-meshing's pedagogical manifestations are the inevitable results of disempowered anti-racist initiatives filtered through a pedagogical imperative.

Proponents of a primacy of identity and, by extension, many proponents of code-meshing pedagogy frame the world based on the erroneous goal of parlaying victimhood into "justice." Activism set on true justice, however, shuns this goal. As discussed in the previous chapter on empowerment, Kenneth Burke's concept of framing, what he calls a "terministic screen," depends on "a selection of reality" adding that, concomitantly, it must depend on "a deflection of reality" as well.[42] Based on how a person or group "selects" or "deflects" reality determines the general makeup of reality—its executive ideology and interpretations of phenomena.

Thus, many "realities" exist, and they shape one's actions in achieving fulfillment. A reality of our American situation is that people of color, especially African Americans, were treated savagely and, to a significant extent, residual effects of that abuse are still present. Another reality of the situation is that LWC is associated with a hegemony wherein aspects of this savagery still exist. Another part of this reality is that LWC's acquisition can and will come in handy in civic and professional contexts; it is a tool to be used. However, what is reflected and deflected depends on one's goals. Taking code-meshing as a primary example, if one's goal is the manipulation of victimhood for the semblance of progress, one will select the racist associations with composition pedagogy and deflect that pragmatic usefulness of LWC as one of many tools for civic and professional success. If one's goals are to provide a pragmatically useful tool for students to use when *kairos* dictates—which, in civic and professional cultures, is often—one will deflect the racist associations with composition pedagogy and reflect the pragmatic efficacy of LWC. This is surely happening among students of color. The results of a study of black community college students by Rosemary Jackson shows that black students understand the efficacy of learning "standard English" and, for that reason, want to learn it despite its associations with white racism. Their only issue is the use of "standard English" as a way to look down on those who do not do this, which, as Jackson discovers, can be remedied with the right pedagogical approach.[43] Perhaps this all comes down to goals and whether the primary term in one's terministic screen is "victim" or "victor." This is the case for many manifestations of a primacy of identity throughout society.

In this context, "deflection" need not be synonymous with "neglect" in a holistic sense. I would never condone ignoring racism or any form of discrimination. However, certain framings center on racism so prominently that pragmatism and productivity go neglected. In composition pedagogy, racism should not be ignored. (Discussing the politics of language and critical language awareness are powerful activities in the classroom.) However, it should not be centered so prominently that the world outside of the classroom is ignored, "deflected," when teaching writing.

As is normal with prefiguration, emotion and what people "want" to see eclipse the actualities we need to acknowledge if we are going to make real progress with race relations in society. In "It Ain't What It Is: Code Switching and White American Celebrationists," Young and Young-Rivera call an attempt by "White American Celebrationists" to teach LWC a "racial micro-aggression"[44] and are "stunned" by the lack of empathy involved in gauging material realities and discerning necessary tools for their navigation.[45] Typical of prefiguration and a primacy of identity—as well as negative emotionality and a stimulus–response orientation toward the world[46]—Young and Young-Rivera write that compositionists "need to allow these students to use their command of multiple Englishes and combine them for the greatest rhetorical effectiveness."[47] Because rhetoric is based on *kairos*, this statement raises a question: Of what "greatest rhetorical effectiveness" do Young and Young-Rivera speak? Their statement is a refusal to accomplish actual societal progression and true societal success in the name of what they would like to see: a narcissistic take on communication that emphasizes the speaker to the utter neglect of audience, context, and anything else considered a fundamental aspect of rhetorical effectiveness. Young and Young-Rivera's take on rhetorical education is a detriment to success, not a benefit. I find it interesting that Young and Young-Rivera insist that what they are doing is meant "not as a retreat to the feel-good, no-failure, boost-your-self-esteem era of the past."[48] The neglect of social realities, the dismissal of pragmatic thought, and the scarcity of reality testing suggests that code-meshing pedagogy is exactly that. It is a retreat into prefiguration.

Make no mistake about what I am saying. Within and beyond the academy, anti-racist initiatives based on a primacy of identity, themselves, are affronts to people of color who do not want to see victims when they look in the mirror. A primacy of identity assumes a lack of agency among individuals and groups. The violence of literacy, as it were, is ultimately self-imposed. To put it simply—because it is simple—learning LWC is tyrannical and oppressive only if one wants it to be. But why would one want it to be? Avenging people of color who were slighted by LWC's historical connection to colonialism is an understandable motivator, but it is by no means a reasonable and pragmatic one, not if fulfillment, success, and real change (not prefigurative change) are the goals.

I will repeat that the main problem may be our blind acceptance of the identification of language with self. I am not saying that people don't strongly identify with language. I am saying that the confluence of a particular identity and a particular language is not a necessary aspect of human being, like the need for food, water, and oxygen are. To many anti-racist proponents in rhetoric and composition, language is seen as ontological, not merely a tool for human interaction and socialization. I want to emphasize the word "tool," here. Carpenters use hammers; they do not identify with their hammers. (If they did, most people would suggest they seek psychological help.) The "pain" of acquiring a language or, worse, the perceived impossibility of doing so, is not unavoidable and is not inevitable.

As I have been arguing, disempowerment is the ultimate cause of the primacy of identity and the terministic screen that interprets the acquisition of LWC as inherently tyrannical. However, that screen produces other phenomena, both purposefully and inadvertently, that need to be addressed. Indeed, anti-racist initiatives could be seen as a tool for perpetuating racism. I will address this in the following chapter.

NOTES

1. Vershawn Ashanti Young, "Nah, We Straight: An Argument Against Code-Switching," *JAC*, 29.1/2, (2009), 53.
2. Young, "Nah, We Straight: An Argument Against Code-Switching."
3. Ibid., 54.
4. Ibid., 111.
5. D. McCrary, "Represent, Representing', Representation: The Efficacy of Hybrid Texts in the Writing Classroom," *Journal of Basic Writing*, 24.2 (2005), 73.
6. Vershawn Ashanti Young, "Linguistic Double Consciousness," *Other People's English: Code-Meshing, Code-Switching, and African American Literacy* (New York: Teachers College Press, 2014), 63.
7. Vershawn Ashanti Young, "Should Writers Use They Own English," *Writing Centers and the New Racism: A Call for Sustainable Dialogue and Change* (Logan, UT: Utah State University Press, 2011), 114.
8. Asao Inoue, "Chapter One: The Function of Race in Writing Assessments," *Antiracist Writing Assessment Ecologies: Teaching and Assessing Writing for a Socially Just Future* (Fort Collins, CO: The WAC Clearinghouse and Parlor Press, 2015) 31. Ebook. https://wac.colostate.edu/books/perspectives/inoue/.
9. Young, "Should Writers Use They Own English," 110.
10. Geneva Smitherman, "'Students Right to Their Own Language': A Retrospective," *The English Journal* 84.1 (1995), 25.
11. Vershawn Ashanti Young and Y'Shanda Young-Rivera, "It Ain't What it Is: Code-Switching and White American Celebrationists," *JAC*, 33.1/2 (2013), 396–401.
12. Laura Greenfield, "The 'Standard English' Fairy Tale: A Rhetorical Analysis of Racist Pedagogies and Commonplace Assumptions about Language Diversity,"

Writing Centers and the New Racism: A Call for Sustainable Dialogue and Change (Logan, UT: Utah State University Press, 2011).

13. Jose Cortez, "History," *Decolonizing Rhetoric and Composition Studies,* ed. Iris Ruiz and Raul Sanchez (New York: Palgrave Macmillan, 2016), 52.

14. Pappas, "The Limitations and Dangers of Decolonial Philosophies: Lessons from Zapatista Luis Villoro," 6.

15. Young, "Should Writers Use They Own English," 63.

16. See the section on "Divergence" in Özlem Atalay, "Accommodation Theory and Language Learning," *Theoretical Considerations in Language Education*, ed. Betil Eröz-Tuğa (Ankara, Çankaya, Turkey: Nuans Publish, 2014), Accessed August 5, 2019. https://www.researchgate.net/publication/291957052_Accommodation_Theory_and_Language_Teaching.

17. See Lisa Ede and Andrea Lunsford, "Audience Addressed/Audience Invoked: The Role of Audience in Composition Theory and Pedagogy," *Cross-Talk in Comp Theory: A Reader*, ed. Victor Villanueva (Urbana, IL: NCTE Press, 2003), 77–95.

18. Gerald Graff, "Code-Meshing Meets Teaching the Conflicts," *Code-Meshing as World English: Pedagogy, Policy, Performance,* ed. Vershawn Ashanti Young and Aja Y. Martinez (Urbana, IL: NCTE Press, 2011), 16.

19. Greenfield, "The 'Standard English' Fairy Tale: A Rhetorical Analysis of Racist Pedagogies and Commonplace Assumptions about Language Diversity," 58.

20. Asao Inoue, *Labor-based Grading Contracts: Building Equity and Inclusion in the Compassionate Writing Classroom* (WAC Clearinghouse, 2019).

21. Inoue, *Labor-based Grading Contracts: Building Equity and Inclusion in the Compassionate Writing Classroom*, 3–4.

22. Young, "Should Writers Use They Own English," 71.

23. Vershawn Ashanti Young, "2019 College Composition and Communication Call for Program Proposals," *NCTE,* 2018, https://cccc.ncte.org/cccc/conv/call-2019.

24. Jabari Asim, *The N-Word: Who Can Say it, Who Shouldn't, And Why* (New York: Houghton Mifflin Company, 2008), 229–30.

25. Young, "Should Writers Use They Own English," 67.

26. Haider, *Mistaken Identity*, Loc 523.

27. Plato, *Gorgias*, in *The Rhetorical Traditions*, ed. Patricia Bizzell and Bruce Herzberg (New York: Bedford, Saint Martin's, 2001), 98.

28. Plato, *Gorgias*.

29. Job Outlook 2018, *National Association of Colleges and Employers* (Bethlehem, PA: N.A.C.E., 2017), 30.

30. Tom Kelleher, *Public Relations* (Oxford, UK: Oxford University Press, 2018), 221–24.

31. Greenfield, "The 'Standard English' Fairy Tale: A Rhetorical Analysis of Racist Pedagogies and Commonplace Assumptions about Language Diversity," 56–57; Asao Inoue, Antiracist Writing Assessment Ecologies: Teaching and Assessing Writing for a Socially Just Future (Collins, CO: The WAC Clearinghouse, 2015), 131–32.

32. Daniel Goleman, *Organizational Awareness: A Primer* (Florence, MA: More Than Sound, 2017), Loc 28.

33. William James, "Pragmaticism's Concept of Truth," *Pragmatism and Other Essays* (New York: Washington Square Press, 1970), 90.

34. Rosemary Robinson Jackson, *The Social Construction of Linguistic Reality: A Case Study Exploring the Relationships Among Poverty, Race, and Remediation in an Urban Community College* (2007) Dissertation.2680. ecommons.luc.edu/luc_diss/2680.

35. Matthew Engelke, *How to Think Like an Anthropologist* (Princeton, NJ: Princeton University Press, 2019), 179–86.

36. Jackson, *The Social Construction of Linguistic Reality*, 208.

37. Richard Rorty, *Philosophy as Cultural Politics* (Cambridge, UK: Cambridge University Press, 2007), 87.

38. Henry Giroux, *Neoliberalism's War on Democracy* (Chicago, IL: Haymarket Books, 2015), 17.

39. Vershawn Ashanti Young, "Nah, We Straight," *JAC* 29.1/2 (2009), 62–63.

40. Vershawn Ashanti Young, *Your Average Nigga: Performing Race, Literacy, and Masculinity* (Detroit, MI: Wayne State University Press, 2007), Loc 710. E-book.

41. Jonathan Matthew Smucker, *Hegemony How-To: A Roadmap for Radicals* (Chico, CA: AK Press, 2017), 132.

42. Kenneth Burke, *Language as Symbolic Action,* in *The Rhetorical Tradition: Readings from Classical Times to the Present*, 2nd ed., ed. Patricia Bizzell and Bruce Herzberg (New York: Bedford St. Martin's Press, 2001), 1341.

43. Jackson, *The Social Construction of Linguistic Reality*, 225.

44. "It Ain't What it Is: Code-Switching and White American Celebrationists," 398.

45. Ibid., 397.

46. Scott O. Lilienfeld, "Microaggression: Strong Claims, Inadequate Evidence," *Perspectives on Psychological Science* 12.1 (2017): 163.

47. Lilienfeld, "Microaggression: Strong Claims, Inadequate Evidence," 398.

48. Ibid., 399.

Chapter 4

The "Soft Bigotry" of Anti-racist Pedagogy

Victims, Tricksters, and Protectors

> They knew too that for such a man's actions it is *not* the case that from good only good, from bad only bad can come, but that often the opposite holds true. Anyone who cannot see that is indeed politically a child.[1]
>
> Max Weber, "Politics as a Vocation"

One of the biggest complaints about identity politics or what I have been calling the primacy of identity (a bastardized version of original identity politics) is that it often proves more dangerous to those it is supposedly trying to help than other tactics that are deemed inappropriate. Some affinity groups are guilty of this, as are their more hegemonically privileged allies. Sometimes, actions done in the name of social justice have consequences that, for all intents and purposes, could have resulted from a racist plan to weaken the minority group or groups in question, like denying their acquisition of valuable resources for the sake of preserving authenticity. Too often, within a primacy of identity, information has been questionably appropriated to justify actions or sentiments.[2] The neglect or evasion of social and material realities to support victimhood and the perpetuation of hegemonic guilt is perplexing.

One can construe anti-racism as a theory and pedagogy of low expectations, but I think this is an oversimplification. Low expectation may be a part of what is happening, but I would like to speculate that other influences come into play, as well. I have labeled these influences victim-framing, "trickster" racism, and protectionism and show how each works to actually perpetuate the problems anti-racists claim to work against. That is, some anti-racist initiatives actually perpetuate racism and perform a "soft bigotry."

VICTIM-FRAMING

An important and unacknowledged reality regarding anti-racist pedagogies (and other manifestations of a primacy of identity) is perception. Let us return to code-meshing pedagogy. Although qualified in some texts on code-meshing and the narratives that surround black identity, a common inference is that black people all feel the same about AAVE and LWC; they see code-meshing as a necessary mission for any self-respecting African American, a mission that will reestablish or maintain black pride in the face of white oppression. However, students of color exist who do not feel oppressed to the point of pathology at having comma-splices pointed out in their writing or being told that a narrative structure is not a part of a particular assignment. Genre conventions do not come across as necessarily stifling.

The race-based arguments against learning LWC ignore the experiences of many minority writers. I am taken aback by the thought that people think the self-esteem of their students of color is in such dire need of bolstering. This victim-framing seems to be an inherent part of anti-racism and a necessary aspect of anti-racist pedagogy. That is, students are framed as disempowered entities in need of enlightenment instead of empowered agents with self-efficacy and a desire to broaden the interactional and behavioral components of empowerment. The possibility that students are empowered self-advocates, not disempowered victims, creates a dissonance so strong that educators who are confronted with the possibility seem to have difficulty processing it, as I will show in this chapter. I have consistently referred to the "allergy" metaphor when discussing anti-racism's aversion to reality. Many scholars and pedagogues of anti-racism may have an allergy to people of color who do not embrace victimhood or who think pragmatically about their futures, which is to say they are disquieted by people of color who have a healthy embrace of empowerment. There seems to be an aversion to a student of color who does not need or want their help in acquiring intraracial enlightenment.

In this book's introduction, I discuss W. E. B. Dubois as an example of an empowered individual, not one who would embrace victimhood for its counterfeit benefits. The words I cited from Dubois' corpus are not the words of a young man suffering from some kind of mental and emotional ailment remediable by victim-framing anti-racist initiatives. Dubois' words are those of a man that knows the value of a repertoire of discourses and knows that, in important and strategic moments, the one he will learn in college will be quite conducive to his goal. These are the words of a man who understands *kairos* and resolves to be prepared for a variety of contexts. Thus, Dubois might have scoffed at statements like "trying to separate the two languages for some is virtually impossible, and makes requirements to do so appear tyrannical, oppressive."[3] Young's following question, "Wouldn't it be better to promote integrating them?"[4] may be answered by the proudly pragmatic and empowered Dubois, "The integration of discourses depends solely on the dictates of the situation and one's particular goals, therein."

Although I understand the attraction of a grade-less writing course, I think Dubois may have seen the rationale behind labor-based grading contracts as especially insulting. Asao Inoue presents grading contracts as a form of assessing hard work in the writing process, not in the writing product. Inoue suggests that this mode of grading can focus on improving student writing without punishing the student for not acquiring standard written English, which is considered a tool of white supremacy. I do not want to rehash the issues with framing such English as inherently oppressive. I do want to share an observation gleaned from part of Inoue's justification for grading contracts. He writes:

> In my experience and research, a grading contract based only on labor is better for all students and undermines the racist and White supremacist grading systems we all live with at all levels of education. But using labor as the only way to grade my students allows my classroom assessment ecologies to engage in larger social justice projects, ones that make up an important agenda *of mine*, ones that interrogate and attempt to dismantle White language supremacy in schools and society.[5] (Emphasis mine)

I generally admire Inoue's work on classroom ecologies, but I think we should pay special attention to the words "an important agenda of mine" in this quote. Inoue may inadvertently show his hand here: Is this pedagogy really for the students? The students' wants and desired outcomes are assumed if considered at all. May this pedagogy be for Inoue and those who share his scholarship and agendas? Perhaps this is about their desires for social justice, not necessarily their students' desires for an education. If they were to focus more clearly on student expectations and desires, they might find more "Duboises" than victims in their classrooms.

Indeed, some students would probably be taken aback in a grade-less writing course. Some students may see grades as markers of progress with which they feel comfortable. They may see the carrot/stick effect of a grade as a necessary driver of their work and attention to style and experience an "academic emptiness" without them.[6] They may understand the civic and professional contexts in which they will enter and want to know how close they really are to being an effective communicator in those spaces. What's more, many would argue that teacher attitude is a bigger concern than grading and that issues of student affect are the biggest determiners of student success.[7] Given our exploration of empowerment to this point, the fundamental question revolves around the assumption that students of color in "white" writing spaces are categorically victims. Would an empowered student want or need labor-based grading?

Another concerning aspect of victim-framing is a structural one. The concept of a victim necessitates some kind of perpetrator. It seems like the primary perpetrator in anti-racist initiatives is white supremacist, hegemonic forces, embodied by white people. However, many do not realize the corollaries to this concept of the perpetrator that do more harm than good to people of color. Victim-framing is often done as a foil to the perpetrators, essentializes both parties, and strongly implies that each is a proprietor of certain behaviors and mindsets diametrically opposed to the other.

The example I will use to illustrate my point is the concept of "whiteliness." Whiteliness, coined by Marilyn Frye, is an ideology of paradigmatic whiteness. Frye's definition of whitely is worth quoting at length:

> Whitely people generally consider themselves to be benevolent and good-willed, fair, honest, and ethical. The judge, preacher, peacemaker, martyr, socialist, professional, moral majority, liberal, radical, conservative, working men and women—nobody admits to being prejudiced, everybody has earned every cent they ever had, doesn't take sides, doesn't hate anybody, and always votes for the person they think best qualified for the job, regardless of the candidates' race, sex, religion or national origin, maybe even regardless of their sexual preferences. The professional version of this person is always profoundly insulted by the suggestion that s/he might have permitted some personal feeling about a client to affect the quality of services rendered. S/he believes with perfect confidence that s/he is not prejudiced, not a bigot, not spiteful, jealous or rude, does not engage in favoritism or discrimination. When there is a serious and legitimate challenge, a negotiator has to find a resolution which enables the professional person to save face, to avoid simply agreeing that s/he made an unfair or unjust judgment, discriminated against someone or otherwise behaved badly. Whitely people have a staggering faith in their own rightness and goodness, and that of other whitely people. We are not crooks.[8]

Frye's concept of whiteliness, per se, is not the problem. It is an interesting observation of a certain kind of hegemonic discourse, a discourse I, myself, have experienced and tacitly discussed in publication.[9] However, the appropriations of Frye's concept of whiteliness for anti-racist initiatives in rhetoric and composition are problematic.

Based on Frye's definition, the problem with whiteliness is not the litany of characteristics Frye spends the paragraph's first half listing (e.g., fairness, honesty, ethics, etc.). The problem is the lack of self-awareness, self-reflexivity, active listening, and genuine empowerment all described in the paragraph's second half that serve as a backdrop for the aforementioned characteristics. Yet, the lack of self-reflexivity, active listening, and genuine empowerment can be found among various people using various rhetorics. So, what is so white about whiteliness? One can glean from the above quote that a profound arrogance is the main characteristic of a whitely person, but, again, no group has a monopoly on arrogance.

Perhaps whiteliness a profound arrogance about particular things, for example, fairness, honesty, and so on. I agree when Frankie Condon describes whiteliness as "an articulation of epistemologies that have been racialized as white; whiteliness is a rhetoric."[10] However, one can reflect Frye's litany of virtues (good-willed, fair, honest, ethical, moral, working, etc.) without abiding by whiteliness, that is, without arrogantly assuming one has a superior handle on those virtues. One can exercise those virtues while maintaining an attitude of open-mindedness, mindfulness, and confidence that is actually sought after by employers.[11] We can infer from Frye's words that whiteliness is the *combination* of characteristics considered virtues across cultures with an arrogance that one's embodiment of these virtues is stronger than that of others. Condon, however, comes dangerously close to suggesting that those virtues, themselves, are whitely and, when expected from people of color, are tools of oppression. Condon explains Frye's words when writing: "Problems must be presented in the right way in order to be processed and addressed. Further, whitely people conceive of themselves as appropriate arbiters of what might constitute the right way."[12] The problem is that Condon only quotes Frye thusly, "Whitely people, Frye writes, 'generally consider themselves to be benevolent and good-willed, fair, honest, and ethical. . . . Whitely people have a staggering faith in their own rightness and goodness, and that of other whitely people.'"[13] Without Frye's full explanation of whiteliness given in the block quote above, one could construe that by "right way" Condon means an expectation of good-will, fairness, honesty, and ethics from others. However, this is a problematic construction. Do people of color embody these virtues without acting out the arrogance inherent in whiteliness, or are people of color just as arrogant but apply that arrogance to different virtues? If so, what are those virtues? Condon brings up whiteliness in an essay that rightly disparages a school district for wanting to remove non-native speakers from language learning classrooms.[14] However, whiteliness has been applied to much less egregious actions like valuing critical thinking and has been used to describe entire writing programs.[15] Who isn't whitely and how does a non-whitely person behave?

This concept of whiteliness points directly at the elephant in the room: What might "blackly" be? Is blackly the harboring of virtues listed in Frye's definition along with a healthy sense of self-reflexivity, rhetorical listening, and self-confidence? Is blackly the embodiment of these virtues combined with a healthy self-regard? Is blackly, like whitely, more of a rhetoric than a vernacular? Or, is blackly simply a mode of being that has escaped reification into a grapholect?

Perhaps we get a hint from Asao Inoue. In *Antiracist Writing Assessment Ecologies: Teaching and Assessing Writing for a Socially Just Future*, Inoue compares a white female writer to a black male writer. The former writer is said to provide "the voice of objective reasoning that she invokes in her essay" and exudes a "hyperindividualism" and an etic distancing from the observed world.[16] In contrast, the black male writer focuses less on the outside world and more on himself in relation. His writing "is contextualized, social in nature, and focused on his own subjective meaning making.[17] Putting aside the fact that Inoue does not talk about the gender distinction, which seems to reverse Elizabeth Flynn's take on the differences between male and female writers (males are more individualistic and objective; females are more communal and interactive[18]), one could glean a clue into what may be considered blackly: subjectivity, context, communality, focus on the self. Is this what is implied by Condon to be the opposite of whitely rhetoric?

Perhaps we can find an answer from another Inoue text: his "Afterward" for *Black Perspectives in Writing Program Administration*. When describing the major characteristics of what he calls a white racial habitus, that is, a space framed and driven by white sensibilities and, by extension, a whitely space, he includes two components with strong implications about what blackly could mean.

- Individual, rational, controlled self—the person is conceived as an individual who is rational, self-conscious, self-controlled, and determined; conscience guides the individual and sight is the primary way to identify the truth or understanding; social and cultural factors are external constraints to the individual.
- Clarity, order, and control—a focus on reason, order, and control; thinking (versus feeling), insight, the rational order, objective (versus subjective), rigor, clarity, and consistency are all valued highly; thinking/rationality and knowledge are nonpolitical, unraced, and can be objective.[19]

Based on this logic, blackly, if it shares a binary relationship to whitely, is irrational; lacking in self-awareness, self-control, and determination; not guided by conscience; lacking in reason, order, control, rigor; feeling-oriented (as opposed to thinking), subjective (as opposed to objective), and irrational; unclear, and inconsistent.

I think it is important to address some considerations regarding Inoue's gloss of whitely spaces. Of course, if we take a post-structuralist viewpoint, we can decide that blackly is everything whitely is not. One may also notice that the characteristics deemed whitely by Inoue, especially those of the first bullet-point, are all prominent aspects of emotional intelligence and, therefore, empowerment. Lastly, the second bullet-point's opposite characteristics are quite indicative of a primacy of identity ideology, suggesting that a primacy of identity is inherently black or, at least, nonwhite. Whatever blackly may be, preparation for the social realities of professional and civic contexts, and critical thinking in general, would be deemed a kind of violence against it.

I want to make clear that I understand the motivations of Frye and Condon; perhaps they want to avoid the *inter se pugnantia* profusely thrown at their own male oppressors. That is, one can assume they do not want to do to people of color what has been done to them. However, I think, in its current iteration, this attempt at allyship is detrimental. In trying to avoid being oppressive and patronizing (whitely?), they may be framing students as victims prematurely and unnecessarily. In trying to avoid coming off as white supremacists, they are afraid to tell students of color to be anything other than themselves, with the mistaken idea that learning to write a standardized vernacular of English or even a more generalized LWC will definitely or, at best, most likely erase their identities and not allow them to be themselves, to be whatever blackly is. In trying to be "woke," they are making sure their students are dead to the world and, therefore, ill-equipped to write in as many professional and civic contexts as possible. Their attempts at goodness are perpetuating harm.

Inoue's scholarship is problematic in similar ways. Beyond what I have addressed above, his scholarship, and the scholarship of other like-minded academics, is inherently essentialist and, therefore, a kind of racism in itself. Inoue, like Young, cannot help presenting black people and white people as separate, monolithic groups, constantly ignoring class and other intersectionalities.[20] I am reminded of Richard Haswell's critique of *Race and Writing Assessment*, where he writes that "any writing assessment shaped by anti-racism will still be racism or, if that term affronts, will be stuck in racial contradictions."[21] Haswell elaborates by writing that the attempt to eradicate racial alignments only creates other racial alignments and that individuality is erased by the anti-racist theories put forth in the book.[22] All this makes for a tricky perpetuation of racism I want to explore in the next section.

TRICKSTER RACISM AND PROTECTIONISM

Victim-framing is the least distressing of the detriments of disempowerment in rhetoric and composition. The other detriments, which I will talk about in tandem, are more insidious and complex. As I have said before and will say again, these concepts may not be done from a place of vindictiveness or a desire to sabotage, but at a closer look, they might as well be.

In order to explain what I mean by both trickster racism and the related concept of protectionism, I have to give a theoretical background to exactly what I mean by the term "trickster." As a graduate student I researched and wrote on the rhetorical merits of the trickster archetype, which represents a "rhetorical virtuoso or a person with tactical knowledge of semantic arbitrariness."[23] The trickster archetype was meant to help people overcome labels, definitions, and interpretations of themselves and others in an attempt to liberate and open minds. The ambiguity of meaning is why the trickster is often seen as a representative of communication and, therefore, human interaction. "If trickster characteristics can be found all throughout language use, and language is what we use to explain the world, then it would make sense that the trickster and all that the trickster represents in the use of language is a fundamental aspect of humanity and the world it tries to describe."[24]

It is no accident that this description smacks of postmodernism; it, too, was embraced for its liberating power. But, like many who would call themselves postmodernists, I embraced the positive aspects of "trickster consciousness" while de-emphasizing, if not ignoring, its negative potential. The fact that the term "trickster" had traditionally negative connotations only fueled my desire to draw out the positive and beneficial aspects of the trickster.

My biggest faux pas, and that of many like-minded people, was to ignore the concept's potential as a tool for those who would use it for more dastardly ends, those who willingly and tactically embrace Plato's "bad rhetoric." Since the election of Donald Trump, many have cited the far Right's use of postmodernism to question objective truth and grand narratives for purposes mostly antithetical to those of the academics who embraced it.

For example, William Doty and William Hynes, when describing their taxonomy of trickster traits, acknowledge the prevalence of "deceiver/trick player," and "situation-inverter," among other traits, in many trickster figures in mythology and folklore.[25] Initially, I saw these traits as ways of resisting essentializing labels and unwarranted stigma. However, these traits are not just available to those resisting hegemonic forces; those hegemonic forces may also take them up. The "situation-inverter" trickster type may be most salient when it comes to what I call trickster racism.

Doty and Hynes thoroughly describe the trickster as "deceiver/trick player" and "situation-inverter." The trickster as "deceiver/trick player" is easy enough to understand. However, Doty and Hynes identify another common aspect of trickster figures with deception and trickery as their salient characteristics. They write: "Once initiated, a trick can exhibit an internal motion all its own. Thus, a trick can gather such momentum as to exceed any control exercised by its originator and may even turn back upon the head of the trickster, so the trick-player is also trickster-tricked."[26] The primacy of identity, with its overemphasis on lived experience, its embrace of sacred victimhood, and its preference for prefiguration over critical thinking, social and material realities, and pragmatic thought may have been a "trick" in the positive sense; it developed a sense of validation and empowerment in groups who traditionally lacked those things in American society. However, the neglect of critical thinking, social conditions, and pragmatic thought works to hinder actual progress in many ways and weakens intellectual legitimacy; it weakens true empowerment. The trick-players have become the tricksters-tricked.

The trickster as "situation-inverter" may be more serious. Doty and Hynes describe the "situation-inverter" when they write: "As situation-inverter, the trickster exhibits typically the ability to overturn any person, place, or belief, no matter how prestigious. . . . What prevails is toppled, what is bottom becomes top, what is outside turns inside, what is inside turns outside, and on and on in an unending concatenation of contingency."[27] The inversion of a situation for racist purposes is nothing new in America. Vance Jones discusses the transition of the lop-sided prison industrial complex into the growing prevalence of house arrest. The prison industry looks to succumb to an outcry against the disproportionate arrest of African Americans and responds with the ankle bracelet to spark a lucrative "house arrest" industry.[28] This situation inversion presents racism, itself, as a shape-shifting captor.

Trickster racism, then, may invert a situation and shape-shift to perpetuate racism in a new and often unrecognizable form. Trickster racists take the wants, desires, and pride of a minority group to use against that very group, and are applauded by that group and their allies for seeing the light, acknowledging the error of their ways, and reemerging as "woke" from a quagmire of ignorance and insensitivity. Racism, in a different form, is allowed to persist.

Thus, trickster racism, especially when understood as purposeful "situation-inversion," may be a kind of "protectionism": the tendency of hegemonic forces to hide or protect social markers of hegemonic identity from marginalized groups. This is what Dubois felt when his white peers at Harvard bristled at his self-confidence, for such a demeanor was the property of whiteness and should not be expressed from a black body.[29] Currently, protectionism does not exist in the ways it has in America's history. No black man is being punished for learning how to read. However, protectionism may be around in subtler and trickier forms.

A common conception is that protectionism gave way to coerced conformity with the onset of desegregation. However, this suggests an either/or situation in which conformity and protectionism cannot coexist. Protectionism did not end with desegregation. In trickster fashion, it may have changed forms. It may be perpetuated by those who embrace language authenticity and the language implications of anti-racist and decolonial pedagogies. Today, we see white people encouraging people of color to dismiss language deemed white in the name of liberation. Protectionism has shifted from something that insists on blacks' ignorance of "white" language to something that incentivizes the evasion of "white" language as a triumph of racial pride. Either way, blacks are encouraged to leave "white" language to white people.

Suddenly, we would have a kind of trickster racism. This manifestation of racism would not only come off as beneficial to minorities, but would also prompt those minorities to embrace it to induce a sense of empowerment and validation. At worst, this trickster racism may praise minority stereotypes that implicitly and insidiously perpetuate ideas of white superiority and inherent racial differences that suggest a hierarchy. While some African Americans, for example, see a standardized English or LWC as something to avoid to enhance racial pride and empowerment, trickster racists see the African American neglect of these Englishes as a way to have them "stay in their lane," and leave the useful and tactical tools of successful societal navigation to whites.

Ralph Ellison was no stranger to such an idea. In *Shadow and Act*, he writes of the black man's need to behave in ways deemed authentically yet acceptably black to those who enjoy and control hegemony. In the chapter titled "Twentieth-Century Fiction and the Black Mask of Humanity," he writes that "whatever else the Negro stereotype might be as a social instrumentality, it is also a key figure in a magic rite by which the white American seeks to resolve the dilemma arising between his democratic beliefs and certain anti-democratic practices, between his acceptance of the sacred democratic belief that all men are created equal and his treatment of every tenth man as though he were not."[30] Toward the end of the chapter, he poignantly writes: "Perhaps the object of the stereotype is not so much to crush the Negro as to console the white man."[31] Incentivizing racial distinctions helps whites maintain a self-image threatened by, say, a black person exuding behaviors coded as white as well as or better than a white person.

This idea is similar to Roland Barthes' concept of inoculation, which he defines as a phenomenon "which consists in admitting the accidental evil of a class-bound institution the better to conceal its principle evil. One immunizes the contents of the collective imagination by means of a small inoculation of acknowledged evil; one thus protects it against the risk of a generalized subversion."[32] In the end, everyone is happy although power dynamics never change.

I argue that protectionism is a motivator worth exploring. Stories like Collin Lamont Craig's, Stacy Perryman-Clark's,[33] Marlene L. Daut's,[34] and my own suggest that successful and capable people of color threaten the ownership of excellence traditionally attributed to whites. According to Perryman-Clark and Craig, it was their success, competence, and confidence that attracted the most negativity. For me, my role as an outsider usurping privileges that "belonged" to my white colleagues at a small liberal arts college threatened the insularity they found comforting.[35] Perryman-Clark and Craig do not explicitly state this in their narratives, but I strongly suspect that if I had acted more "black" (i.e., taught "black" courses while letting the white people do "white" things), I would have had a much easier time.

But the above situations are all about situations within higher education. This protectionism goes on beyond the Ivory Tower and, interestingly enough, it often revolves around language. As an adult, my education and, frankly, grasp of a discourse coded white while within a white context has rubbed more than a few white people in the wrong way. There is a bar and grill in York County, PA, that I no longer attend because, on three separate occasions, three different white men harassed me because I didn't act like a "real" black man. From discomfort to anger, these people vocalized their issue with my Discourse. To them, I am supposed to have lower social status, not an equal or even higher status. Code-meshing, for instance, may have been more pleasant and less threatening for them; a black man using English coded as white would be construed as a kind of cultural appropriation. This is why "respectability politics," the idea that conformity to mainstream standards and values will inevitably result in better treatment from hegemonic powers, is not a part of my issue with code-meshing or any aspect of anti-racism. In many situations, code-meshing can enhance the acceptance of black presence in white spaces, making a black man speaking LWC or Standard American English a kind of usurper, an example of an egregious cultural appropriation of whiteness. To many whites, a black person speaking AAVE or a code-meshed dialect is both a delightful novelty and proof of a sought-after distinction between races.

With the above instance, I am reminded of Patrick Finn's reading of Paolo Freire, recognizing a Machiavellian/Freirean motivation in which hegemonic tools and skills are acquired in the spirit of insurgency and speaking truth to that hegemony.[36] Although my take on this is admittedly snide, I believe that if traditionally hegemonic people are nervous about a marginalized person's acquisition of a particular tool or skill they feel they *own*, this should be taken as a definite sign that the marginalized person should, indeed, acquire that skill.

The above situation reminds me of white composition instructors whose insistence on centering their students of color in ways they deem empowering (e.g., encouraging code-meshing) inadvertently manifests as trickster racism and is effectively (not intentionally) similar to the results of protectionism. Kim Brian Lovejoy relays a story in which African American colleagues and some of his students were concerned that, by discussing and allowing code-meshing in his class, he was secretly trying to stifle African American progress.[37] Similarly, Melinda J. McBee Orzulak describes the push back white instructors received from African American students when discussing

AAVE. One middle school student's charge that expecting or even allowing AAVE in student writing was "racist" strongly suggests a suspicion of protectionism.[38] The student's instructor was right to inform the student that the language the student herself called ghetto or sloppy was a bona fide dialect that should be respected as much as any other dialect. However, the instructor's surprise at the student's desire to write in LWC and not AAVE or something like it speaks to a framing of student identities not as empowered (perhaps the student wanted to enhance her interactional component of empowerment), but as disempowered and unaware.

Though harboring good intentions, Lovejoy and Orzulak reflect a kind of "I know what's good for you" pedagogy derived from framing students as disempowered and too ignorant of language issues for their own good. Ironically, both pedagogues may illustrate what Paul C. Gorski and Noura Erakat call a "cause theme" of burnout for people of color doing anti-racism work. The cause-theme of "harboring unevolved or racist views"[39] describes the tendency of white allies to think they know all they need to know about a situation; sometimes more than the people with more experience in that situation. Based on a survey, Gorski and Erakat attribute burnout among people of color to "white activists who were resistant to learning from activists of color who often perceive themselves as more racially conscious than they actually were."[40] A survey participant, when talking about this phenomenon in activist circles, wrote: "It's just crazy to me. How can you represent a community that you don't derive from or have done some extensive work in—fieldwork, on the ground grassroot work? I don't understand it. . . . They just read a couple books and did a couple of workshops and it validates their expertise. That's just crazy to me."[41] Lovejoy and Orzulak have clearly done research on race and pedagogy, but the incredulity regarding students of color refusing to embrace AAVE or code-meshed language *because they came to learn something else* is concerning. Their victim-framing, in general, is challenged by students who may not embrace such victimhood and may value something akin to empowerment, if not empowerment outright.[42]

Lovejoy, a white man, is taken aback when a colleague informs him that his black students saw his encouragement to write in AAVE or code-meshed language as an attempt to hold them down or a sign that he thought they weren't capable.[43] He was told this after reading positive teacher evaluations for the class in question, but his colleague informed him that students later shared their true assumptions with her. Lovejoy's ultimate response was to attribute this contradictory information to Smitherman's concept of push-pull,[44] and ultimately writes in a way that paints students as tortured victims stuck in a dilemma between self-love and self-hate. The possibility that the students did not need a class to tell them to be proud to be black, or the possibility that they were there for the express purpose of receiving a skill they had yet to acquire and not exercise a skill they already had, did not seem to enter his mind. His insistence that he knew the students better than the students knew themselves can, itself, be construed as a kind of racism.

I want to be clear that I am not criticizing Lovejoy for critical inquiry. When discussing pedagogy with his colleagues of color, I believe he was right to engage in a conversation about what is and is not proper when using code-meshing as a pedagogy. I reference this section of his work to show an instance of victim-framing and inadvertent trickster racism. Studies show that white liberals are much more concerned about the detriments of anti-black racism than black people, themselves.[45] The tendency of white pedagogues to see victims when looking at students of color, particularly black students, may be a part of this same trend

Also, as I said before and may say again, protectionism is alive and well today. Even if protectionism is not the motivation for white-led anti-racist initiatives, the effects of those initiatives could be quite similar. Code-meshing pedagogy could be construed as an insidious move to placate users of alternative dialects and encourage a neglect of the aspects of the culture of power that are needed to understand and successfully navigate society. In other words, this movement can look like incentivized ignorance; when misused, it can be seen as encouraged immobility ensuring that hegemonic forces maintain the lion's share of social capital in professional contexts. The three York County men I described above may be happy to hear that white teachers are letting African Americans write *their own way*, not for the liberation of the students, but for the protection of white cultural property. Lovejoy may inadvertently enact the ignoble sentiments of these men.

All this being said, a counterargument to my experience with three York men exists, and it is put forth by Laura Greenfield when she describes the phenomenon of whites disliking blacks or other minorities for sounding "white."[46] Greenfield seems to say that the acquisition of LWC does not help minorities and, on occasion, may actually hinder them and get them labeled as a "contradiction."[47] Although hatred or confusion toward minorities for sounding white is a real phenomenon, it is by no means a reason to dismiss the acquisition of LWC. *Kairos* and pragmatism must still be central concepts in any communicative consideration. I have experienced situations similar to those three incidents in that York restaurant, but, ultimately, they are few and far between. Men like these are decidedly disempowered and act from a disempowered standpoint; they do not represent all whites in positions of power, definitely not enough whites to warrant the evasion of LWC. But, as I suggested before, the bristling of some white people at the sound of LWC coming from a black body is a sign that becoming acquainted with this dialect or any hegemonic code is a powerful thing to do.

Just to be clear, I do not think that trickster racism and protectionism are the motivations of organizations like NCTE, CCCC, or other comparable institutes. My point is that, regardless of intention, some anti-racist initiatives can come off as more suppressive than progressive, and a fertile ground for insidious results. For example, whether or not it is inadvertent, code-meshing pedagogy can be construed as a pedagogy of trickster racism.

I am surprised that I have to reference Lisa Delpit's *Other People's Children* to make my point, especially since the pro-code-meshing collection, "Other People's English," clearly riffs off Delpit's title. In the chapter titled "The Silenced Dialogue," Delpit says this about what she calls the "Culture of Power": "If you are not already a participant in the culture of power, being told explicitly the rules of that culture makes acquiring power easier."[48] Although this is said in a context in which Delpit laments the fact that a culture of power is an inherent part of the classroom, the aforementioned quote suggests a pragmatic attitude necessary for upward mobility. Donald Lazere, talking about nonacademic cultures of various ethnicities, makes a similar point when he asks this question:

> Are we doing a service to members of communities traditionally deprived of college education by telling them that their own culture is just as good as academic culture and that they shouldn't want the kind of education that *we* have been privileged with? Shouldn't we instead be doing everything we can to enable them to gain access to academic discourse for their own empowerment?[49]

When it comes down to it, emphasizing code-meshing in first-year writing courses could be understood less as an empowerment of students and more as a restriction. Let's put it this way: if one wanted to devise a plan to squelch the social mobility of a minority group without that group realizing the plan, code-meshing pedagogy and other anti-racist initiatives may offer some keen pointers. Trickster racism—whether intended or unintended—is alive, well, and thriving in the pedagogical circles of rhetoric and composition.

I, for one, would have been taken aback if a teacher had told me to mesh all I wanted, as long as I exercised the more "global" aspects of academic discourse (Thesis statement, counterargument, etc.), or that I could write a narrative sans the aforementioned aspects if it felt more authentic. I probably would have taken issue with a grade-less writing course. This is similar to Lovejoy's students who thought his encouragement to write in AAVE or code-meshed language was an attempt to hold them down or a sign that he thought they weren't capable.[50] As a student, I may have said to myself, "Does this teacher think I can't do it? Does she not know I am as skilled, if not more so, than the other students in this class?" If the teacher conveyed that he or she wanted me to maintain pride in my ethnicity, I would have thought "I *do* have pride in my ethnicity. I don't need to *not* be taught what I came here to learn in order to feel good about my ethnicity. If I needed my composition teacher to help me feel better about being black, I'd have bigger problems than first-year composition. I feel great about being black. Now teach me parallelism!"

What is most blatant about code-meshing's pedagogical inefficacy is that minority writers have written brilliant, canonical, and world-changing texts in a language that is, apparently, tyrannical and dangerous for their mental and emotional well-being. We know what W. E. B. Dubois thought about the *Lingua Franca* of academic and civic discourse. I wonder if James Baldwin felt oppressed when writing *The Fire Next Time*. I wonder if Martin Luther King, Jr. felt like his voice was being stifled because he had to write "Letter From Birmingham Jail" in the code most familiar to his target audience. I wonder if they felt wrong for acquiring this mode of writing, or if they used it as a tool to convey necessary content to the necessary readers for necessary reform.

Combating something like trickster racism and its semantic and situational trickery is itself tricky. Discerning the necessary steps to do so will take time, energy, and willingness. However, the first necessary step is clear; proponents of a primacy of identity must recognize its detriments to progress. The dearth of reality testing, the "allergy to the real" must be acknowledged. A willingness to move from prefigurative politics to a more tactical and effective strategy for progress is imperative.

As pedagogues, we need to stop projecting ourselves (our wants, our "agenda") onto students and their educations. Then again, as many have discussed in their own scholarship, perhaps the classroom is always already too contrived, too unrealistic for real learning to take place. I will write more about this in the next chapter.

NOTES

1. Max Weber, "Politics as a Vocation," *Max Weber: Selections,* ed. W. G. Runciman (New York: Cambridge University Press, 1978), 220.
2. Haider, *Mistaken Identity*, Loc 485–515.
3. Vershawn Ashanti Young, "Nah, We Straight: An Argument Against Code-switching," *JAC,* 29.1/2, (2009), 63.
4. Ashanti Young, "Nah, We Straight: An Argument Against Code-switching."
5. Asao Inoue, *Labor-Based Grading Contracts: Building Equity and Inclusion in the Compassionate Writing Classroom* (Boulder, CO: University Press of Colorado, 2019), 3–4.
6. David A. Tomar, "Eliminating the Grading System in College: The Pros and Cons," *The Quad,* accessed 7 August 2019. https://thebestschools.org/magazine/eliminating-grading-system-college-pros-cons/.

7. See Jason Goulah, "Cultivating Chrysanthemums: Tsunesaburo Makiguchi on Attitudes toward Education," *Schools: Studies in Education*, 12.2 (2015), 252–60; Jeff Gentry, "Why Grades Still Matter," *Chronicle of Higher Education* 20 November 2018, accessed 7 August 2019. https://www.chronicle.com/article/Why-Grades-Still-Matter/245100; Jackson, *The Social Construction of Linguistic Reality*; Stephen D. Krashen, *Principles and Practices in Second Language Acquisition* (New York: Pergamon Press, 1982).

8. Marilyn Frye, *Willful Virgin: Essays in Feminism* (Freedom, CA: The Crossing Press, 1992), 154.

9. See "A Barbarian Within the Gates: The Detriments of Insularity at a Small Liberal Arts College," *Defining, Locating, and Addressing Bullying in the WPA Workplace*, ed. Cristyn L. Elder and Bethany Davila (Logan, UT; University State University Press, 2019).

10. Frankie Condon, "A Place Where There Isn't Any Trouble," *Code-Meshing as World English*, ed. Vershawn Ashanti Young and Aja Y. Martinez (Urbana, IL: NCTE, 2011), 3.

11. Tom Kelleher, *Public Relations* (Oxford, UK: Oxford University Press, 2018).

12. Condon, "A Place Where There Isn't Any Trouble," 3.

13. Ibid.

14. Ibid.

15. Asao Inoue, "Afterward," *Black Perspectives in Writing Program Administration: From the Margins to the Center* (Urbana, IL: NCTE, 2019), 150.

16. Asao Inoue, "Antiracist Writing Assessment Ecologies," *Antiracist Writing Assessment Ecologies: Teaching and Assessing Writing for a Socially Just Future* (Collins, CO: WAC Clearinghouse and Parlor Press, 2015), 96–97. Ebook. https://wac.colostate.edu/books/perspectives/inoue/.

17. Inoue, "Antiracist Writing Assessment Ecologies," 100.

18. Elizabeth Flynn, "Composing as a Woman," *College Composition and Communication*, 39.4 (1988), 423–35.

19. Inoue, "Afterward," 150.

20. This is very prominent in *Labor-Based Grading Contracts: Building Equity and Inclusion in the Compassionate Writing Classroom*. Perspectives on Writing, where he considers the personae of the rap artists Dead Prez as exemplars of black maleness, deeming any student successful in school as "brainwashed." Inoue, *Labor-Based Grading Contracts: Building Equity and Inclusion in the Compassionate Writing Classroom*, 35.

21. Richard Haswell, "Writing Assessment and Race Studies Sub Specie Aeternitatis: A Response to Race and Writing Assessment," *The Journal of Writing Assessment Reading List* (2013). http://jwareadinglist.ucdavis.edu/index.php/2013/01/04/writing-assessment-and-race-studies-sub-specie-aeternitatis-a-response-to-_race-and-writing-assessment_/.

22. Haswell, "Writing Assessment and Race Studies Sub Specie Aeternitatis: A Response to Race and Writing Assessment."

23. Erec Smith, *A Rhetoric of Mythic Proportions: Rhetorical and Messianic Trickster Consciousness and Its Effects on Society*. Dissertation, 2003, v.

24. Smith, *A Rhetoric of Mythic Proportions*, 25.
25. William Doty and William Hynes, *Mythical Trickster Figures: Contours, Contexts, and Criticism* (Tuscaloosa, AL: University of Alabama Press, 1997), 34.
26. Doty and Hynes, *Mythical Trickster Figures*, 35.
27. Ibid., 37.
28. *The 13th*, Dir. Ava DuVernay, Kandoo Films, 2016.
29. W. E. B. Dubois, "A Negro Student Goes to Harvard at the End of the 19th Century," *W.E.B Dubois: A Reader*, ed. David Levering Lewis (New York: Henry Holt and Company 1995), 274.
30. Ralph Ellison, *Shadow and Act* (New York: Vintage International, 1964), Loc 592. E-book.
31. Ellison, *Shadow and Act*, Loc 780.
32. Roland Barthes, *Mythologies* (New York: Farrar, Strauss, and Giroux, 1972), 150.
33. Staci Perryman-Clark and Collin Lamont Craig, "Introduction: Black Matters: Writing Program Administration in Twenty-First Century Higher Education," *Black Perspectives in Writing Program Administration: From the Margins to The Center* (Urbana, IL: NCTE, 2019).
34. Marlene L. Daut, "Becoming a Full Professor While Black," *Chronicle of Higher Education*, July 28, 2019. https://www.chronicle.com/article/Becoming-Full-Professor-While/246743.
35. Smith, "A Barbarian Within the Gate."
36. Patrick Finn, *Literacy With An Attitude: Educating Working Class Children in Their Own Interests*, 2nd ed. (New York: SUNY Press, 2009).
37. Kim Brian Lovejoy, "Code-Meshing: Teachers and Students Creating Community," *Other People's English: Code-Meshing, Code-Switching, and African American Literacy* (New York: Teachers College Press, 2014), 124.
38. Melinda J. McBee Orzulak, "Disinviting Deficit Ideologies: Beyond 'That's Standard,' 'That's Racist,' and 'That's Your Mother Tongue," *Research in the Teaching of English* 50.2 (November 2015), 185.
39. Paul C. Gorski and Noura Erakat, "Racism, Whiteness, and Burnout in Anti-racism Movements: How White Racial Justice Activists Elevate Burnout in Racial Justice Activists of Color in the United States," *Ethnicities* 0.0 (2019), 11.
40. Gorski and Erakat, "Racism, Whiteness, and Burnout in Antiracism Movements: How White Racial Justice Activists Elevate Burnout in Racial Justice Activists of Color in the United States."
41. Ibid., 11–12.
42. For statistics on the number of students of color who do not feel unsafe or oppressed in predominately white institutions, see Knight Foundation, *Free Expression on Campus: What College Students Think about First Amendment Issues: A Gallup/Knight Foundation Survey* (Washington, DC: Gallup, 2018), 19. Also, studies show that students of color score higher on emotional intelligence tests than their white peers. See Steven J. Stein, Howard E. Book, Korrel Kanoy, *The Student EQ Edge: Emotional Intelligence and Your Academic and Personal Success* (San Francisco, CA: Jossey-Bass, 2013), 22–24. Lastly, national trends seem to suggest that

whites see blacks as victims of racism more than blacks see themselves as such. See Thomas B. Edsall, "The Democrats' Left Turn Is Not an Illusion," *The New York Times*, October 18, 2018, accessed 19 August 2019. https://www.nytimes.com/2018/10/18/opinion/democrat-electorate-left-turn.html?fbclid=IwAR0TMqpnrpr-rlmAwLQQiyIKmTru3lRitsBt5rGfcRigyqrAS4rLvUyziLw.

43. Lovejoy, "Code-Meshing: Teachers and Students Creating Community," 124.

44. Ibid., 125.

45. Edsall, "The Democrats' Left Turn Is Not an Illusion."

46. Laura Greenfield, "The 'Standard English' Fairy Tale: A Rhetorical Analysis of Racist Pedagogies and Commonplace Assumptions about Language Diversity," *Writing Centers and the New Racism: A Call for Sustainable Dialogue and Change* (Logan, UT: Utah State University Press, 2011), 51–54.

47. Greenfield, "The 'Standard English' Fairy Tale: A Rhetorical Analysis of Racist Pedagogies and Commonplace Assumptions about Language Diversity," 53.

48. Lisa Delpit, "The Silenced Dialogue: Power and Pedagogy in Teaching Other People's Children," *Harvard Educational Review,* 58.3 (1988), 282.

49. Donald Lazere, *Political Literacy in Composition and Rhetoric: Defending Academic Discourse Against Postmodern Pluralism* (Carbondale, IL: Southern Illinois University Press, 2015), 97.

50. Lovejoy, "Code-Meshing: Teachers and Students Creating Community," 124.

Conclusion

Getting Over Ourselves and Centering Empowerment

So what is the lesson in all of this, so far? We see that lack of empowerment—a pseudo-empowerment—causes many rhetoric and composition scholars to grasp at the semblance of power by adopting an ideology that emphasizes identity—a primacy of identity—that lionizes marginalized identities into "sacred" victims. This semblance of empowerment creates a terministic screen that seems to benefit marginalized bodies but, in reality, promotes a lack of power by incentivizing the victim mentality of marginalized groups and the genuflection of hegmonic groups. This lesson is not meant to suggest that discriminatory practices like racism do not exist; this book was never meant to be a critique of anti-racism, per se. The lesson is about the fact that the ideology and tactics used to fight racism and promote anti-racism can do more harm than good. It perpetuates disempowerment and, potentially, a lack of academic rigor.

The field of rhetoric and composition is no stranger to what I've been calling a semblance of empowerment. What is to be done?

Applying empowerment theory to anti-racism initiatives in the field of rhetoric and composition, or, rather, observing these initiatives for instances of empowerment, reveals a dearth of empowerment that implies, among other things, a neglect of rhetoric and academic discourse, themselves. It also reveals a systemic disempowerment that has resulted in the defense mechanisms I have described as a primacy of identity, a corresponding sacred victim narrative, and prefigurative politics which, in turn, has worked to shape the field in ways that weaken writing pedagogy and perpetuate the very discriminatory practices anti-racists work to discourage. In this concluding chapter, I hope to identify a way of improving anti-racism initiatives, and rhetoric and composition in general, by adequately engaging in social and material realities and, in a sense, getting over ourselves and into true empowerment.

The common, traditional conception of rhetoric and composition as a field is that it is focused on the art of persuasion and argumentation and its written manifestations in several genres.[1] However, rhetoric and composition as it is currently understood has been seen as one that perpetuates Eurocentric sentiments. I believe that, coming from a sense of empowerment, rhetoric's concept of *kairos* transcends that characterization and moves into a pragmatic space where rhetoric—as a kairotic disposition and a conduit of fair-minded critical thinking—can produce not just effective (and affective) communication, but also productive and fulfilling collaboration. As I will show in this concluding chapter, an empowered attitude and an authentic engagement with social and material reality can show rhetoric's efficacy as a field that emphasizes a discovery of the available means of persuasion beneficial to all people.

Rhetoric and composition—the theory and practice of persuasion, shaping discourse, and practical instruction in writing[2]—are imperative in playing out the three components of empowerment. What's more, the components and competencies of emotional intelligence implicit in empowerment are decidedly rhetorical. Consider the rhetorical skill necessary in acquiring and maintaining Conflict Management, Organizational Awareness, Teamwork, etc. Also, notice how rhetoric is enhanced by emotional intelligence, for example, the role of Empathy and Social Awareness in rhetorical listening and gauging one's *kairos*. Rhetoric and empowerment are tightly linked.

However, in anti-racism circles, this link is downplayed. I argue that a dearth of empowerment has had the field's identity give way to a "secure base" concept, denoting a place where victimized people can feel safe. Of course, any field should be considered a safe space for those who inhabit it, as has been argued by scholars and professionals alike. However, I argue, the pendulum has swung too far. The secure base is emphasized to the point where rhetoric and composition, as explained earlier, are not centralized but are usurped by those who embrace a primacy of identity, prefiguration, and victimhood.

This secure base is defined by George Kohlrieser as a place that offers caring and protection while also providing inspiration and encouragement.[3] This secure base can be human or nonhuman, events or ideologies. Ultimately, it serves as a protection against societal "elements" like loss of power, discrimination, disenfranchisement, precarity, and so on. The secure base is both an energizer and motivator, a safe space in which vulnerable groups and groups trying to stave off vulnerability can find security, and from which they can safely navigate the world. Having such a space threatened can literally feel like an attack on one's general safety.[4] Kohlrieser et al write:

> To understand why we all need secure bases, consider how the human brain works. When an actual or perceived threat to survival emerges, the primal brain

will prompt the individual to resist change or avoid risk to protect the self. However, when a person has a secure base, he can turn the focus from pain, danger, fear and loss to focus on reward, opportunity and benefit. . . . The stronger the secure base, the more resilient the person becomes in the face of adverse or stressful circumstances.[5]

For the marginalized who harbor feelings of disempowerment, a secure base can be an oasis of sorts. Smucker's claim that many people see activists' groups as therapeutic spaces most importantly is the result of "secure base" politics.

Cynthia Willett discusses the concept of home in similar ways. She writes that vulnerable populations, specifically African American people, embrace a sense of community more than their Anglo-American peers who value the individual rationality of Enlightenment thinking.[6] As we have seen throughout this work, a primacy of identity demonizes rationality and individual agency as "white" and, therefore, oppressive. Aspects of whiteliness can be defined in ways that smack of Enlightenment values, as well. Thus, the bildungsroman motif of leaving the security of the home for an adventurous and heroic life—an apparent sentiment of Enlightenment thinking—is replaced by a narrative of building and maintaining a secure base where there is power in numbers and where pain is both shared and assuaged by working together. Regarding social justice proponents in rhetoric and composition, a threat to the secure base of anti-racism proponents can be seen as another "colonial" attack singing the praises of individuality, pragmatism, and reason.

Fortunately, empowerment theory combines the individuality of the bildungsroman with the secure base ideology. The intrapersonal component secures self-efficacy and self-esteem while the interactional and behavioral components emphasize understanding and working with community. Empowerment thinking is not a panacea for healthy and effective change, but it is a necessary starting point toward effecting societal progress. Empowerment thinking is a threat to the primacy of identity and sacred victim narratives, but it can also constitute strong building blocks for another kind of secure base, one I see as more effective in all aspects.

To explore this further, I want to discuss the communal aspect of anti-racism as it is put forth by Inoue's appropriation of Buddhist thought in anti-racist pedagogy. First, I should make something clear. Buddhist thought is unlike the religiosity I discuss when describing the sacred victim narrative and the collective sentiment of many social justice circles. The latter is more akin to an evangelistic and even fundamentalist take on "right" or "wrong," "good" or "bad," that promotes "us versus them" thinking. Buddhist philosophy as I use it here is just that: philosophy. It does not revolve around the concepts of righteousness and sin. Thus, to criticize evangelistic religiosity but argue for the efficacy of Buddhist thought is not a hypocritical move.

Conclusion

In *Antiracist Writing Assessment Ecologies: Teaching and Assessing Writing for a Socially Just Future*, Inoue references the Buddhist monk and author, Thich Naht Hahn, whose concept of a sangha—a Buddhist term for community—is likened to Inoue's use of the term "ecosystem" to describe the classroom. Inoue cites Hahn's concept of interbeing which denotes the consubstantiality or interdependence of people with each other and their material environment. He uses this concept to discuss how a classroom, if conceptualized as a sangha (a community of practitioners that embrace the interbeing concept), can move toward anti-racism. Inoue writes:

> Interconnection as a way to explicitly understand the relationship between and among people, their labors, drafts, practices, and environments is vital to a fully functioning antiracist writing assessment ecology. It offers students ways out of simply disagreeing, simply seeing difference, or "agreeing to disagree." Seeing difference is a good start, but ultimately, we must work together, help each other in writing classrooms and beyond. We must see how we all inter-are, how we can be a Sangha. Once we act in ways that acknowledge the fluid boundaries between ourselves and others, between our writing and others' judgments of it, we become fuller.[7]

I share Inoue's fondness for the idea of inherent interconnection. I have also published on the relationship between Buddhism and writing pedagogy and cite interbeing as a useful concept, seeing interbeing as an effective methodology for tutoring practice.[8] However, I take a more intricate look at interbeing (a writing center session is, by nature, more intimate than a classroom ecology). When applying interbeing to Inoue's purposes, it manifests differently.

Hanh calls interbeing "Tiep Hien," "'which translates to being in touch with' (Tiep) and 'realizing' or 'making it here and now' (Hien)."[9] He then parses this concept out into what he calls the "Charter of Interbeing," consisting of the following four concepts: nonattachment from views, direct experimentation, appropriateness, and skillful means. "Nonattachment from views" is a warning against dogmatic and acontextual thinking. "Direct experimentation" is a concept that "emphasizes the direct experience of reality, not speculative philosophy." "Appropriateness" denotes the belief that "a teaching, in order to bring about understanding and compassion, must reflect the needs of people and realities of society," which is an idea that aligns with the concept of reality testing. Lastly, "skillful means" is a term synonymous with "rhetoric" understood as the proper mode of communication to lead people to enlightenment.[10] Hanh writes: "Skillful means consist of images and methods created by intelligent teachers to show the Buddha's Way and guide people in their efforts to practice the Way in their own particular circumstances."[11] When thinking about this four-point Charter of Interbeing, we see that open-mindedness and direct interaction must coexist with reality testing and rhetoric. Ultimately, it is an appreciation of *kairos*. All this seems to work well with Inoue's use of interbeing to justify his concept of the classroom as sangha, but I feel his use of the concept is too limited for what Hanh intended.

To illustrate this, let's look at the concept of a sangha. Hanh cites interbeing as an incorporation of the charge to make it "here and now." However, how are we defining "here" and "now"? We may find an answer to this question in the third component of the Charter of Interbeing: appropriateness. I have already equated this concept to reality testing, citing Hanh's charge that a good teaching "must reflect the needs of people and realities of society."[12] This concept also raises the question of the sangha regarding its size and scope, which must also take into consideration the goals of the students involved. I can synthesize all this in this way: students seek the ability to communicate in the world, not in the narrow confines of a classroom. Thus, their audience, if we are to consider "the needs of people and realities of society," must move beyond the classroom as ecosystem to a larger audience as ecosystem. I believe Hanh's conception of interbeing is more cosmopolitan than Inoue lets on. To apply Hanh's work to the charge of first-year composition is to take seriously the trends of civic and professional spaces and, by extension, the usefulness of a Language of Wider Communication.

I also think that Hanh's concept of interbeing and the four-part Charter of Interbeing provide an understanding of identity that aligns less with anti-racist notions of an essentialist identity necessarily cathected to language and more with a kairotic disposition in which one's identity is always intertwined—that is, in interbeing—with one's surroundings. This notion of identity, the idea rendered in Buddhism as nonbeing and nonattachment, seems to contradict that tacit notion that students are and should be attached to a particular way of speaking and writing. The implicit idea that one must behave in a certain way to authentically embody a designated race is as non-Buddhist as it is racist.

Let us consider the words of the poet Ai, a woman who was part Japanese, black, white, and Native American:

> The insistence that one must align oneself with this or that race is basically racist. And the notion that without a racial identity a person can't have any identity perpetuates racism. . . . I wish I could say that race isn't important. But it is. More than ever, it is a medium of exchange, the coin of the realm with which one buys one's share of jobs and social position. This is a fact which I have faced and must ultimately transcend. If this transcendence were less complex, less individual, it would lose its holiness.[13]

This quote captures a desire to get over the multivalent trap of race. It also contains an apparent contradiction to one of my most common refrains throughout this work: the detriments of religiosity in anti-racism movements.

However, no contradiction really exists. Again, I, like Inoue, see merit in a Buddhist approach to pedagogy. Thus, I cite the *philosophical* aspects of Buddhism and refrain from a kind of dogma that can potentially deem people as zealots or heretics for not abiding by certain named and unnamed rules. My ultimate goal in synthesizing Buddhism and rhetorical theory and practice is to transcend the primacy of identity and, therefore, the victim narrative, by moving beyond identity as it is understood in social justice circles. That is, I resolve to shake loose the fetters of race and identity without necessarily losing sight of their ongoing symbolic relevance in society and higher education. One can study an object without being cathected to it. According to Buddhist thought in general, identity is not and cannot be set in stone.

Although my work on Buddhism and writing pedagogy began with Thich Naht Hanh, my subsequent work in this area focuses on a Japanese form of Buddhism called "Nichiren." This form of Buddhism prioritizes the *Lotus Sutra*, understood by Nichiren Buddhists as the last major sutra given by the Buddha, as the primary Buddhist text, rendering all previous sutras as provisional and designed for an audience relatively ignorant of true Buddha nature. The prior sutras were seen as "expedient means," a term synonymous with skillful means (rhetoric), used to meet uninformed audiences at their current mental, emotional, and intellectual standpoints. The *Lotus Sutra*, however, provides the "one vehicle" or "the true aspect of all phenomena."[14] Identity is included within the aegis of "all phenomena."

In "Buddhism's Pedagogical Contribution to Mindfulness," I discuss the concepts in the *Lotus Sutra* that denote an understanding of identity that is inherently kairotic. I conclude that Buddhism's concept of simultaneous being and nonbeing suggests that we, as living beings, do not just consider and experience *kairos*; we *are kairos*.[15] This is to say that we are our actions and interactions. Interbeing is a description of our identities. We "inter-are" as Inoue might say. So, if identity is not a solidified concept, if it is a nebulous and always becoming thing, it cannot be essentialized. Whether proponents of anti-racism admit it or not, much anti-racist ideology relies on an essentialized concept of race; to be black or white is to be a particular kind of person. Yes, constant experience in a particular environment with particular people will interpellate particular identities, but interpellation is the key term here. Interpellation is an action and a call to action, not a reification.

Interpellation, being called forth by particular kairotic dynamics, is a key aspect of the *Lotus Sutra*'s concept of the "true aspect of all phenomena." We do not embody a racial essentialism. Ultimately, we embody *kairos,* which is to say we *are* mindfulness of ourselves, others, our environment, and the goals that move us. In turn, this is to say that, whether consciously or not, we *are* empowerment: we are effective agents (intrapersonal) aware of our surroundings (interactional) that prompt us to behave in certain ways for certain ends (behavioral). It is our lack of awareness of this phenomenon that gets us in trouble. Awareness allows us to effectively navigate this way of being without projecting essentialized ideas of identity, negative emotionality, or stimulus-response interpretations that do not correlate to the moment. We do not let preconceived narratives *necessarily* frame our experiences. We are mindful of narratives, how and why they work, and why we are motivated to have them. We are social epistemic rhetoricians, as James Berlin may say.[16] Empowerment theory's foundation is mindfulness and a kairotic disposition.

I think it is telling that a Nichiren Buddhist who founded a lay Buddhist organization called Soka Gakkai (Value-creation society), Tsuneseburo Makiguchi, got into Buddhism because, as an educator, he believed Buddhist philosophy was strongly conducive to true education.[17] Soka Gakkai is considered the most diverse Buddhist organization in the United States and takes seriously the concept of "dependent origination"—what Hanh and Inoue would call interbeing. As opposed to most American Buddhist organizations that are predominately white and relatively aloof to societal issues like race,[18] Soka Gakkai embraces diversity, a sentiment captured in their maxim, "many in body, one in mind" wherein "One in mind" refers to all members sharing a respect for individual dignity and empowerment.[19] The most diverse Buddhist organization in the country emphasizes empowerment comparable to the kind I have been touting throughout this book.

Makiguchi, as an educator heavily influenced by Buddhism, was interested in composition pedagogy.[20] His value-creating pedagogy emphasized "individual happiness, independent thinking, criticality, and social self-actualization."[21] Combine these things with dependent origination (interbeing) and we have components similar to empowerment theory. Nichiren Buddhists do not see themselves as railing against society in ways indicative of anti-racist proponents. The world is an interaction that empowered beings can improve through collaboration and mutual respect. Like empowerment theory, such thinking is not a panacea of change; it is *the place from which* people must work to effect change. Makiguchi felt that this attitude was the most important aspect of pedagogy. Jason Goulah, a specialist in Soka Gakkai, writes:

> Makiguchi asserts that a teacher's attitude is of utmost importance in determining the ends of education. Teachers must demonstrate an attitude totally focused on the students before them, set entirely on fostering, or guiding, these students' growth and development into creative and critically engaged individuals. From such an attitude everything emerges and, further, only after understanding and endeavoring to foster the proper attitude can one meaningfully engage in a discussion on which methods to use.[22]

I relay this not to dismiss the effect of structural racism in education, but to display a lack of victim mentality and a primacy of identity in a value-creating pedagogy. I admire Inoue's use of Buddhism as a lens through which to see the classroom as an ecology, but his emphasis on the detriments of whiteness, to the point of demonizing aspects of critical thinking for their Eurocentric origins, actually does not align with Buddhist sentiments. Inoue's take is not a true engagement with the world as much as it is engagement with *some* against a structural *other* that is necessarily oppressive: "Many in Body, One in Mind . . . except for when it comes to white stuff," is not the maxim.[23] Yes, Nichiren Buddhism and Soka Gakkai represent just one of many sects and not the one to which Hanh belongs. However, the sect that emphasizes and practices diversity while promoting value-creating pedagogy (Soka Gakkai has two universities and various high schools founded on Makiguchi's principles[24]) should receive more attention from pedagogues interested in Buddhism and education than it does.

Makiguchi's words about attitude also denote the need for teachers to "see" their students. Critical Language Awareness and respect for student cultures and languages reflect the attitude of which Makiguchi speaks. Thinking that the home dialects of marginalized groups are a deficiency that needs to be eradicated is antithetical to Makiguchi's ideal attitude. However, Makiguchi, who openly shared a fondness for American Pragmatism and John Dewey, would see the clear tactical significance of learning writing styles for civic and professional contexts.[25] An attitude that embraces the understanding of where students are while working to get them to acquire skills indicative of a place they have yet to be is not contradictory. A value-creation attitude is not one of supremacy and indoctrination. It is pragmatic, it is kairotic, it is empowerment, and one could add that it is Buddhist.

Makiguchi's emphasis on attitude is shared by others interested in anti-racism and rhet/comp instruction and can contribute to a more productive secure base in education. Delpit cites teacher attitude as the primary consideration when teaching writing, citing Stephen Krashen's "affective filter," for example, when a classroom environment is too judgmental for students to strive, as a way to understand how an attitude of openness and positive regard can create a secure base conducive to both learning and all-around self-esteem.[26] In "Topsy-Turvies: Teacher Talk and Student Talk," Herbert Kohl insists that being aware of one's environment and adopting an attitude of "patient, intelligent, and sensitive speaking, reading, and listening" is more essential than "questions of test scores and covering the curriculum."[27] Rosemary Jackson shows, through the results of a study of black community college students, that black students understand the efficacy of learning "standard English" and, for that reason, want to learn it despite its associations with white racism. Their only issue is the use of "standard English" as a way to look down on those who do not do this, which, as Jackson discovers, can be remedied with the right pedagogical approach, that is, the right teaching attitude.[28] When LWC or even standard English is taught in the right way, the dialect's origins in colonialism are, a la Burke,[29] deflected and its pragmatic and rhetorical efficacy is selected to better engage social and material realities.

And let us not forget the attitudes that many students bring with them to the classroom. From Dubois to Jackson's aforementioned students, many students entering writing classrooms are there to acquire a beneficial skill and only ask to be respected while doing so. Many students bring a strong sense of reality testing and an enthusiasm, or what Goleman and other scholars of emotional intelligence may call Positive Outlook, that de-emphasizes negative emotionality and stimulus-response modes of interpreting the world. Many students do not see victims when they look in the mirror.

So, Inoue's appropriation of Buddhism is a worthwhile endeavor, but it does not go far enough. The understanding of Buddhism I put forth is more in line with the empowerment theory I have been discussing throughout this work. A deep discussion of Buddhist pedagogy goes beyond the general purpose of this book. For now, I want to identify a pedagogy that is conducive to the Buddhist pedagogy put forth by Makiguchi and Soka Gakkai as an organization and to the general theory of empowerment that is the framework of this book.

PROBLEM-BASED LEARNING: A THEORY AND PEDAGOGY OF EMPOWERMENT

Taking deliberate steps to engage the public in ways that enhance student and faculty knowledge could be the best way to get over an aversion to the other, get over disempowerment and its results, and, generally, get over ourselves. That being said, I think a specific kind of civic engagement would best serve this purpose. I believe Problem-Based Learning (PBL), having students take on authentic local problems, could help as both a pedagogy of empowerment and an illustration of how transcending the primacy of identity can enhance rhetorical savvy and promote anti-racism. I am not presenting PBL as something completely distinct from service learning and other forms of civic engagement. However, unlike those initiatives, PBL more definitely necessitates an embrace of *kairos*. It promotes a kairotic disposition that, in turn, necessitates the embrace of empowerment theory. The three components of empowerment—intrapersonal, interactive, and behavioral—will both enhance and be enhanced by PBL initiatives. The problem is not anti-racism; it is victim-based anti-racism. We need to more deliberately promote an empowerment-based anti-racism. PBL may help.

PBL works to enhance the ability to acquire the following skills:

- Think critically and be able to analyze and solve complex, real-world problems;
- Find, evaluate, and use appropriate learning resources;
- Work cooperatively in teams and small groups;
- Demonstrate versatile and effective communication skills, both verbal and written;
- Use content knowledge and intellectual skills acquired at the university to become continual learners.[30]

These outcomes reflect the three components of empowerment and the important considerations for rhetorical effectiveness. PBL incorporates what Inoue calls the seven elements of anti-racist writing ecologies (Power, Parts, Purpose, People, Processes, Products, and Places)[31] while also going beyond the classroom ecosystem. The authentic, real-world issues that shape all PBL initiatives leave behind arguments about what to teach and/or allow in a writing class and solves the problem of contrived assignments; social and material realities both within and beyond the classroom will dictate what is to be learned. Because most PBL assignments work in contexts in which a Language of Wider Communication (as opposed to "standard" written English) is written and expected,[32] having students practice writing in this dialect would be a pragmatic move on our part as instructors.

That being said, students—individually or in groups (which is more typical)—may find themselves writing primarily in a dialect other than LWC or SWE if *kairos* dictates it. Students, as researchers and problem solvers, are interpellated by the particulars of the problem to be solved. Who needs to read the finished product? What do they value in rhetoric and dialect? What do clients expect from written documents? All these questions—not contrived assignments or counterhegemonic agendas—will determine the language used in a project.

PBL promotes instrumental motivation as well as expressive motivation, whereas other anti-racism initiatives, sans pragmatic consideration, de-emphasize the former. According to political scientist Kurt Burch, "Problems are vehicles for learning. . . . Problems transport students from the classroom to tangible, real-world situations that stimulate their curiosity and creativity."[33] Instrumental motivation, based on real-life actualities and not classroom fabrications (not to mention classroom assumptions about students' intrapersonal attitudes), is sufficiently present; the "active and applied"[34] nature of PBL takes students out of themselves and toward their audiences in a way that automatically transcends a primacy of identity. In this way, what Inoue may call "the conditions that operationalize our assessment ecologies"[35] are discovered kairotically and not from purposeful framing from the teacher. A primacy of social, material, and kairotic reality would be a more accurate, and a more rhetorically sound, description of PBL. In short, PBL necessitates that we get over ourselves to better accomplish our goals.

In fact, and perhaps most importantly, PBL addresses each component of empowerment while also doing anti-racist work. Discussing how each component relates to PBL will show its efficacy as a tool of both empowerment and rhetorical pedagogy. Also, it will show how anti-racism can be done without resorting to the semblance of empowerment put forth by current leaders of anti-racism in rhetoric and composition studies.

Regarding the intrapersonal component, one's perceived beliefs about self-competence and self-efficacy, PBL, by nature, allows students to see exactly how they can begin to contribute to solving a problem and, for our purposes, communicating discovered tactics to others. Regarding the interactional component, students will discover the imperative to work and communicate with others, discovering their audiences inside a group—if the project is group-oriented—and beyond the group. This brings us to the behavioral component, which emphasizes the ability to influence outcomes with strategic action.[36] This represents the solution to the problem on which the project is based and necessitates the fundamentals of rhetoric—audience consideration, *kairos*—and the resulting product to be read (or heard, or viewed, or all simultaneously).

Most importantly, from an anti-racist standpoint, PBL can enhance diversity and equality as they are connected to ideas of participatory democracy that are implicitly rhetorical. Kurt Burch explicitly states that, because of its democratic and interpersonal nature, PBL will improve "the participation, achievement, and enthusiasm of women, minorities, introverts, and those frustrated by the competitiveness and alienating isolation fostered by typical classroom instruction."[37] Burch believes that the relationship between participation and diversity is reciprocal; each enhances the other.[38] This will necessarily counter the often antidemocratic nature of anti-racist spaces in rhetoric and composition wherein differing viewpoints are silenced.

PBL must utilize what architects call tensegrity. Coined by Buckminster Fuller, tensegrity is the process of integrating opposing forces into a structure to help it maintain integrity.[39] Tensegrity, then, is a metaphor for dialectical collaboration. Collaboration based on the concept of tensegrity would rarely see dissenting voices silenced or ostracized. Such voices will be incorporated into the conversation, their audibility dictated, like everyone else's, by *kairos*, pragmatism, and the end goal.

PBL unavoidably necessitates the five major components of emotional intelligence: Self-Awareness, Social Awareness, Self-Management, and

Relationship Management. Working with others on real societal issues demands an awareness of self, others, stakeholders, and the social and material realities of a situation; these components and their corresponding competencies, then, will come up automatically in unpredictable ways that, again, must necessitate a rhetorical savvy and a kairotic awareness.

Ultimately, Burch seems to see PBL as a tool of empowerment, agency, and anti-racism. He writes about the processes and outcomes of PBL: "First, a contemporary philosophical debate rages over the merits of communitarian and individualist principles of social interaction. For students to participate in cooperative groups is a valuable tonic for the often lonely, asocial individualism of our contemporary society and education systems."[40] He concludes with the idea that PBL promotes a "radically multicultural democracy" that "challenges interlocking forms of oppression—such as ageism, racism, sexism, and resources inequalities—by seeking to overcome narrow 'identities' in favor of multiple and fluid identities. PBL groups foster both communitarian interactions and multicultural, pluralistic participation."[41] PBL aligns with studies that suggest cross-racial interaction enhances cognitive functioning, especially because students are forced to deal with any cognitive disequilibrium that comes with experiencing different standpoints in productive ways because the end result, the problem to be solved, necessitates it. By not rejecting newfound standpoints, students can process the innovative information and revise their viewpoints accordingly.[42]

Burch's take is indicative of the Buddhist concepts of interbeing and "the true aspect of all phenomena" in that it naturalizes consubstantiality and the "multiple and fluid" concept of identity put forth in Buddhist philosophy. What's more, Burch seems to be describing a pedagogy that flies against the conception of students by which proponents of anti-racism would have us abide. In PBL, agency, voice, and empowerment are shared by all involved. Among other things, PBL *is* anti-racism.

Of course, PBL will manifest in different ways based on the specifics of a particular educational domain. I have used PBL for group writing projects and individual projects. Obviously, the results are different but each scenario is psychologically empowering in its own way. Also, assessment will depend on particular partnerships and the weight of stakeholder input. Perhaps Inoue's labor-based grading could be of benefit when assessing PBL projects, especially when a "real world" client with no pedagogical training is involved in the evaluation process.[43] A full discussion of PBL assessment is beyond the scope of this book. However, resources on ways to implement PBL abound. Ultimately, I hope PBL can ground and empower academics and students. The learning can enhance anti-racist initiatives and can also involve issues of race as the very problem to be solved.

Centering Empowerment

PBL both actualizes rhetorical theory, putting it into authentic practice, and centers empowerment. As both a process and outcome, empowerment is honed through acknowledging the social and material realities of a particular project, its kairotic characteristics, and a realistic sense of one's own agency. PBL is something that should be explored further, especially in rhetoric and composition.

However, the issues I go over throughout this book go beyond the classroom and into rhetoric and composition as a field. Based on this, I conclude that we, as scholars, pedagogues, and administrators center empowerment in our endeavors. How can we think about and enhance the intrapersonal, interactive, and behavioral components explicitly? How might a true respect and embrace of empowerment transform the racist bully cultures discussed in books like *Defining, Locating, and Addressing Bullying in the WPA Workplace* and *Black Perspectives in Writing Center Administration*? How may attitudes toward grading, assessment, rubrics, and other considerations of teaching change? I do not have the answer to these questions. I only want to ask them and work together to answer them.

Of course, in order to adequately work together, one can argue that one's sense of empowerment must already be intact. However, this is not the case. As PBL suggests and empowerment theorists explain, empowerment is a process *and* an outcome. In other words, one can use empowerment theory to acquire empowerment and, eventually, concrete change. Zimmerman writes that "empowering processes are ones in which attempts to gain control, obtain needed resources, and critically understand one's social environment are fundamental. The process is empowering if it helps people develop skills so they can become independent problem-solvers and decision-makers."[44] It would seem that, when acquiring empowerment, the journey *is* the destination. That is, one has to constantly perform empowerment; it is always becoming.

Regarding empowerment as an outcome, Zimmerman writes, that outcomes "refer to operationalization of empowerment so we can study the consequences of citizens' attempts to gain greater control in their community, or the effects of interventions designed to empower participants."[45] So, outcomes, final products, let empowered agents know how well they are doing and/or what needs to be done to improve efficacy. One can see how PBL and empowerment theory are a good match.

When it comes to the empowerment of academics, then, we must take on the attitude of PBL students and think kairotically. Zimmerman says as much:

> Empowering processes will vary across levels of analysis. For example, empowering processes for individuals might include organizational or community involvement; empowering processes at the organization level might

include shared leadership and decision-making; empowering processes at the community level might include assessable government, media, and other community resources. . . . Empowerment outcomes also differ across levels of analysis. When we are concerned with individuals, outcomes might include situation-specific perceived control, skills, and proactive behaviors. When we are studying organizations, outcomes might include organizational networks, effective resource acquisition, and policy leverage. When we are concerned with community-level empowerment, outcomes might include evidence of pluralism, the existence of organizational coalitions, and accessible community resources.[46]

Empowerment is not a one-size-fits-all endeavor. How it looks and feels will depend on the institution, the specific project, and the kinds of people involved. Thus, a prescription for empowerment that fits specific needs is necessarily kairotic, although theorists do provide examples as well as their own experiences.[47]

As I have argued throughout this work, empowerment is a necessary skill for creating self-actualizing academics (students and scholars) who can work with others to make concrete and progressive changes in the world. The three components of empowerment have substantial overlap with rhetorical theories and the encompassing concept of *kairos*. The components of emotional intelligence that necessarily coexist with empowerment can also inform theories and practices regarding emotional labor. What's more, it synthesizes rhetoric and pragmatism in ways that better ensure tangible outcomes that affect the social and material realities in which we and our students enter, that is, the world beyond the ivory tower. In fact, as one can glean from my fondness for PBL, I believe the "real" world may be the key to how rhetoric and composition, its anti-racist methodologies in particular, can best incorporate theories of empowerment into scholarship and pedagogy.

I believe a major distinction that needs to be made clear—in academia and society alike—is a teleological one. Is the goal of anti-racism group esteem and societal validation, or is the goal group esteem, societal validation, *and actual societal progress*? Not only do I believe in the latter *telos*; I also believe such progress necessitates very different tactics from those of esteem and validation alone. Unlike esteem and validation, which can be approached through celebration, memorial recognition (holidays and events), and idealistic performance, I believe progress necessitates an empowered attitude that willingly gauges the world as it is and acts accordingly. Whereas esteem and validation politics work on idealism and moral propositions, actions toward societal progress are more kairotic in nature. That is, they take in particular situations, gauge the social and material realities accordingly, and devise actions based on that gauge. Politics of esteem and validation, then, are relatively egocentric and narcissistic (this includes a collective egocentrism and narcissism) and indicative of a primacy of identity. The pragmatics of *kairos*, on the other hand, go beyond the self and one's group, taking into consideration all involved to ensure progress.

An exploration of how empowerment theory can manifest in specific contexts, especially with an anti-racist telos grounded in social and material reality, could change the landscape of rhetoric and composition in ways that go far beyond racial equality on an interpersonal and structural level. But, admittedly, we will not really know until we remove ourselves from a deficit model of empowerment—the semblance of empowerment—and center empowerment in our theory, pedagogy, and interactions.

NOTES

1. Steven Lynne, "The Open Hand: Meet Rhetoric and Composition," *Rhetoric and Composition: An Introduction* (New York: Cambridge University Press, 2010), 1–35.
2. Lynne, "The Open Hand: Meet Rhetoric and Composition."
3. Kohlrieser, Goldsworthy, and Coombe, *Care to Dare*, 8.
4. Daniel Goleman, "Emotional Self-Awareness: An Introduction," *Emotional Self Awareness: A Primer* (Florence, MA: More Than Sound, 2017), Loc 145.
5. Goleman, "Emotional Self-Awareness: An Introduction," 9.
6. Cynthia Willett, *The Soul of Justice: Social Bonds and Racial Hubris* (Ithaca, NY: Cornell University Press, 2001).
7. Inoue, *Antiracist Writing Assessment Ecologies*, 104.
8. Erec Smith, "Writing Under the Bodhi Tree," *Academic Exchange Quarterly* 9.2 (2005).
9. Thich Nhat Hanh, *Interbeing: Fourteen Guidelines for Engaged Buddhism* (Berkeley, CA: Parallax Press, 1998), 1.
10. Hanh, *Interbeing*, 8
11. Ibid.
12. Ibid.
13. "Ai," *The Poetry Foundation*, accessed 1 August 2019, https://www.poetryfoundation.org/poets/ai.
14. Erec Smith, "The *Lotus Sutra* as Rhetorical Doctrine: Toward a Spiritual Paradigm Shift in Academia," *The Journal of South Texas English Studies*, 1.1 (2009), accessed 9 August 2019. https://docs.google.com/a/ycp.edu/document/d/1hAXTwywbAfxwIVY9PHHKCX9Ow-YkodQGrdKTx3yUjd8/edit.
15. Smith, "Buddhism's Pedagogical Contribution to Mindfulness," 36–46.
16. Berlin, *Rhetorics, Poetics, and Cultures*, 80–84.
17. Goulah, "Cultivating Chrysanthemums: Tsuneseburo Makiguchi on Attitudes toward Education," 255.
18. For a narrative take on lack of diversity and antiracism in Buddhist organizations, see Angela Kyodo Williams, *Being Black: Zen and the Art of Living with Fearlessness and Grace* (New York: Penguin Books, 2000).

19. "Many in Body, One in Mind," *SGI-USA,* accessed 3 August 2019. https://www.sgi-usa.org/study-resources/core-concepts/many-in-body-one-in-mind/.

20. See *Makiguchi Tsunesebaro in the Context of Language, Identity, and Education,* ed. Jason Goulah (New York: Routledge, 2017).

21. Goulah, "Cultivating Chrysanthemums: Tsuneseburo Makiguchi on Attitudes toward Education," 255.

22. Ibid., 256.

23. To be clear, Makiguchi did speak truth to power and paid for it with his life for the "thought crime" of speaking against Japanese imperialism and chauvinism. The fatal result of his protest speaks to my point. The oppression of the Japanese government during WWII is not comparable to the effects of being a person of color in what Inoue calls a white habitus. Compared to the former, the latter is more of an inconvenience than oppression.

24. Other Buddhist institutes of higher education do exist. However, Soka University of America expressly put forth the values of "peace, education, and cultural exchange." See Tanya Storch, "Buddhist Universities in the United States of America," *International Journal of Dharma Studies,* 1.4 (2013). https://link.springer.com/article/10.1186/2196-8802-1-4.

25. Jason Goulah, "Makiguchi Tsunesaburo and Language, Value-Creative Composition Instruction, and the Geography of Identity in Community Studies: A Response to Politicized Imagining and Ineffective Critical Approaches," *Makiguchi Tsunesaburo in the Context of Language, Identity, and Education,* ed. Jason Goulah (New York: Routledge, 2017), 34–35.

26. Delpit, "No Kinda Sense," 55–56.

27. Herbert Kohl, "Topsy-Turvies: Teacher Talk and Student Talk," *The Skin that We Speak: Thoughts on Language and Culture in the Classroom,* ed. Lisa Delpit and Joanne Kilgour Dowdy (New York: The New Press, 2018), 210.

28. Jackson, *The Social Construction of Linguistic Reality,* 225.

29. Kenneth Burke, *Language as Symbolic Action,* in *The Rhetorical Tradition: Readings From Classical Time to the Present* 2nd ed., ed. Patricia Bizzell and Bruce Herzberg (New York: Bedford St. Martin's Press, 2001), 1341.

30. Barbara J. Duch et al., *The Power of Problem-Based Learning,* ed. Barbara J. Duch, Susan E. Groh, Deborah E. Allen (Sterling, VA: Stylus Publishing, 2001), 6.

31. Inoue, *Antiracist Writing Assessment Ecologies,* 120–76.

32. Geneva Smitherman, *Talking that Talk: Language, Culture, and Education in African America* (New York: Routledge, 2001), 38–39.

33. Kurt Burch, "PBL, Politics, and Democracy," *The Power of Problem-Based Learning,* ed. Barbara J. Duch, Susan E Groh, Deborah E. Allen (Sterling, VA: Stylus Publishing, 2001), 194.

34. Burch, "PBL, Politics, and Democracy," 195.

35. Asao Inoue, "Writing Assessment as the Conditions for Translingual Approaches: An Argument for Fairer Assessments," *Crossing Divides: Exploring Translingual Writing Pedagogies and Programs,* ed. Bruce Horner and Laura Tetreault (Logan, UT: Utah State University Press, 2017), 124.

36. Zimmerman, "Psychological Empowerment: Issues and Illustrations," 590.

37. Burch, "PBL, Politics, and Democracy," 197.
38. Ibid.
39. Matheus Pereira, "Tensegrity Structures: What They Are and What They Can Be," trans. Guilherme Carvalho, *Arch Daily*, 3 June 2018, https://www.archdaily.com/893555/tensegrity-structures-what-they-are-and-what-they-can-be.
40. Burch, "PBL, Politics, and Democracy," 199.
41. Ibid.
42. Mitchell J. Chang, Alexander W. Austin, and Dongbin Kim, "Cross-Racial Integration Among Undergraduates: Some Consequences, Causes, and Patterns," *Research in Higher Education*, 45.5 (2004), 545.
43. Even though the "real world" would be a white racial habitus at the "macro" level for Inoue, what he considers the confining nature of grades could be eluded and genuine partnerships with authentic clients beyond the classroom can create a better understanding of the connections between one's thought processes and one's particular ecology.
44. Marc A. Zimmerman, "Empowerment Theory: Psychological, Organizational, and Community Levels of Analysis," *Handbook of Community Psychology*, ed. Julian Rappaport and Edward Seidman (New York: Plenum Publishers, 2000), 46.
45. Zimmerman, "Empowerment Theory: Psychological, Organizational, and Community Levels of Analysis."
46. Ibid.
47. For illustrations of how to practice empowerment with downtrodden populations, see Judith A. B. Lee, *The Empowerment Approach to Social Work: Building the Beloved Community,* 2nd ed. (New York: Columbia University Press, 2001); As it applies to people with physical disabilities, see S. B. Fawcett et al., "A Contextual-Behavioral Model of Empowerment: Case Studies Involving People with Physical Disabilities," *American Journal of Community Psychology,* 2 (1994) 471–86.

Epilogue

Am I Overreacting?
(A Humble Request for Your Input)

Okay, I have a question. I've had this question for a long time and I think answering it or merely asking it can help us explore and understand the dearth of empowerment in rhetoric and composition. In order to adequately ask the question, however, I have to provide a bit of context. Bear with me.

As a graduate student, I collaborated with my peers and a professor to publish a collection of our own literacy narratives—really, short autoethnographies about our erstwhile attitudes toward writing and rhetoric—to display different viewpoints toward literacy.[1] In my narrative, I speak of my experience as a child between two cultures, and how I acted in racist contexts in order to survive mentally and emotionally. In my initial environment, a predominately White suburb of Philadelphia, I speak of acquiring a "black identity," but "acquire" is not quite accurate; it was projected onto me by others, actually. I describe instances in which I would be met with amusement when saying something coded as black and mockery whenever I dared to act like everyone else. The struggle was real, but I did not feel like I needed to abandon AAVE, nor did I harbor any shame from it, but "clowning" it got me through some tough situations. This tactic was pragmatic in nature.

My narrative takes an interesting turn when it describes my transition to a more diverse high school, where I held expectations of a long-awaited sense of belonging. Instead, I suffered severe rejections from my black peers for acting and sounding too white. My Discourse, as James Gee may describe it (values, behaviors, and paralinguistic tendencies, etc.) was not acceptably black. I found even stranger the tendency of black students to trivialize their own race in the form of insults. This was not just the basic "dozens." These were blatant attempts to degrade blackness, for example, ridiculing people for having dark complexions. I write:

> What was confounding was that this was done amidst fellow African Americans, and not amidst Whites, as a pathetic attempt to fit in. A very popular insult was to comment on how *African* one's physical features were, or how dark one's complexion was. The telling of these jokes every so often would have been one thing, but their frequency was blatant testimony to their tellers' inherent lack of racial pride. I did not fit in with my African-American peers because I wasn't 'Black' enough, yet one's racial characteristics could summon cruel insults I had only previously heard from White people, and not nearly as frequently.[2]

At the time of writing this autoethnography, a harsh twofold realization resulted from these memories: 1. Empowerment was needed among minorities in both predominantly white spaces *and* predominately black spaces; 2. Adopting ready-made codes designated for particular races, including code-meshed language, was intrinsically stifling and, therefore, was not going to bring about this empowerment.

At the end of the autoethnography, I discovered the arbitrary nature of identity and its correlations to dialect and Discourse. One's mode of speaking need not be intertwined into one's sense of being. I write:

> I resolved, then, as I do now, to perpetuate a selfhood of my own and dismiss any sense of personhood forced upon me by someone else. Ethnicity is not natural, but a manmade construct. . . . *Freedom is not having a way (read 'ethnicity'), and adopting a particular way for every given situation.* If one is to understand me, or feel more comfortable around me if I comply to a certain ideology of being, so be it. There is no deception here. The only deception is to think that ethnicity is a rigid, natural, and vital truth. Indeed, ethnicity, even one constructed for the proposed uplifting of a people, can be just as blind, limiting, and robbing of freedom.[3] (Emphasis mine)

The italicized sentence basically served as my thesis statement for the narrative and the primary motivation for my dissertation. Traces of it can be seen in my publications about the confluence of Buddhism and rhetoric. It is kinda my thing.

But I have to show you something.

Vershawn Young was one of the collaborators on the aforementioned collection of literacy narratives. So, one would be right to assume he was well aware of my story and my intentions. However, when citing my literacy narrative in his book *Your Average Nigga: Performing Race, Literacy, and Masculinity*, my words are altered for whatever reason.

Remember the above quote that can serve as a thesis to my early work, "Freedom is not having a way (read 'ethnicity'), and adopting a particular way for every given situation." Now, notice Young's rendition of the quote here:

I know the personal pain that Smith experienced in school, which is why I understand his motivation for wanting to problematize the ideas of ethnicity and identity. We both realize that our world is committed to these ideas, but we differ in that he believes that *"freedom" from them "is not having [one] way (read 'ethnicity') [but] adopting a particular way [read ethnicity and race] for every given situation.*[4] (Emphasis mine)

The changes in this quote may seem subtle at first, but upon a closer look, they are quite significant. In case you missed it, here is the original quote followed by Young's rendering.

Freedom is not having a way (read "ethnicity"), and adopting a particular way for every given situation.
"freedom" from them "is not having [one] way (read 'ethnicity') [but] adopting a particular way [read ethnicity and race] for every given situation.[5]

He changed the words, y'all. I mean, homeboy replaced "and" with "but"! "And" and "but" are very different conjunctions, am I right? Bracketed words usually signal that a word or phrase is replaced with a word or phrase that does not alter meaning but works better in a compositional context. Young didn't do that. He even added a word that isn't supposed to be there. Mind you, this was not a "hit and run" quote on Young's part; his treatment of my work is a substantial part of the chapter in which he "quotes" me. Because of the new meaning derived from Young's "treatment" of my quote, he was now justified to say other things about me that were wildly inaccurate (and kinda insulting, but whatever). With my words changed, I look more like a black person suffering from a kind of racial schizophrenia or sybil syndrome and, therefore, personify one of Young's major scholarly theses. What we have here is the straw man fallacy on steroids. Is this cool?

This is the main question driving this epilogue: am I overreacting to think this is wrong? Maybe I'm just too close to it. That's why I ask you, the readers, for your input on this one. Is Young's rendering not a big deal? At any rate, what does it say about empowerment in the field, the inability or refusal to address the world as is? What's more, don't most of us have sections in our syllabi warning students not to be academically dishonest, which "includes any form of cheating, plagiarism, falsification of records, collusion, or giving false information"?[6] I mean, if a student did this, I would make that student revise and resubmit. At the very least, I would talk to the student/students about his/her/their justifications for altering the quote.

But maybe I am overreacting. I don't know. When I think about whether I am or not, I can't help thinking that, either way, this says a lot about empowerment. Let's look at the possible conclusions and their implications.

If I *am* overreacting, then changing another author's words to the point where the meaning is changed is totally acceptable. *And the meaning was changed.* As I said above, Young's use of brackets is a bit off. For one, "A" and "one" are not really interchangeable. If they mean the same thing, why change "a" to "one" in the first place? "One" does a better job of denoting an essential and definite identity, whereas "a" is less essentializing and more indefinite, as the article is commonly understood to be, but you already know that. Next, replacing "and" with "but" totally changes the meaning of my sentence. "And" denotes addition and "but" denotes contrast. The last situation, when he tells readers to read my use of "way" as "ethnicity and race" is less egregious; although that is not what I was going for, his interpretation isn't entirely unreasonable.

If I am overreacting and Young's behavior is okay, it means that, when we come across an idea antithetical to our own—and, reading Young's work, one can see clearly that my conclusions are antithetical to his—we can just go ahead and pretend the author said something else. How's *that* for insufficient reality testing?

I had a person once tell me that Young's take was just "his truth." After scrunching my face in disbelief and counting to ten to control my anger, I asked myself (I was still too upset to speak aloud), what about my truth? What about *the* truth? I had a very prominent scholar in English studies tell me "everybody does that. It's no big deal." I can only assume this person did not quite understand that Young's rendering of my quote was not merely a misinterpretation, but a *dis*interpretation. Both guys were white and considered themselves allies and accomplices for people of color. Hmm. (Of course, because I do not embrace victimhood, my status as a black man is forfeited; allyship to *me* would have little if any cultural capital.) I think this all speaks to an inability or unwillingness to engage fair-mindedly and realistically. I think this all reflects a primacy of identity and a lauding of the sacred victim. I think this all exemplifies disempowerment.

If I *am not* overreacting, Young got away with a serious lack of academic integrity, which raises questions: Why did this happen? How did this happen? Is there a blind spot in our publication practices? Young had to have some serious hutzpah to even attempt this. He had to be pretty sure no one would catch it or care if they did. If no one caught it, that is fine; who's Erec Smith, anyway? But if people see this, believe I am justified in overreacting, but shrug and move on, what does that say about our field? It seems to expose sophistic critical thinking, looking the other way when the facts don't match our ideas or our preferred narratives. It, too, shows a lack of true empowerment.

I see the primacy of identity working here: what the author wants to see is all that counts, even if not grounded in reality. I see the sacred victim narrative as well: the injured party cannot be questioned and the narrative has to be preserved at all costs. Did this happen because Young's rendering is seen as doing more for anti-racism than my original quote? Did this happen because Young's rendering perpetuates the vic.

No, I am not happy that my words were changed to mean something I see as diametrically opposed to the intended meaning, but that is not why I ask this question. I write this epilogue because I am wondering how connected this is to a lack of theoretical empowerment (and I don't feel like revising the book to incorporate this question).

So, am I making too big a deal out of this? I don't know. That's why I am stepping back from this and asking you, the reader, to decide. If you would be so kind, send your thoughts on this matter to tell.me.if.i.am.overreacting@gmail.com. Am I overreacting? Why or why not? I'm listening.

I don't seek retribution, but I do seek closure. When I predict the charges of pettiness I will receive for broaching this subject, I can't help but think about Andrea Dardello's narrative about surviving bullying and fierce attempts from her colleagues to erase her. She shares her experience: "Knowing that if I give power to shame with my silence, it erases the horrendous act—and others like it—and I forfeit the change that can happen if I but dare to speak. . . . I write to become part of a conversation."[7] I no longer want to be silent about this issue, for silence is consent. Frankly, I really just want to know if I'm overreacting or not.

That is, I want to know how I should think about this and what it means for scholarship. I want to know if this issue truly is a result of the primacy of identity and victim narrative I mentioned a few times throughout this book. I think this can be a very productive conversation about interpretation, subjectivity, epistemic standard, the values of our field, etc. Based on the anti-racist scholarship I have read, I suppose my biggest fear is that my desire to be quoted without literally having my words and message changed is a "whitely" expectation.

In the end, I have the same hope for this question that I do for this book, that it will start a dialogue about the importance of true empowerment in our field and beyond.

NOTES

1. Cohen et al. "Culture Wise: Narrative as Research, Research as Narrative," *Remapping Narrative: Technology's Impact on the Way We Write,* ed. Gian Pagnucci and Nick Mauriello (Hampton Press, 2009).
2. Cohen et al. "Culture Wise: Narrative as Research, Research as Narrative."
3. Ibid.
4. Young, *Your Average Nigga,* Loc. 1672.
5. Ibid.

6. "Profile 2—Centering Students in the First-Year Composition Classroom: Engagement, Improvement, and Pedagogical Practices," *Black Perspectives in Writing Program Administration: Companion Resources*, accessed 9 August 2019. http://www2.ncte.org/black-perspectives-in-writing-program-administration-web-resources/.

7. Andrea Dardello, "Breaking the Silence of Racism and Bullying in Academia," *Defining, Locating, and Addressing Bullying in the WPA Workplace* (Logan, UT: Utah State University Press, 2019), 104.

References

"Ai." *The Poetry Foundation.* Accessed 1 Aug 2019. https://www.poetryfoundation.org/poets/ai.
Allen, Sarah. "The Making of a Bully Culture (And How One Might Transform It)." *Defining, Locating, and Addressing Bullying in the WPA Workplace.* Ed. Cristyn L. Elder and Bethany Davila. Logan, UT: Utah State University Press, 2019. 69–85.
Appiah, Antony. *As If.* Cambridge, MA: Harvard University Press, 2017.
Appiah, Kwame Anthony. *The Ethics of Identity.* Princeton, NJ: Princeton University Press, 2005.
Appiah, Kwame Anthony. "The Politics of Identity." *Daedalus* 135.4 (2006), 15–22.
Arendt, Hannah. *The Origins of Totalitarianism.* New York: Meridian Books, 1960.
Aristotle. *Aristotle on Rhetoric: A Theory of Civic Discourse.* Trans. George Kennedy. *The Rhetorical Tradition: Readings from Classical Times to the Present.* Ed. Patricia Bizzell and Bruce Herzberg. New York: Bedford/St. Martin's Press, 2001. 179–240.
Asim, Jabari. *The N-Word: Who Can Say it, Who Shouldn't, And Why.* New York: Houghton Mifflin Company, 2008.
Atalay, Ozlem. "Accommodation Theory and Language Learning." *Theoretical Considerations in Language Education.* Ed. Betil Eröz-Tuğa. Ankara, Çankaya, Turkey: Nuans Publish, 2014. Accessed 5 August 2019. https://www.researchgate.net/publication/291957052_Accommodation_Theory_and_Language_Teaching.
Barthes, Roland. *Mythologies.* New York: Farrar, Strauss, and Giroux, 1972.
Berlin, James. *Rhetorics, Poetics, and Cultures: Refiguring College English Studies.* Urbana, IL: NCTE, 1996.
Bizzell, Patricia. "Hybrid Academic Discourse: What, Why, How." *Composition Studies*, 27.2 (1999), 7–21.
Booth, Wayne. *The Rhetoric of Rhetoric: The Quest for Effective Communication.* Hoboken, NJ: Wiley-Blackwell, 2004.
Boyatzis, Richard. "Emotional Self-Control: What It Looks Like, How to Develop It." *Emotional Self-Control: A Primer.* Florence, MA: More Than Sound, 2017. Loc 197–223.

Boyatzis, Richard. "Influence in Action." *Influence: A Primer.* Florence, MA: More Than Sound, 2017. Loc 152–79.

Boyatzi, Richard. "The Basis for Inspirational Leadership." *Inspirational Leadership: A Primer.* Florence, MA: More Than Sound, 2017. 143–62.

Burch, Kurt. "PBL, Politics, and Democracy." *The Power of Problem-Based Learning.* Ed. Barbara J. Duch, Susan E Groh, Deborah E. Allen. Sterling, VA: Stylus Publishing, 2001. 193–205.

Burke, Kenneth. *Language as Symbolic Action.* In *The Rhetorical Tradition: Readings From Classical Times to the Present*, 2nd ed. Ed. Patricia Bizzell and Bruce Herzberg. New York: Bedford St. Martin's Press, 2001.

Campbell, Bradley and Jason Manning. *The Rise of Victimhood Culture: Microaggresions, Safe Space, and the New Culture Wars.* New York: Palgrave Macmillan, 2018.

Chang, Mitchell J., Alexander W. Austin, and Dongbin Kim. "Cross-Racial Integration Among Undergraduates: Some Consequences, Causes, and Patterns." *Research in Higher Education*, 45.5 (2004), 529–253.

Christen, Briand D., Christina Hamme Peterson, and Paul W. Speer, "Psychological Empowerment in Adulthood." *Encyclopedia of Primary Prevention and Health Promotions.* Ed. T.P. Gullotta and M. Bloom. New York: Springer Science+Business Media, 2014. 1766–76.

Clark, Carol Lee. *Praxis: A Brief Rhetoric*, 3rd ed. Southlake, TX: Fountainhead Press, 2016.

Cohen, et al. "Culture Wise: Narrative as Research, Research as Narrative." *Remapping Narrative: Technology's Impact on the Way We Write.* Ed. Gian Pagnucci and Nick Mauriello. New York: Hampton Press, 2009.

Combahee River Collective. "Combahee River Collective Statement." *African American Rhetoric.* Ed. Vershawn Ashanti Young. New York: Routledge, 2019. 352–58.

Condon, Frankie. "A Place Where There Isn't Any Trouble." *Code-Meshing as World English.* Ed. Vershawn Ashanti Young and Aja Y. Martinez. Urbana, IL: NCTE, 2011.

Corrigan, Paul T. "White People are a Problem: A Conversation with Asao Inoue." *Teaching and Learning in Higher Ed*, 30 July 2019. Accessed 4 August 2019. https://teachingandlearninginhighered.org/2019/07/30/White-teachers-are-a-problem-a-conversation-with-asao-inoue/?fbclid=IwAR2RjUSCt6QTTyq-a95dLLnH_rWjBTeSUH31uE1ATxyhm6cA_ofauan1yr0.

Cortez, Jose. "History." *Decolonizing Rhetoric and Composition Studies.* Ed. Iris Ruiz and Raul Sanchez. New York: Palgrave Macmillan, 2016.

Coutu, Diane. "How Resilience Works." *Resilience: HBR Emotional Intelligence Series.* Boston, MA: Harvard Business Review Press, 2017.

Crawford, Jarret T. and Jane M. Pilanski. "Political Intolerance, Right *and* Left." *Political Psychology* 35.6 (2014) 841–51.

Dardello, Andrea. "Breaking the Silence of Racism and Bullying in Academia: Leaning in to a Hard Truth." *Defining, Locating, and Addressing Bullying in the WPA Workplace.* Ed. Cristyn L. Elder and Bethany Davila. Logan, UT: Utah State University Press, 2019. 102–23.

Daut, Marlene L. "Becoming a Full Professor While Black." *Chronicle of Higher Education*, 28 July 2019. Accessed 10 August 2019. https://www.chronicle.com/article/Becoming-Full-Professor-While/246743.

Delpit, Lisa. "No Kinda Sense." *The Skin That We Speak: Thoughts on Language and Culture in the Classroom*. Ed. Lisa Delpit and Joanne Kilgour Dowdy. New York: The New Press, 2018. E-book.

Delpit, Lisa. "The Silenced Dialogue: Power and Pedagogy in Teaching Other People's Children." *Harvard Educational Review*, 58.3 (1988), 280–98.

Dewey, John. *The Philosophy of John Dewey*. Ed. Joseph Ratner. New York: Henry Holt and Company, 1928.

Doty, William and William Hynes. *Mythical Trickster Figures: Contours, Contexts, and Criticism*. Tuscaloosa, AL: University of Alabama Press, 1997.

Dubois, W. E. B. "A Negro Student Goes to Harvard at the End of the 19th Century." *W.E.B Dubois: a Reader*. Ed. David Levering Lewis. New York: Henry Holt and Company 1995. 271–86.

Dubois, W. E .B. "The Negro College." *W.E.B Dubois: A Reader*. Ed. David Levering Lewis. New York: Henry Holt and Company 1995. 68.

Douglass, Frederick. "What to the Slave is the Fourth of July." *Teaching American History*. Accessed 4 August 2019. https://teachingamericanhistory.org/library/document/what-to-the-slave-is-the-fourth-of-july/.

Druskat, Vanessa. "Emotional Self Control in Team." *Emotional Self-Control: A Primer*. Florence, MA: More Than Sound, 2017. Loc 163–97.

Duch, Barbara, Susan E Groh, and Deborah E. Allen. "Why Problem-based Learning: A Case Study of Institutional Change in Undergraduate Education." *The Power of Problem-Based Learning*. Ed. Barbara J. Duch, Susan E. Groh, and Deborah E. Allen. Sterling, VA: Stylus Publishing, 2001. 3–11.

Ede, Lisa and Andrea Lunsford. "Audience Addressed/Audience Invoked: The Role of Audience in Composition Theory and Pedagogy." *Cross-Talk in Comp Theory: A Reader*. Ed. Victor Villanueva. Urbana, IL: NCTE Press, 2003. 77–95.

Edsall, Thomas B. "The Democrats' Left Turn is Not an Illusion." *The New York Times*, 18 October 2018. Accessed 19 August 2019. https://www.nytimes.com/2018/10/18/opinion/democrat-electorate-left-turn.html?fbclid=IwAR0TMqpnrpr-rlmAwLQQiyIKmTru3lRitsBt5rGfcRigyqrAS4rLvUyziLw.

Ellison, Ralph. *Shadow and Act*. New York: Vintage International, 1964, Loc 592. E-book.

Engelke, Matthew. *How to Think Like an Anthropologist*. Princeton, NJ: Princeton University Press, 2019.

Epictetus. *Enchiridion*. Trans. Thomas Wentworth Higginson. *Project Gutenberg*. Accessed March 10, 2014. https://www.gutenberg.org/files/45109/45109-h/45109-h.htm.

Fawcett, Stephen B., Glen W. White, Fabricio E. Balcazar, and John F. Smith. "AContextual-Behavioral Model of Empowerment: Case Studies Involving People with Physical Disabilities." *American Journal of Community Psychology*, 2 (1994), 471–86.

Finn, Patrick. *Literacy With An Attitude: Educating Working Class Children in Their Own Interests*, 2nd ed. New York: SUNY Press, 2009.

Fisch, William B. "Hate Speech in the Constitutional Law of the United States." *American Journal of Comparative Law*, 50 (2002), 463–92.
Flynn, Elizabeth. "Composing as a Woman." *College Composition and Communication*, 39.4 (1988), 423–35.
Frazier, Demita. "Rethinking Identity Politics: An Interview with Demita Frazier." Interview by Karen Kahn. *Sojourner: The Women's Forum*, 21.1 (1995), 12.
Frost, Diane and Samantha Coole. *New Materialism: Ontology, Agency, and Politics*. Raleigh, NC: Duke University Press, 2010.
Frye, Marilyn. *Willful Virgin: Essays in Feminism*. Freedom, CA: The Crossing Press, 1992.
Garfinkel, Harold. "Conditions of Successful Degradation Ceremonies." *American Journal of Sociology*, 61.5 (1956), 420–24.
Gates, Jr. Henry Louis. "Breaking the Silence." *The New York Times*, 24 August 2004, accessed 17 July 2019. https://www.nytimes.com/2004/08/01/opinion/breaking-the-silence.html.
Gee, James. *Social Linguistic and Literacies: Ideology in Discourses*, 3rd edition. New York: Routledge, 2008.
Gentry, Jeff. "Why Grades Still Matter." *Chronicle of Higher Education*, 20 November 2018. Accesses 7 August 2019. https://www.chronicle.com/article/Why-Grades-Still-Matter/245100.
Gilyard, Keith. "Introduction." *African American Rhetoric(s): Interdisciplinary Perspectives*. Ed. Elaine B. Richardson and Ronald L. Jackson II. Carbondale, IL: Southern Illinois University Press, 2004. 1–18.
Giroux, Henry. *Neoliberalism's War on Democracy*. Chicago, IL: Haymarket Books, 2015.
Goleman, Daniel. "Achievement Orientation: An Introduction." *Achievement Orientation: A Primer*. Florence, MA: More Than Sound, 2017. Loc 116–51.
Goleman, Daniel. "Adaptability: An Introduction." *Adaptability: A Primer*. Florence, MA: More Than Sound, 2017. Loc 117–36.
Goleman, Daniel. "Coach and Mentor: An Introduction." *Coach and Mentor: A Primer*. Florence, MA: More Than Sound, 2017. Loc 122–51.
Goleman, Daniel. "Conflict Management: An Introduction." *Conflict Management: A Primer*. Florence, MA: More Than Sound, 2017. Loc 106–29.
Goleman, Daniel. "Emotional Intelligence Competencies: An Introduction." *Emotional Self-Awareness: A Primer*. Florence, MA: More Than Sound, 2017. Loc 30–102.
Goleman, Daniel. "Emotional Self-Awareness: An Introduction." *Emotional Self Awareness: A Primer*. Florence, MA: More Than Sound, 2017. Loc 198–222.
Goleman, Daniel. "Emotional Self-Control: An Introduction." *Emotional Self-Control: A Primer*. Florence, MA: More Than Sound, 2017. Loc 115–31.
Goleman, Daniel. "Empathy: An Introduction." *Empathy: A Primer*. Florence, MA: More Than Sound, 2017. Loc 117–41.
Goleman, Daniel. "Influence: An Introduction." *Influence: A Primer*. Florence, MA: More Than Sound, 2017. Loc 115–52.
Goleman, Daniel. "Organizational Awareness: An Introduction." *Organizational Awareness: A Primer*. Florence, MA: More Than Sound, 2017. Loc 112–51.

Goleman, Daniel. "Positive Outlook: An Introduction." *Positive Outlook: A Primer.* Florence, MA: More Than Sound, 2017. Loc 114–35.

Goleman, Daniel. "Teamwork: An Introduction." *Teamwork: A Primer.* Florence, MA: More Than Sound, 2017. Loc 116–44.

Gordon, Uri. "Prefigurative Politics Between Ethical Practice and Absent Promise." *Political Studies* 66.2 (2018): 521–37.

Goodnight, G. Thomas. "The Personal, Technical, and Public Spheres of Argument: A Speculative Inquiry into the Art of Public Deliberation." *Contemporary Rhetorical Theory: A Reader.* Ed. Mark J. Porrovecchio and Celeste Michelle Condit. New York: Guilford Press, 2016. 199–209.

Gorski, Paul C and Noura Erakat. "Racism, Whiteness, and Burnout in Antiracism Movements: How White Racial Justice Activists Elevate Burnout in Racial Justice Activists of Color in the United States." *Ethnicities* 0.0 (2019), 1–25.

Goulah, Jason. "Cultivating Chrysanthemums: Tsunesaburo Makiguchi on Attitudes toward Education." *Schools: Studies in Education*, 12.2 (2015) 252–60.

Goulah, Jason. "Makiguchi Tsunesaburo and Language, Value-Creative Composition Instruction, and the Geography of Identity in Community Studies: A Response to Politicized Imagining and Ineffective Critical Approaches." *Makiguchi Tsunesaburo in the Context of Language, Identity, and Education.* Ed. Jason Goulah. New York: Routledge, 2017.

Graff, Gerald. "Code-Meshing Meets Teaching the Conflicts." *Code-Meshing as World English: Pedagogy, Policy, Performance.* Ed. Vershawn Ashanti Young and Aja Y. Martinez. Urbana, IL: NCTE Press, 2011. 9–20.

Grand Scholar Wizard. "The Cs Chairs Address." Writing Program Administrator's Listserv Archive." March 22, 2019, https://lists.asu.edu/cgi-bin/wa?A2=ind1903&L=wpa-l&F=&S=&P=224918.

Greenfield, Laura. "The 'Standard English' Fairy Tale: A Rhetorical Analysis of Racist Pedagogies and Commonplace Assumptions about Language Diversity." *Writing Centers and the New Racism: A Call for Sustainable Dialogue and Change.* Logan, UT: Utah State University Press, 2011. 33–60.

Haider, Asad. *Mistaken Identity: Race and Class in the Age of Trump.* Brooklyn, NY: Verso Press, 2018. E-book.

Haidt, Jonathan and George Lukianoff. "The Coddling of the American Mind." *The Atlantic* (2015). Accessed 10 August 2019. https://www.theatlantic.com/magazine/archive/2015/09/the-coddling-of-the-american-mind/399356/#Cognitive%20Disorders.

Hanh, Thich Nhat. *Interbeing: Fourteen Guidelines for Engaged Buddhism.* Berkeley, CA: Parallax Press, 1998.

Haswell, Richard. "Writing Assessment and Race Studies Sub Specie Aeternitatis: A Response to Race and Writing Assessment." *The Journal of Writing Assessment Reading List* (2013). Accessed 10 August 2019. http://jwareadinglist.ucdavis.edu/index.php/2013/01/04/writing-assessment-and-race-studies-sub-specie-aeternitatis-a-response-to-_race-and-writing-assessment_/.

Haswell, Richard and Min-Zhan Lu. *Comp Tales: An Introduction to College Composition Through Its Stories.* New York: Longman, 2000.

Holiday, Ryan. *Trust Me, I'm Lying: Confessions of a Media Manipulator,* 3rd ed. New York: Penguin, 2017.

Inoue, Asao. "Afterward." *Black Perspectives in Writing Program Administration: From the Margins to the Center*. Urbana, IL: NCTE 2019. 141–53.

Inoue, Asao. *Antiracist Writing Assessment Ecologies: Teaching and Assessing Writing for a Socially Just Future*. Fort Collins, CO: The WAC Clearinghouse and Parlor Press, 2015. Ebook. https://wac.colostate.edu/books/perspectives/inoue/.

Inoue, Asao. "How Do We Language So People Stop Killing Each Other, Or What Do We Do About White Language Supremacy?" Conference on College Composition and Communication Annual Convention, March 14, 2019. Accessed 10 August 2019. https://docs.google.com/document/d/11ACklcUmqGvTzCMPlETChBwS-Ic3t2BOLi13u8IUEp4/edit.

Inoue, Asao. *Labor-Based Grading Contracts: Building Equity and Inclusion in the Compassionate Writing Classroom*. Perspectives on Writing. Fort Collins, CO: The WAC Clearinghouse and University Press of Colorado, 2019. Accessed 19 August 2019. https://wac.colostate.edu/books/perspectives/labor/.

Inoue, Asao. "Writing Assessment as the Conditions for Translingual Approaches: An Argument for Fairer Assessments." *Crossing Divides: Exploring Translingual Writing Pedagogies and Programs*. Ed. Bruce Horner and Laura Tetreault. Logan, UT: Utah State University Press, 2017. 119–34.

Jackson, Rosemary Robinson. *The Social Construction of Linguistic Reality: A Casestudy Exploring the Relationships Among Poverty, Race, and Remediation in an Urban Community College* (2007) Dissertation.2680. Accessed 10 August 2019. ecommons.luc.edu/luc_diss/2680.

James, William. "Pragmatism's Concept of Truth." *Pragmatism and Other Essays*. New York: Washington Square Press, 1970.

"Job Outlook 2018." *National Association of Colleges and Employers*. Bethlehem, PA: N.A.C.E., 2017.

Kay, Frances and Neilson Kite. *Understanding Emotional Intelligence: Strategies for Boosting your EQ and Using it in the Workplace*. Philadelphia: Kogan Page, 2011.

Kelleher, Tom. *Public Relations*. Oxford, UK: Oxford University Press, 2018.

Knight Foundation. *Free Expression on Campus: What College Students Think about First Amendment Issues: A Gallup/Knight Foundation Survey*. Washington, DC: Gallup, 2018.

Kohl, Herbert. "Topsy-Turvies: Teacher Talk and Student Talk." *The Skin that We Speak: Thoughts on Language and Culture in the Classroom*. Ed. Lisa Delpit and Joanne Kilgour Dowdy. New York: The New Press, 2018.

Kohlrieser, George. "A Mindset of Adaptability." *Adaptability: A Primer*. Florence, MA: More Than Sound, 2017. Loc 3o2–313.

Kohlrieser, Georege. "How Secure Base Leaders Maintain Differences Without Breaking Bonds." *Conflict Management: A Primer*. Florence, MA: More Than Sound, 2017. Loc 129–58.

Kohlrieser, George, Susan Goldsworthy, and Duncan Coombe. *Care to Dare: Unleashing Astonishing Potential Through Secure Base Leadership*. San Francisco, CA: Jossey-Bass, 2012.

Kopelson, Karen. "Dis/integrating the Gay/Queer Binary: 'Reconstructed Identity Politics' for a Performative Pedadagogy." *College English* 65.1 (2002) 17–35.

Krashen, Stephen D. *Principles and Practices in Second Language Acquisition.* New York: Pergamon Press, 1982.

Lazere, Donald. *Political Literacy in Composition and Rhetoric: Defending Academic Discourse Against Postmodern Pluralism.* Carbondale, IL: Southern Illinois University Press, 2015.

Leff, Michael C. "What is Rhetoric?" *Rethinking Rhetorical Theory, Criticism, and Pedagogy.* East Lansing, MI: Michigan State University, 2016. 471–81.

Lilienfeld, Scott O. "Microaggression: Strong Claims, Inadequate Evidence." *Perspectives on Psychological Science* 12.1 (2017) 138–69.

Lilla, Mark. *The Once and Future Liberal: After Identity Politics.* New York: Harper Collins, 2017. E-book.

Lovejoy, Kim Brian. "Code-Meshing: Teachers and Students Creating Community." *Other People's English: Code-Meshing, Code-Switching, and African American Literacy.* New York: Teachers College Press, 2014.

Lynne, Steven. *Rhetoric and Composition: An Introduction.* New York: Cambridge University Press, 2010.

"Many in Body, One in Mind." *SGI-USA,* accessed 3 August 3, 2019. https://www.sgi-usa.org/study-resources/core-concepts/many-in-body-one-in-mind/.

Marguia, Edward and Kim Diaz. "The Philosophical Foundations of Cognitive Behavioral Therapy: Stoicism, Buddhism, Taoism, and Existentialism." *Journal of Evidence-Based Psychotherapies* 15.1 (2015) 37–50.

Martin, Brian and Florencia Pena Saint Martin. "Public Mobbing: A Phenomenon and its Features." *Organización social del trabajo en la posmodernidad: salud mental, ambientes laborales y vida cotidiana.* Ed. Norma González González. Guadalajara, Jalisco, México: Prometeo Editores, 2014. https://www.bmartin.cc/pubs/14Gonzalez.html.

McBee, Melinda J. Orzulak. "Disinviting Deficit Ideologies: Beyond 'That's Standard,' 'That's Racist,' and 'That's Your Mother Tongue." *Research in the Teaching of English,* 50.2 (2015), 176–98.

McCrary, D. "Represent, Representin', Representation: The Efficacy of Hybrid Texts in the Writing Classroom." *Journal of Basic Writing,* 24.2 (2005), 72–91.

McIntyre, Lee. *Post-Truth.* Cambridge, MA: MIT Press, 2018.

McWhorter, John. "Virtue Signalers Won't Change the World." *The Atlantic.* December 23, 2018. https://www.theatlantic.com/ideas/archive/2018/12/why-third-wave-anti-racism dead-end/578764/.

Pappas, Gregory Fernando. "The Limitations and Dangers of Decolonial Philosophies: Lessons from Zapatista Luis Villoro." Academia.edu. Accessed 19 Aug 2019. https://tamu.academia.edu/gregorypappas.

Patel, Eboo. "Chicago's New Black Lesbian Mayor and the Power/Privilege/Oppression Paradigm." *Inside Higher Ed,* 11 April 2019. https://www.insidehighered.com/blogs/conversations-diversity/chicago%E2%80%99s-new-black-lesbian-mayor-and-powerprivilegeoppression.

Patel, Eboo. Whom Do Activists of Color Speak For?" *Inside Higher Ed.* 2 April 2019. Accessed 10 August 2019. https://www.insidehighered.com/blogs/conversations-diversity/whom-do-activists-color-speak.

Paul, Richard. *Critical Thinking: What Every Person Needs to Survive in a Rapidly Changing World.* Tomales, CA: The Foundation for Critical Thinking, 2012.

Pereira, Matheus. "Tensegrity Structures: What They Are and What They Can Be." Trans. Guilherme Carvalho. *Arch Daily,* 3 June 2018. Accessed 10 August 2019. https://www.archdaily.com/893555/tensegrity-structures-what-they-are-and-what-they-can-be.

Perkins, Douglass and Marc Zimmerman. "Empowerment Theory, Research, and Application." *American Journal of Community Psychology,* 23.5 (1995), 569–79.

Plato. *Gorgias.* In *The Rhetorical Traditions: Readings from Classical Times to the Present.* Ed. Patricia Bizzell and Bruce Herzberg (New York: Bedford, Saint Martin's, 2001.

"Profile 2—Centering Students in the First-Year Composition Classroom: Engagement, Improvement, and Pedagogical Practices." *Black Perspectives in Writing Program Administration: Companion Resources.* Accessed 9 August 2019. http://www2.ncte.org/black-perspectives-in-writing-program-administration-web-resources/.

Raekstad, Paul. "Revolutionary Practice and Prefigurative Politics: A Clarification and Defense." *Constellations* (2017), 362. https://onlinelibrary.wiley.com/doi/epdf/10.1111/1467-8675.12319.

Rorty, Richard. *Philosophy as Cultural Politics.* Cambridge, UK: Cambridge University Press, 2007.

Royster, Jacqueline Jones. "When The First Voice You Hear Is Not Your Own." *College Composition and Communication* 47.1 (1996), 29–40.

Schoepflin, Todd A. "On Being Degraded in Public." *The Qualitative Report,* 14.2 (2009), 361–73.

"Shakubuku." *The Nichiren Buddhism Library,* accessed 8 August 2019. https://www.nichirenlibrary.org/en/dic/Content/S/108.

"Shoju." *The Nichiren Buddhism Library,* accessed 8 August 2019. https://www.nichirenlibrary.org/en/dic/Content/S/148.

Smith, Christian. "Higher Education is Drowning in BS." *Chronicle of Higher Education.* January 9, 2018, https://www.chronicle.com/article/Higher-Education-Is-Drowning/242195.

Smith, Erec. "A Barbarian Within the Gate: The Detriments of Insularity at a Small Liberal Arts College." *Defining, Locating, and Addressing Bullying in the WPA Workplace.* Ed. Cristyn L. Elder and Bethany Davila. Louisville, CO: University Press of Colorado, 2019. 138–50.

Smith, Erec. *A Rhetoric of Mythic Proportions: Rhetorical and Messianic Trickster Consciousness and Its Effects on Society.* University of Illinois-Chicago. Dissertation, 2003.

Smith, Erec. "Buddhism's Pedagogical Contribution to Mindfulness." *Journal of the Assembly for the Expanded Perspectives on Learning,* 21 (2016), 36–46.

Smith, Erec. "The *Lotus Sutra* as Rhetorical Doctrine: Toward a Spiritual Paradigm Shift in Academia." *The Journal of South Texas English Studies,* 1.1 (2009),

Accessed 9 August 2019. https://docs.google.com/a/ycp.edu/document/d/1hAXT wywbAfxwIVY9PHHKCX9Ow-YkodQGrdKTx3yUjd8/edit.

Smith, Erec. "Writing Under the Bodhi Tree." *Academic Exchange Quarterly*, 9.2 (2005), 16–21.

Smitherman, Geneva. "'Students Right to Their Own Language': A Retrospective." *The English Journal*, 84.1 (1995), 21–27.

Smitherman, Geneva. *Talking that Talk: Language, Culture, and Education in African America.* New York: Routledge, 2001.

Smucker, Jonathan Matthew. *Hegemony How-To: A Roadmap for Radicals.* Chico, CA: AK Press, 2017.

Stein, Steven J., Howard E. Book, and Korrel Kanoy. *The Student EQ Edge: Emotional Intelligence and Your Academic and Personal Success.* San Francisco, CA: Jossey-Bass, 2013.

Storch, Tanya. "Buddhist Universities in the United States of America." *International Journal of Dharma Studies*, 1.4 (2013). Accessed 10 August 2019. https://link.springer.com/article/10.1186/2196-8802-1-4.

The 13th, Dir. Ava DuVernay, Kandoo Films, 2016.

The Oxford Companion to Consciousness. Ed. Tim Bayne, Axel Cleeremans, and Patrick Wilken. New York: Oxford University Press, 2009.

Weber, Max. "Politics as a Vocation." *Max Weber: Selections.* Ed. W.G. Runciman. New York: Cambridge University Press, 1978. 212–25.

White, Eric Charles. *Kaironomia.* Ithaca, NY: Cornell University Press, 1987.

Wiarda, Howard J. *Political Culture, Political Science and Identity Politics: An Uneasy Alliance.* Farnham, Surrey: Ashgate, 2014.

Willett, Cynthia. *The Soul of Justice: Social Bonds and Racial Hubris.* Ithaca, NY: Cornell University Press, 2001.

Williams, Angela Kyodo. *Being Black: Zen and the Art of Living with Fearlessness and Grace.* New York: Penguin Books, 2000.

Young, Vershawn Ashanti. "2019 College Composition and Communication Call for Program Proposals." *NCTE*, 2018. Accessed 10 August 2019. https://cccc.ncte.org/cccc/conv/call-2019.

Young, Vershawn Ashanti. "Linguistic Double Consciousness." *Other People's English: Code-Meshing, Code-Switching, and African American Literacy.* New York: Teachers College Press, 2014. 55–65. E-book.

Young, Vershawn Ashanti. "Nah, We Straight." *JAC* 29.1/2 (2009), 49–76.

Young, Vershawn Ashanti. "Should Writers Use They Own English." *Writing Centers and the New Racism: A Call for Sustainable Dialogue and Change.* Logan, UT: Utah State University Press, 2011. 61–72.

Young, Vershawn Ashanti. *Your Average Nigga: Performing Race, Literacy, and Masculinity.* Detroit, MI: Wayne State University Press, 2007.

Young, Vershawn Ashanti, Rusty Barret, Y'Shanda Young-Rivera, and Kim Brian Lovejoy. *Other People's English: Code-Meshing, Code-Switching, and African American Literacy.* New York: Teachers College Press, 2014. Ebook.

Young, Vershawn Ashanti and Y'Shanda Young-Rivera, "It Ain't What it Is: Code-Switching and White American Celebrationists." *JAC*, 33.1/2 (2013), 396–401.

Zimmerman, Marc A. "Empowerment Theory: Psychological, Organization, and Community Levels of Analysis." *Handbook of Community Psychology*. New York: Plenum Publishers, 2000. 43–64.

Zimmerman, Marc A. "Psychological Empowerment: Issues and Illustrations." *American Journal of Community Psychology,* 23.5 (1995), 581–99.

Zizek, Slavoj. *The Year of Dreaming Dangerously*. Brooklyn, NY: Verso Books, 2015. E-book.

Index

AAVE. *See* African American Vernacular English
abstraction, 14
academia, 124–26; disciplines in, 21; minority accompaniment in, 32, 60n30; primacy of identity in, 15–17; sacred victim in, 20–21. *See also* code-meshing pedagogy; code-meshing teaching
academic entrepreneurship, 79
academics, 3–4, 6, 9
Achievement Orientation, 39–40
"acting white," xxii–xxiii
Adaptability, 38–39
"affective filter," xvii
African, 124
African American Vernacular English (AAVE), xvii, 74; LWC with, 72; of Obama, 66; protectionism and, 97–98
agency, 10, 82
Ai, 109
Alt-Right, 21–22
ambiguity, 45–46
anti-intellectualism, 6
anti-racism. *See specific topics*
anti-racist initiatives, xxvii, 39
Antiracist Writing Assessment Ecologies (Inoue), 92, 108

Appiah, Kwame Anthony, 18, 58, 63n95; on identity, 12–13; on negation of affirmation, 55–56
appropriateness, 108
Arendt, Hannah, 52
argumentation, viii
Aristotle, 5
Asim, Jabari, 75
attention to appropriateness of place and audience (*prepon*), 23n10
authenticity, 71; in primacy of identity, 7–13
autoethnography, 124
awareness: of identity, 110–11, 123–24. *See also* Emotional Intelligence

Baldwin, James, 101
"A Barbarian at the Gate" (Smith, E.), 57
Barthes, Roland, 96
behavioral component, 34; in empowerment theory, 32, 58n9, 59nn12–13, 59n28
Berlin, James, 50
Beyond the Choir, 10
Black lesbian activists, 2–3, 11
blackly, 91–92
blackness, 123–24

Black Perspectives in Writing Program Administration(Inoue), 92–93
bond, 47–48
Boyatzis, Richard, 37, 43, 44
"to break and subdue" (*shakubuku*), vii–viii
Buddha, 110
Buddhism, xxvii–xxviii, 110–12
Buddhist thought: empowerment theory and, 111; Hanh on, 108–10; Inoue on, 107–8, 112, 113; PBL and, 116
bully cultures, 117
Burch, Kurt, 115–16
Burke, Kenneth, 41–42, 81

capability, trickster racism and, 100–101
capacity (*facultas*), 6
Catalonia (Spain), xvi
change, 38–39
"charismatic passivism," 20
Charter of Interbeing, 108–9
"Chicago's New Black Lesbian Mayor and the Power/Privilege/Oppression Paradigm" (Patel), 12
"civic humanistic rhetoric," 5–6
civil rights activism, 19, 101
"clubhouse," 46
Coach and Mentor, 44–45
coalition building, 2–3
code-meshing, 65; LWC as, 67–68; in sacred victim and minority writer, 69
"Code-meshing Meets Teaching the Conflicts" (Graff), 72
code-meshing pedagogy, xiv, xx–xxi; examples from, 66–67; identity and, 65–66, 68; professional and civic world related to, 66–67; "racial schizophrenia" in, 65–66; slang in, 67–68; victim-framing in, 87–93
code-meshing teaching: AAVE in, 72, 74; context in, 74; empowerment from, 77–78; evaluation in, 72–73; feedback in, 74–75; as heuristic, 71–72; illusion in, 77, 79; *kairos* in, 72, 76, 80–82; labor-based grading in, 73, 74, 89; LWC in, 67–68, 71–74, 78, 81; N-word in, 75; oppression in, 73; organic process in, 75–76; power in, 79; pragmatism in, 78–79; primacy of identity in, 76–77, 80–81; progress in, 77; public relations related to, 77–78; register in, 75; rhetoric in, 76–77; sacred victim and, 80; segregationism in, 75; SE in, 74; symbolism in, 73–74; truth in, 78–79
code-switching, xviii, 65–66
cognitive/noncognitive binary, 62n90
cognitive transactional models, 55
Combahee River Collective, 2–3, 11, 13, 18
communication: with academics, 3–4; *kairos* and, 77–78; persuasion in, 4–5. *See also* Language of Wider Communication
community: empowerment of, 117–18; home as, 107; sangha as, 108–9
compliance, 44–45
Condon, Frankie, 91
conference, viii
Conference on College Composition and Communication, xiii
conflict, 47–48, 50, 72
Conflict Management, 47–48, 51
control, 32
Coole, Samantha, xxiv
Craig, Collin Lamont, xxvi, 96–97
Critical Language Awareness, 44, 112
critical thinking, xiv, 20–21, 32, 33; about empowerment, 31
critiques, viii, 21
cultural appropriation, 97
cultural differences, 42
culture, 102n20; bully, 117; Hip Hop music, 66–67
culture of power, 100

DanDennet, 18, 63n95
Dardello, Andrea, 127
Daut, Marlene L., 96
Dead Prez, 102n20

"dealing swords," viii
decolonialism, 8–9
deficit-model, of empowerment, 57
deliberative rhetoric, viii
Delpit, Lisa, xvii, 39, 100, 112
Delpit, Maya, xxixn19, xvii–xviii, 39
desegregation, xxii
Dewey, John, 37
dialects, xvi–xvii, xix–xx, 7, 51; slang in, 67–68. *See also* Language of Wider Communication
direct experimentation, 108
disciplines, 21
Discourse, 49
disempowerment, xiv, xxv–xxvi, xxvii; in academics, 9; EQ and, 48; primacy of identity and, 105; in victim-framing, 87–88. *See also* code-meshing pedagogy
*dis*interpretation, 124–26
Doty, William, 94–95
Douglass, Frederick, xxvi–xxvii
Druskat, Vanessa, 37
Dubois, W. E. B., xv, xvii, 101; empowerment of, xx–xxi; failure of, xviii–xx; pragmatism of, xix–xxi; sense of self of, xx–xxii; victim-framing and, 88–89; Young and, xx–xxi, xxii
Duboisian Attitude, xxi–xxii, 40
Dyspeptics, 55–56

Ellison, Ralph, 96
Emotional Intelligence (emotion quotient) EQ, 49, 103n42, 106; Achievement Orientation in, 39–40; Adaptability in, 38–39; Coach and Mentor in, 44–45; Conflict Management in, 47–48, 51; cultural differences in, 42; disempowerment and, 48; Emotional Self-Control in, 36–38; Empathy Awareness in, 35; influence in, 43–44; IQ compared to, 34, 48; "noncognitive" competencies compared to, 62n90; Organizational Awareness in, 35–36; PBL related to, 115–16; Positive Outlook in, 40–42, 113; Relationship Management in, 43–48; Rhetoric and Composition in, 43–44; Self-Awareness in, 34–35; Self-Management in, 36; Social Awareness in, 35–36; "Social Intelligence" in, 34; Teamwork in, 47–48
Emotional Intelligence tests, 51
emotional quotient. *See* Emotional Intelligence
Emotional Self-Control, 36–38
emotions, 50; trickster racism and, 100–101. *See also* negative emotionality
empathy, 50
Empathy Awareness, 35
empowerment, xvii, 125–27; applications of, 27–28; centering of, 117–19; from code-meshing teaching, 77–78; of community, 117–18; control in, 32; critical thinking about, 31; deficit-model of, 57; definition of, 27, 28; of Dubois, xx–xxi; lack of, 29; lived experience in, 3; from PBL, 117; persuasion and, 106; prefiguration and, xxv; as process and outcome, 28; rhetoric of, 28; through SE, xxii–xxiii; term use of, 48–49. *See also* disempowerment; Emotional Intelligence; rhetoric of empowerment
empowerment, true, 52–54, 57–58; negation of affirmation in, 55–56
empowerment theory, 27, 33–34, 78, 105, 117; Buddhist thought and, 111; morality of, 57–58
empowerment theory components, 37, 118; behavioral component in, 32, 58n9, 59nn12–13, 59n28; interactional component in, 30–32, 58n9, 59nn12–13; intrapersonal component in, 28–30, 58n9, 59nn12–13, 107
Engelke, Matthew, xv–xvi

English. *See* standardized English
Enlightenment thinking, 107
Erakat, Noura, 98
essentialism, 7–8
ethic of responsibility, xxv
ethic of ultimate ends, xxv
The Ethics of Identity (Appiah), 55–56
"ethics of intention," 20
ethnicity, 124–26
ethos, 43
evangelical rhetoric, 18–21

Facing Unpleasant Truths (Orwell), xiii
facultas (capacity), 6
fair-minded critical thinking, 31–32
feedback, 74–75
fictional affinity group, 55–56
Finn, Patrick, 97
Fish, Stanley, 67
Flynn, Elizabeth, 92
Frazier, Demita, 2–3
freedom, 124–25
Frost, Diana, xxiv
Frye, Marilyn, 90–91, 93
Fuller, Buckminster, 115

Gates, Henry Louis, Jr., 9
Gee, James, 49, 123
gender, 37, 50n49, 92
Gilyard, Keith, 80
Giroux, Henry, 79
Goleman, Daniel. *See* Emotional Intelligence
Goodnight, G. Thomas, viii
Gorgias (Socrates), 77
Gorski, Paul C., 98
Goulah, Jason, 111
graduate student, vii, 123
Graff, Gerald, 72, 74
Greenfield, Laura, 73, 74, 99

Haidt, Jonathan, 54
Hanhn, Thich Naht, 108–10
Hart, Albert Bushnell, xviii
Harvard University, xviii–xix

Haswell, Richard, 93
hegemony: in primacy of identity, 21–22; protectionism and, 97
Hegemony How-To (Smucker), xxiv–xxvi, 10
"Higher Education is Drowning in BS" (Smith, C.), 17
Hip Hop music, 66–67
home, 107
"homie," 75
honesty, 125–26
hooks, bell, 7
hopelessness, xxiv
How to Think Like an Anthropologist (Engelke), xv
Hynes, William, 94–95

identity, 14; Appiah on, 12–13; awareness of, 110–11, 123–24; code-meshing pedagogy and, 65–66, 68; *kairos* and, 110; language related to, xiv–xvii, 82–83; negation of affirmation and, 55–56; nonattachment and, 109–10; PBL and, 116; personal experience with, 57; primacy of, 57; racism related to, 109; in sacred victim and minority writer, 68–69, 71
identity politics: Combahee River Collective on, 2–3, 11, 13, 18; conception of, 2, 11; definition of, 11; escape from, 2; powerlessness in, 1–2. *See also* primacy of identity
"ideology of anonymity," xv–xvi
illusion, vii–viii, 77, 79
individual, 29–30
influence, 43–44
inoculation, 96
Inoue, Asao, 30, 62n90, 66–67, 73, 74; on Buddhist thought, 107–8, 112, 113; "real world" of, 116, 121n43; victim-framing and, 89, 92–93
Inspirational Leadership, 45–46
integrity, 124–26
intelligence quotient (IQ), 34, 48

"intentional strategy," 63n95
interactional component, 30–32, 58n9, 59nn12–13
interbeing, 108–9
interconnection, 108
intrapersonal component, 28–30, 58n9, 59nn12–13, 107
IQ. *See* intelligence quotient
"It Ain't What It Is" (Young and Young-Rivera), 82

Jackson, Rosemary, 81, 112–13
James, William, xviii, xx, 78
Japanese, 47
Japanese government, WWII, 120n23
Jones, Vance, 95

Kaironomia (White), 5
kairos, 23n10, 39, 43; in code-meshing teaching, 72, 76, 80–82; communication and, 77–78; definition of, 5; identity and, 110; PBL and, 113, 115; rhetoric and, 6, 106; in sacred victim and minority writer, 70
Kelleher, Tom, 77–78
King, Martin Luther, Jr., 101
Kohl, Herbert, 112
Kohlrieser, George, 38–39, 47–48, 106–7
Kopelson, Karen, 8
Krashen, Stephen, xvii, 112

labor-based grading: in code-meshing teaching, 73, 74; victim-framing and, 89–90
language: "affective filter" for, xvii; in Catalonia, xvi; code-switching in, xviii; Critical Language Awareness, 44, 112; dialects of, xvi–xvii; identity related to, xiv–xvii, 82–83; "ideology of anonymity" and, xv–xvi; of reality, 41–42
Language of Wider Communication (LWC), xxviiin5; AAVE with, 72; as

code-meshing, 67–68; in code-meshing teaching, 67–68, 71–74, 78, 81; in protectionism, 99
laws, xxvi–xxvii
Lazere, Donald, 100
"leading another to correct teaching" (*shoju*), vii–viii
Lee, Judith A. B., 29–30, 33, 34, 36, 38
Leff, Michael, 5–6
Lightfoot, Lori, 56
Lilienfeld, Scott O., 52–53, 55
Lilla, Mark, 1, 15, 16, 18
lived experience, 3–4, 50
Lotus Sutra (Buddha), 110
Lovejoy, Kim Brian, 97–99
Lukianoff, George, 54
LWC. *See* Language of Wider Communication
Lynne, Steven, 5

Makiguchi, Tsuneseburo, 111–12, 120n23
marginalization, 70; in Catalan, xvi; in primacy of identity, 3, 12; of right, 22
marginalized bodies, xiv
McBee Orzulak, Melinda J., 97–98
McIntyre, Lee, xiii, xiv
McWhorter, John, 19, 20
"Men," 37, 50n49
Mentor, 44–45
middle class white students, xix
minority accompaniment, 32, 60n30
minority writer, 68–71
misrepresentation: of ethnicity, 124–26
morality: of empowerment theory, 57–58; in primacy of identity, 13–14
Muhammad, the Prophet, xv
music, Hip Hop, 66–67

narcissism, 14, 16–17
National Council for the Teaching of English, xiii
NE. *See* negative emotionality
negation of affirmation, 55–56

negative emotionality (NE), 55;
definition of, 52; Lilienfeld on, 52–53;
stimulus-response model and, 54
"A Negro Attends Harvard in the
Nineteenth Century" (Dubois),
xviii–xix
New Materialisms (Frost and Coole),
xxiv
Nichiren Buddhism, vii, 110–12
nonattachment: identity and, 109–10;
from views, 108
noncognitive competencies, 62n90
N-word, 75
The N-Word (Asim), 75

Obama, Barack, 66
Occupy Wall Street movement, xxiv–
xxv, 15
The Once and Future Liberal (Lilla),
1, 16
optimism, 41, 42
orality, writing compared to, 70
Organizational Awareness, 35–36
Orwell, George, xiii
Other People's Children (Delpit, L.),
100
Other People's English (Young),
xiv–xv
outcomes, 117–18
outsiders, 56

Pappas, Gregory Fernando, 8–9, 33, 70
Patel, Eboo, 12, 58
Paul, Richard, 31, 33, 35
PayScale, 77
PBL. *See* problem-based learning
Perryman-Clark, Staci, xxvi, 96–97
persuasion: in communication, 4–5;
empowerment and, 106
Philosophy as Cultural Politics (Rorty),
79
Plato, 18, 77, 94
political correctness, 31
politics of recognition, 71
Positive Outlook, 40–42, 113
postmodernism, 94
Post-Truth (McIntyre), xiii, xiv

power, 100; in code-meshing teaching,
79; of silence, 127; truth and,
viii. *See also* disempowerment;
empowerment
powerlessness, 1–2
pragmatism, xviii, xxii–xxiii
prefiguration, xxv, 19–20, 82
prefigurative politics, 10–13, 15
prepon (attention to appropriateness of
place and audience), 23n10
primacy of identity, 50–51, 126;
abstraction in, 14; in academia, 15–17;
agency in, 10, 82; appropriation
in, 87; authenticity in, 7–13; "civic
humanistic rhetoric" in, 5–6; in
code-meshing teaching, 76–77,
80–81; critiques in, 6; decolonialism
in, 8–9; disempowerment and, 105;
distraction in, 17; essentialism in,
7–8; hegemony in, 21–22; lived
experience in, 3–4; marginalization
in, 3, 12; meaning in, 16; morality
in, 13–14; narcissism in, 14,
16–17; narrative filter in, 11,
17; performance of, 12, 14–15;
prefigurative politics in, 10–17,
19–20, 22; recognition in, 12–13;
rhetorics in, 14; sacred victim in,
18–21; self-admiration in, 15, 17;
self-expression in, 4–6;
self-reflection in, 16; stereotypes
in, 12–13; trickster and, 94–95;
validation in, 9–10; victim as rightful
king in, 21–22; victimhood in,
14–15; virtue signaling in, 19; voices
in, 7
prison industry, 95
problem-based learning (PBL): Buddhist
thought and, 116; empowerment
from, 117; EQ related to, 115–16;
identity and, 116; *kairos* and, 113,
115; "real world" and, 116, 118,
121n43; skills from, 114; tensegrity
and, 115
protectionism, xxvii; AAVE and,
97–98; cause-theme and, 98; cultural
appropriation and, 97; culture of

power in, 100; hegemony and, 97; incentivized ignorance in, 99; insularity in, 96–97; intention in, 99–100; LWC in, 99; push-pull in, 98–99; trickster racism and, 95–100; victim-framing and, 98–99; white spaces and, 97
psychology, 55
public relations, 77–78

Queer theory, 8

Race and Writing Assessment (Haswell), 93
"racial schizophrenia," xv, xvii, 39, 65–66
racism, xiv, xxvi–xxvii, 81–82, 103n42; identity related to, 109. *See also* trickster racism
Raekstad, Paul, 10–11
realism, xxv
realist pragmatism, xviii
reality, language of, 41–42
"real world," 116, 118, 121n43
recognition: politics of, 71; in primacy of identity, 12–13
"recruitment" (*shakubuku*), vii–viii
register, in code-meshing teaching, 75
Relationship Management, 43–48
repentance, eternal, 19
resilience, 50
rhetoric and composition, 43–44
rhetoric of empowerment, 28; conflict in, 50; Discourse in, 49; emotions in, 50; empathy in, 50; lived experience in, 50; resilience in, 50; secure base in, 51, 106–7; self-perception in, 49
rhetorics, 4–5, 43, 66; argumentation in, viii; Buddha and, 110; in code-meshing teaching, 76–77; *kairos* and, 6, 106; in primacy of identity, 14; in sacred victim and minority writer, 70–71
right, 21–22
Robinson Jackson, Rosemary, 78

Rorty, Richard, 79
Royster, Jacqueline Jones, 3, 7

sacred victim and minority writer: authenticity and, 71; code-meshing in, 69; expectations in, 69; identity in, 68–69, 71; *kairos* in, 70; non-Western marginalization in, 70; personal experience with, 69–70; rhetoric in, 70–71; validation in, 68–69
sacred victims: in academia, 20–21; code-meshing teaching and, 80; in primacy of identity, 18–21; safety of, 56–57; validation of, 19, 68–69
safety, 56–57
sangha (community), 108–9
scholarship, 124–27
SE. *See* standardized English
secure base, in rhetoric of empowerment, 51, 106–7
segregationism, xxiii, 75
self-actualization, 118
self-admiration, 15, 17
Self-Awareness, 34–35
Self-Control, 36–38
self-expression, 4–6
Self-Management, 36
self-perception, 49
self-reflection, 16
self-reflexivity, 90–91
self-segregation, xxiii
sense of belonging, 55
sense of self, xx–xxi
Shadow and Act (Ellison), 96
shakubuku ("to break and subdue," "recruitment," "suppression of others' illusions"), vii–viii
shoju ("leading another to correct teaching"), vii–viii
"Should Writers Use They Own English" (Young), 67, 72, 74
"situation-inverter," trickster as, 95
skillful means, 108
slang, 67–68

Smith, Christian, 17
Smith, Erec, 57
Smitherman, Geneva, 67, 98
Smucker, Jonathan, xxvi, 10–11, 14, 56; on ambiguity, 45–46; on Occupy Wall Street movement, xxiv–xxv, 15; "sidelines" of, 80; on social justice activism, 53–54
"social and material," xxviiin2, xiv
social awareness, 35–36
"Social Intelligence," 34
social justice, 87
social justice activism, 53–54
societal progress, 118–19
sociolinguistic naturalism, xv–xvi
Socrates, 77
Soka Gakkai (Value-creation society), 111–12, 120n24
sophistic critical thinking, 31–32, 33
Spain, xvi
standardized English (SE), xviiin5, viii–xix, xvii; as "acting white," xxii–xxiii; in code-meshing teaching, 74; as compliance, 44; empowerment through, xxii–xxiii; sacred victim and minority writer and, 70; Young on, xx–xxi, 65–67, 72, 74
stereotypes, 12–13
stimulus-response model, 54–55
"strategies," xiv
structural racism, xiv
subjectivity, 126–27
"suppression of others' illusions" (*shakubuku*), vii–viii
symbolism, 73–74

teacher attitude, 111, 112–13
teamwork, 47–48
teleology, 118–19
tensegrity, 115
transactional model, 55
transcendence, 109
trickster: primacy of identity and, 94–95; as "situation-inverter," 95
trickster archetype, 94
trickster racism: capability and, 100–101; description of, 95; Ellison on, 96; emotions and, 100–101; progress from, 101; protectionism and, 95–100
truth, viii, 124–26; in code-meshing teaching, 78–79

"unprincipled opportunism," xxv–xxvi

Vaihinger, Hans, 54
validation: in primacy of identity, 9–10; of sacred victims, 19, 68–69; teleology and, 118–19
value-creation society (Soka Gakkai), 111–12, 120n24
victim as rightful king, 21–22
victim-framing: blackly in, 91–92; in code-meshing pedagogy, 87–93; disempowerment in, 87–88; Dubois and, 88–89; gender in, 92; Inoue on, 92–93; labor-based grading and, 89–90; protectionism and, 98–99; self-reflexivity and, 90–91; whiteliness in, 90–91
victimhood, xxiii–xxiv, 18–21
victim narrative, xxi, xxii
Villoro, Luis, 8–9, 33
virtues, 91
"The Virtue Signalers Won't Change the World" (McWhorter), 19
virtue signaling, 19
voices, 7

Weber, Max, xxv, 20, 87
Wendell, Barret, xx
"What to the Slave is the Fourth of July" (Douglass), xxvi
"When the First Voice You Hear is Not Your Own" (Royster), 3
White, Eric Charles, 5
whiteliness, 89, 127; in victim-framing, 90–91
white protectionism, xxvii
white racism, xxvii

white spaces, 97
white students, xix, xxii
Willett, Cynthia, 107
Wing, Bob, 29
wishful thinking, 41
Woolard, Kathryn A., xvi
writing, 70, 89–90. *See also specific topics*
Writing Centers and the New Racism, 73
writing crisis, xix
WWII Japanese government, 120n23

The Year of Dreaming Dangerously (Zizek), 15

Young, Vershawn, xiv–xv, xviii, 80, 124–26; Dubois and, xx–xxi, xxii; "homie" from, 75; on SE, xx–xxi, 65–67, 72, 74; on self-segregation, xxiii; victim-framing and, 88–89; victimhood and, xxiii–xxiv
Young-Rivera, Y'Shanda, 82
"Your Average Nigga" (Young), 80, 124–25

Zimmerman, Marc A., 117–18; on empowerment theory components, 28–29, 30–32, 37, 58n9, 59nn12–13, 59n28
Zizek, Slavoj, 15, 17

About the Author

Erec Smith is associate professor of rhetoric and composition at York College of Pennsylvania. He has published on size acceptance activism, social media rhetoric, race, and the confluence of rhetorical theory and Buddhist philosophy. His current scholarship focuses on anti-racist ideology and issues of emotional intelligence and empowerment in academia and beyond.

Made in the USA
Columbia, SC
19 July 2021